Economics Reading Lists, Course Outlines, Exams, Puzzles & Problems

Compiled by Edward Tower, *Duke University*, July 1981

Vol. 4

Macroeconomics, Monetary Economics and Money & Banking Exams, Puzzles & Problems

including the University of Chicago M.A. comprehensive exams in micro and macroeconomic theory, Ph.D. core exams in the theory of income, and M.A. & Ph.D. preliminary exams in money and banking 1967-1981

eno river press

Economics Reading Lists, Course Outlines, Exams, Puzzles & Problems

Compiled by Edward Tower, *Duke University*, July 1981

Vol. 4

Macroeconomics, Monetary Economics and Money & Banking Exams, Puzzles & Problems

including the University of Chicago M.A. comprehensive
exams in micro and macroeconomic theory,
Ph.D. core exams in the theory of income, and M.A. & Ph.D.
preliminary exams in money and banking 1967-1981

eno
river
press

Box 4900
Duke Station
Durham, NC 27706 USA

NOTES TO USERS AND POTENTIAL CONTRIBUTORS

These teaching materials are drawn from both undergraduate and graduate reading programs at 68 major colleges and universities. They are designed to widen the horizons of individual professors and curriculum committees. Some include suggestions for term paper topics, and many of the lists are useful guides for students seeking both topics and references for term papers and theses. Thus, they should enable *faculty members* to advise students more effectively and efficiently. They will also be useful to prospective *graduate students* seeking more detailed information about various graduate programs; to those currently enrolled in programs who are preparing for field examinations; and to *librarians* responsible for acquisitions in economics. Finally, they may be interesting to *researchers* and *administrators* who wish to know more about how their own work and the work of their department is being received by the profession.

The exams, puzzles and problems include both undergraduate and graduate exams contributed by economics departments and individual professors. They should be especially useful to professors making up exams and problem sets and to students studying for comprehensive exams. They may also serve as the focus for study groups.

From time to time we will reprint updated and expanded versions. Therefore, we would welcome new or updated teaching materials, especially those which complement material in this collection or cover areas we missed. Potential contributors should contact Edward Tower, Economics Department, Duke University, Durham, N.C. 27706, U.S.A.

While Eno River Press has copyrighted the entire collection, authors of the various parts retain the right to reproduce and assign the reproduction of their own materials as they choose. Thus, anyone wishing to reproduce particular materials should contact the author of them. Similarly, those wishing to make verbatim use of department-wide examinations, except as teaching materials for one's own class, should contact the department chairman concerned.

Acknowledgement

The cover was designed by Robert Steiner, and the volumes were printed by Chapel Hill Printing Co.

Eno River Press
Box 4900, Duke Station
Durham, North Carolina 27706, U.S.A.

ISBN for this volume 0-88024-031-8
ISBN Eno River Press for this series 0-88024-027-X

Library of Congress Catalog Number 81-69302

CONTENTS

1. BEN S. BERNANKE and ROBERT E. HALL, Stanford University
   Examinations in the Theory of Income and
   Economic Fluctuations 3

2. JACOB A. FRENKEL, University of Chicago
   Examinations in Macroeconomics 17

3. ROBERT J. GORDON, Northwestern University
   Examination in Macroeconomics 26

4. EARL A. THOMPSON, U.C.L.A.
   Examinations in Money and Macroeconomics 28

5. CLAREMONT GRADUATE SCHOOL
   Qualifying Examinations in Monetary Analysis 34

6. UNIVERSITY OF CHICAGO
   Core Examinations in the Theory of Income 43

7. UNIVERSITY OF CHICAGO
   Money and Banking Preliminary Examinations 152

8. UNIVERSITY OF CHICAGO
   Comprehensive Examinations for the A.M. Degree in Price
   Theory, the Theory of Income, Employment, and
   the Price Level 192

9. UNIVERSITY OF MICHIGAN
   Monetary Theory and Stabilization Policy
   Preliminary Examinations 313

10. UNIVERSITY OF WASHINGTON
    Macroeconomics Field Examinations 327

Economics 210

THEORY OF INCOME AND ECONOMIC FLUCTUATIONS

Final Examination

Answer all three parts. You may assume all material from lectures and readings--
no credit is given for mere repetition of this material in your answers. Please
be brief. Answer each question in a separate book.

PART I (one hour)

1. "Automation and other improvements in productivity are good for the worker.
   They increase wages and output and lower the price level."

2. "Automation and other improvements in productivity are bad for the worker.
   Firms need less workers and so unemployment increases and wages are kept
   low."

This question is designed to analyze the above statements in an IS-LM context.
Assume the aggregate production function is $Y = AF(K,N)$; there is an unexpected
permanent increase in A .

(i) Suppose the economy is Walrasian (i.e., prices are perfectly flexible).
     Describe the effects of the productivity increase on the three major markets
     of the economy. Specify any special elasticity assumptions that you make.

     Is it possible that aggregate consumption can be reduced by the productivity
     increase? If so, would this make the economy worse off?

(ii) Suppose the economy is Keynesian (i.e., prices and wages adjust slowly).
     Under what conditions will the productivity increase initially add to unem-
     ployment? Describe the adjustment process of the economy. Are real wage
     cuts required to reduce unemployment?

(iii) Summarize the arguments for and against automation from the point of view
      of the worker. Bring in considerations from outside this model, if you
      wish. Do not exceed one page in answering (iii).

PART II (45 minutes) Answer one question.

1. With a fixed labor force, the Ripoff Oil Co. produces output in each period
   according to

   $$y_t = K_t - aK_t^2 \qquad\qquad 0 < a \ll 1$$

-3-

The price of output is set to equal 1 in each period. The price of new capital in terms of the output good in period t is q_t. q_t is known to be declining by a constant percentage each year; that is,

$$q_t = x q_{t-1} \qquad\qquad 0 < x < 1 \quad \text{(for all } t \text{)}$$

Capital physically depreciates at rate d. The constant real interest rate is r. There are no taxes.

(a) Find the Ripoff Oil Co.'s desired capital stock in period t, K_t^*. Explain how this can be derived either through a marginal product rule or by solving the capital scheduling problem.

(b) In order to capture windfall profits, the Congress (in secret session) agrees to an explicitly temporary, one-period tax on oil company profits, at rate u. It is desired to minimize the reduction in investment caused by the tax. Congrsswoman A suggests that the tax should be announced, as a surprise, at the beginning of the period in which it is effective. Gongressman B wants to announce the tax far in advance.

Assume that all capital is ordered one period in advance, so that investment in period t is chosen to make capital equal to its expected desired level in $t+1$. Compare A's and B's plans in their effects on desired capital and investment. What happens if the way the tax is levied affects oil company expectations about how taxes will be levied in the future?

2. Here are data on real income and consumption for a large industrial country. (see next page.) With reference to the data and your knowledge of the theory of consumption:

(a) Why does consumption consistently fall short of income?

(b) Why did consumption decline in 1958?

(c) Why did consumption decline in 1974? Relate your answer to part (b).

(d) Can aggregate data tell us whether the lifecycle-permanent income model is correct? Could other data?

	Disposable Income Per Capita 1972 Dollars	Consumption Per Capita 1972 Dollars
1956	2643	2415
1957	2650	2421
1958	2636	2406
1959	2696	2493
1960	2697	2507
1961	2725	2516
1962	2796	2589
1963	2849	2649
1964	3009	2755
1965	3152	2872
1966	3274	2982
1967	3371	3035
1968	3464	3156
1969	3515	3234
1970	3619	3265
1971	3714	3342
1972	3837	3510
1973	4062	3648
1974	3973	3589
1975	4025	3627
1976	4136	3808
1977	4271	3955

PART III (45 minutes) Answer one question.

1. Robert Barro repeats his analysis for Argentina and finds much smaller real effects from monetary surprises than in the U.S. What kinds of differences would you expect to find in the Argentinian economy that explained his findings? You need not know anything about Argentina to answer this question. Consider Lucas' and at least one other explanation of monetary non-neutrality.

2. Here are data for the U.S. in 1974 and 1975:

	Rate of Change of Wages	Unemployment Rate	Real GNP
1974	9.1%	5.6	1213
1975	9.9	8.5	1202

(a) "This experience refutes the Phillips curve." Comment. Identify any shifts in the Phillips curve that may have taken place.

(b) How do the ideas in Lucas' model help explain these data, if at all?

(c) Why does such a small drop in real GNP go with a large increase in unemployment?

SAMPLE EXAM QUESTIONS

1. Macro textbooks are currently making great use of
    an "aggregate demand--aggregate supply" diagram that
    looks like this:

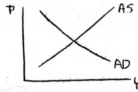

    P is the aggregate price level, Y is real output.

a) Explain the slopes of the AD (aggregate demand) and AS
    (aggregate supply) curves, assuming that the components of
    nominal wealth (M,B) and expectations of inflation are
    held fixed.

b) What is the pitfall in thinking of this diagram as
    analogous to the usual microeconomic supply and demand
    diagram?

c) Show how this diagram can explain the observation of a
    Phillips curve in macro-data. What happens to the
    diagram and to the derived Phillips curve over time, as
    price-level expectations adjust?

d) A former member of the Council of Economic Advisors
    suggests that the Fed's strongest weapon against
    inflation is its credibility--the ability to make the
    public believe that it is going to pursue restrictive
    monetary policies. Evaluate this in terms of the AD-AS
    diagram.

2. Opponents of increased government spending for economic expansion often argue that such spending merely soaks up savings that would otherwise have been available for investment. (This is sometimes called "crowding out".)

a. Analyze this position using the IS-LM model. Be sure to discuss the effects of the way the government chooses to finance its spending. Why is the speed at which markets clear in the aggregate an important consideration?

b. How do the more detailed analyses of the investment sector we have seen bear on this question? Discuss the relevance of i) expectations of aggregate demand and the cost of capital ii) delivery lags iii) the putty-clay hypothesis.

3. The IS-LM theory was constructed for, and probably is most relevant to, the Depression of the 1930s. Using this framework, evaluate the following statements about (as Friedman calls it) "the Great Contraction". (This question can be answered with practically no knowledge of economic history from outside the model--which goes to show how hard it is to distinguish economic history and economic analysis.)

a. The stock market crash was a dramatic event, but its effects did not extend much beyond people who actually had large holdings of stocks.

b. As suggested by the "needs of trade" doctrine, the Fed acted properly in reducing the money stock as output fell.

c. The absence of social insurance (e.g., unemployment insurance) probably made the Depression more severe.

d. High tariffs to improve the balance of trade were expansionary.

e. The fact that interest rates were at a fraction of 1% in the mid-'30s greatly weakened the potential of monetary policy to expand the economy.

f. There was too much real capital in the U.S. in the 1930s.

g. A fall in real wages would have permitted a reduction of the 24% unemployment rate.

h. The failure of the economy to re-collapse after World War II was due to the Pigou effect.

4. "There is nothing wrong with the assumption of rational expectations itself, nor with its fruitful application to financial markets. But in the light of widespread evidence that, except in a few scattered auction markets, prices adjust sluggishly to the market-clearing level in response to demand and supply shocks, it is hard to avoid the conclusions that for short-run analysis, the Lucas supply function . . . should be relegated to the same scrap heap of discarded ideas where lie the earlier classical models of perfect market clearing laid to rest by Keynes forty years ago." (Robert J. Gordon, AER, February 1977, p. 132). Write a balanced evaluation of this remark, emphasizing what Lucas has and has not contributed to our understanding of fluctuations.

5. It is widely thought that the oil price increase of 1973-74 brought about the deep recession of 1974-75. Sketch your own beliefs about how an exogenous price increase can depress output. What relation does monetary neutrality have to your answer?

6. "The life cycle-permanent income theory says that tax policy cannot affect consumption. The theory is well supported by the evidence. Therefore, we cannot stimulate the economy during a recession through tax cuts for consumers." Criticize this statement, paying equal attention to each link in its logic.

1. Suppose that there is an influx of "boat people" to the U.S. All are able-bodied and have labor skills equal to the average American's. They have no wealth. Those who cannot find work are to be supported by the government. Analyze the macro-implications of the immigration in a) Walrasian (full-employment) and b) Keynesian contexts. Specify your additional assumptions.

2. Discuss the neutrality of money in each of the following situations (using full-employment model):

   a) Everyone is acutely aware that increased government borrowing now means higher taxes later.

   b) There is no wealth effect on consumption.

   c) Income taxation is progressive in nominal income.

3. Predict the effect of the following events on a given firm's a) average $u_q^\sim u$ b) marginal $u_q^\sim u$

   i) a radical increase in energy prices
   ii) the loss of a multi-million dollar lawsuit
   iii) a rise in real estate rates
   iv) a new technology for producing the firm's product is invented and cheaply marketed
   v) a graduate of Econ 210 finds a way to avoid recession without inducing inflation

Economics 210
Homework #3

1. Imagine an economy in which
   a) production is Cobb-Douglas with capital exponent α
   b) the price of capital goods (in real terms) is always constant at q.
   c) there is a corporate income tax rate u, but no depreciation
      deductions (z = 0)
   d) there is an investment tax credit k which may be varied by the
      government over time.

   Show that desired capital stock K* is given by

   $$K^* = \frac{\alpha(1-u)y}{q[(r_n - \pi^e + \delta)(1-k) + \overset{\bullet}{k}^e]}$$

   Where $r_n - \pi^e$ is the real rate of interest and $\overset{\bullet}{k}^e = (dk/dt)^{expected}$

   Suppose that investment adjusts toward K* via a flexible accelerator
   and that, initially, k = 0. Assess qualitatively the differential
   effects on the path of investment of the following policies:
   i) a permanent and perfectly anticipated investment tax credit
   ii) a permanent tax credit imposed as a surprise
   iii) a tax credit both perfectly anticipated and known to be temporary
   iv) a credit which is known to be temporary but is imposed as a surprise

   The tax credit rate is the same in each case

2. A firm has the following putty-clay technology: New capacity (y) in a
   given period can be created by any combination of capital (K) and labor
   force (N) that satisfied the relation

   $$y = AK^\alpha N^{1-\alpha} \qquad A, \alpha \text{ constant}$$
   $$0 < \alpha < 1$$

   However, once capacity is in place, the initially chosen capital-labor
   ratio can not be varied for the life of the capital.
   Each machine (unit of capital) initially costs q, works for T periods
   without operating costs or depreciation, then is scrapped. The real

-11-

wage (per worker per period) may vary but is known with certainty for
each future period. There are no taxes.
The real interest rate is r.

i) Briefly discuss the realism of the specification of the technology.

ii) Find the capital-labor ratio that minimizes the average cost of
capacity. How does this ratio react to a longer capital working life
or higher expected wages?

iii) What is the competitive supply curve for capacity by this firm?

Economics 210

Fall 1980

Instructions

Answer Parts I, II, and III. Note that you are to choose between
questions 1 and 2 in Part II.

Separate your answers to Bernanke's questions (Part I and question 1 in
Part II) in one bluebook and your answers to Hall's questions (question
2 in Part II and question III) in a second bluebook.

Read these instructions again. We cannot grade any exams that contain
Bernanke and Hall answers in the same book. Be sure to answer all
three parts and to choose between questions 1 and 2 in Part II.

ECONOMICS 210 EXAM (Bernanke)

PART I (one hour)

Advisors to the new President have advocated income tax
cuts as an anti-inflation tool. In this question you are
asked to evaluate their proposal.

(i) Using the general equilibrium macro-model with <u>flexible</u>
prices which we set forth in class, analyze the short-run
impact of a cut in the tax rate on the price level and the
other major variables. You may assume a constant tax rate t,

that is, $t(Y)=tY$. <u>Briefly</u> describe the long-run effect of
the tax cut on the price level.

(ii) The model used in (i) could correctly be criticized
for ignoring the effects of income taxes on the supply of
output. Show that a tax rate of t on income implies the
identical tax rate on wages and capital rentals. How is
the basic macro-model modified by the assumption that
workers and investors consider only <u>after-tax</u> returns in
supply decisions?

(iii) Repeat (i) using the model as modified in (ii).
Again, assume flexible prices and describe long-run impacts
only briefly. On what assumptions about empirical magnitudes
does the tax-cutters' case depend?

(iv) Ignoring political considerations, what is the general
form of the tax scheme that would be optimal from the
"supply-side" point of view?

PART II (40 minutes) Answer <u>one</u> question.

1. In class we defined the functions

$$S(I_t) = \text{the total real cost of gross investment}$$
$$\text{I at time t, including adjustment costs}$$

$$F(K_t, N_t) = \text{the production function}$$

Now consider a firm for which

$$S(I_t) = I_t + bI_t^2 \qquad b > 0$$

$$F(K_t, N_t) = \theta K_t \qquad \theta > 0$$

That is, production requires no labor. Let r be the constant
real interest rate and d the rate of capital depreciation.
There are no taxes.

(a) The firm wishes to invest so as to maximize the present
discounted value of cash flows. Show how the solution to
this problem can be expressed both in terms of "Tobin's q"
and the Hall-Jorgenson optimal scheduling criterion.

(b)   What is the value of an additional unit of installed capital at each instant?

(c)   Give explicitly the optimal investment path and the long-run optimal capital stock.   This does not require any complex mathematics.

ECONOMICS 210 EXAM (Hall)

II. 2 (Choose between this and Bernanke's question II.1)

Real income obeys the process

$$y_t = y_{t-1} + e_t$$

where e_t is completely unpredictable: $E_{t-1} e_t = 0$.

a)   What is the best forecast of future income, y_{t+i}, given information available at time t?

b)   Under the life cycle-permanent income hypothesis, what will be the consumption function relating consumption, c_t, to information available at time t?   (if you omit interest rate effects, justify the omission)

c)   Does the consumption function satisfy the property that c_{t-1} is the only predictor of c_t?

d)   The government introduces a temporary tax cut.   What will happen to consumption?   State your assumptions explicitly.

III.   (40 minutes)   Answer the following question.

Consider an economy where real output, y_t fluctuates around a normal level of 1.0.   Its price level is p_t.   There are monetary shocks x_t and real shocks z_t whose average values are zero.   The economy is described by

$$\log y_t = a \, x_t - (1-a) \, z_t$$

$$\log p_t = (1-a) \, x_t + (1-a) \, z_t + \log m_{t-1}$$

where a is a parameter between 0 and 1 and m_{t-1} is known to the public.

a)   Relate this economy to the one described by Lucas.   How would you characterize the economy with a=0?

b)   How does the nominal value of output respond to the nominal and real shocks?

c)   What characteristics of the economy determine the value of a?

d)   Describe the "Phillips curve" relating y_t and p_t/m_{t-1}.   Is it a deterministic relation?   What do you infer about a point with high p/m and high y?   About a point with high p/m and low y?

-15-

Professor Bernanke
Professor Hall

Sample examination questions

1. Many schemes have been advanced for stabilization of the price level. Compare and critically evaluate at least four of these.

2. "The Friedman/Sargent-Wallace argument for a steady rate of growth of the money supply is empirically faulty. For example, money growth was stable in the face of the 1973-74 oil price shock, and the result was a disastrous recession." Comment.

3. The early stages of the Great Depression were marked by severe and roughly simultaneous drops in income, M1, and prices. This period also saw many bank failures, and increased ratios of both reserves and currency holdings to deposits. The stock of high-powered money changed little.

    a. Friedman and Schwartz have argued that the falling stock of money resulted from the impact of exogenously-caused bank failures on money supply. Explain how bank failures could have this effect.

    b. Temin has countered that the monetary collapse came from the demand side of the money market. What mechanism does he have in mind?

    c. What sorts of evidence could help you decide which of these two interpretations is historically correct?

4. The permanent reduction in government spending proposed by the new Administration is supposed to result in lower interest rates. Analyze this in an equilibrium context. What is the role of the accompanying tax cuts? What are the implications of reduced government spending for GNP?

5. In a Tobin-Baumol inventory model of transactions demand, show that even spacing of transactions is optimal for n=3.

6. "Even if prices are sticky in the short run, Barro-Grossman-type models are rendered empirically irrelevant by the life-cycle/permanent-income hypothesis." Comment.

7. Does Blinder's econometric study of temporary tax cuts avoid the Lucas critique? Why or why not?

8. The economy of Langia has no fiat money; the only financial assets are shares in the national mutual fund, which owns all Langian industry. Transactions are computerized, so that a sale of goods is immediately reflected in the transfer of fund shares from one citizen to another.

    a. Is there a determinate price level in this economy? If not, how could one be established?

    b. The government of Langia finances itself by issuing additional shares in the national mutual fund. What are the implications of this practice for the economy?

-16-

Two Hours

Jacob A. Frenkel
Spring, 1980

1. (30 minutes) Assume a fully employed economy in which output is produced by a Cobb-Douglas production function (using capital and labor) and in which savings depend positively on the rate of interest and negatively on the value of marketable wealth, investment depends negatively on the rate of interest while the desired ratio of real balances to marketable wealth depends negatively on the rate of interest. Marketable wealth is defined as the sum of the real value of cash balances and equities (which in turn correspond to the value of claims on the return to capital); Assume that labor income can not be capitalized in the capital market, and that the supply of labor depends positively on the (after tax) real wage. Denote the corporate tax rate by τ and the personal income tax rate by t.

Analyse the effects of a rise in the quantity of money that is brought about through an open market purchase of equities on the equilibrium values of

   (i) the rate of interest

   (ii) the real value of cash balances.

In your answer assume that in order to maintain a balanced budget, the government lowers the tax rate when it conducts the open market purchase. Explain in detail how your answers to questions (i) and (ii) depend on whether the tax rate that is being reduced is the corporate income tax or the personal income tax?

2. (20 minutes) Using a Cagan-type demand for money show

   (i)   that the steady-state revenue maximizing rate of monetary expansion is $1/\alpha$ where $\alpha \equiv d\ell n\, m/d\pi$, m denotes real balances and π denotes the steady-state expected (and realized) rate of inflation.

   (ii) How do you explain the fact that the revenue maximizing rate of monetary expansion is independent of the rate of growth of income?

   (iii) How does the steady state revenue maximizing rate of inflation depend on the rate of growth of income?

-17-

3. (10 minutes) Consider the steady-state growth path of an economy which produces output according to a constant returns to scale Cobb-Douglas production function (using capital and labor), and suppose that the economy always follows the "golden rule." Comment on the proposition that

> "The higher the elasticity of output with respect to the input of labor, the lower must be the economy's average savings ratio"

4. (10 minutes) "The existence of personal income tax implies that the equilibrium difference between the nominal and the real rates of interest exceeds the expected rate of inflation." Comment

5. (20 minutes) Define briefly the following concepts and outline their significance

      (i)   modified golden rule

      (ii)   welfare cost of inflation

      (iii) crowding out

      (iv) inside money

      (v)   long-term contracts

6. (25 minutes) "Rational behavior implies that as long as the marginal rate of time preference is constant, changes in the percentage rate of monetary expansion will not affect the <u>steady-state</u> stock of capital or consumption (per head) since the equilibrium marginal product of capital must equal the given <u>fixed</u> marginal rate of time preference."

Analyse critically the above proposition using a formal neoclassical model with rational individuals who maximize utility subject to a constant marginal rate of time preference.

Jacob A. Frenkel

1-3/4 hours   Final Examination   Winter, 1978

(25 minutes)
1. Consider an economy that is composed of two generations--the "young" generation and the "retired" generation--and assume that the economy is growing along the steady state growth path. The government considers the introduction of a new "social security" system by which each member of the young generation contributes 10 percent of his income to a fund that is distributed equally among members of the retired generation. The contribution carries with it the promise that when members of the young generation reach their retirement age they will receive 10 percent of the income of the new young generation.

   (i) Should the current young generation favor the introduction of the new system?

   (ii) How would you modify your answer to part (i) if you were given the information that output is produced by a Cobb-Douglas production function (using capital and labor), and that the economy's average savings ratio exceeds the elasticity of output with respect to the input of capital.

(20 minutes)
2. Did France suffer one of the most drastic deflations in history in the late 1950's when 100 of old francs were converted after 1958 into 1 new franc and prices fell to one percent over their previous level? In your answer, discuss the issues of whether monetary reforms are an extreme way for the imposition of inflation tax.

(25 minutes)
3. "The monetary authority controls the nominal money supply, but cannot use this control to peg real quantities." Discuss this statement in relation to (1) the trade-off between inflation and unemployment and the natural rate of unemployment; (2) nominal versus real interest rates (3) does this statement mean that monetary policy is powerless and can therefore be ignored

(20 minutes)
4. Comment on the following statements assuming a Cagan-type demand for money.

   (i) As long as the real rate of interest exceeds the rate of growth of output the revenue maximizing rate of inflation is reached at the point where the elasticity of the demand for real cash balances with respect to the nominal rate of interest exceeds unity.

   (ii) Independent of the rate of growth of output, increasing the stock of money at a percentage rate μ per year and distributing the increased supply among individuals proportionally to their current money holdings, amounts to paying interest on money at a rate that is equal to the nominal rate of interest.

(15 minutes)
5. Comment on the following statements:

   (i) The rational expectations hypothesis is unreasonable since it assumes that individuals have much more information than what is realistically sensible.

   (ii) The rational expectations hypothesis does not make sense since it ignores the cost of acquiring information. If information is costly, it is reasonable to assume that individuals will not possess all the relevant information and therefore one should not be surprised when forecasts are not always realized.

minutes)   1. Consider a growing economy in which the nominal money supply
                grows at an annual rate of six percent per year and the rate
                of inflation is fully anticipated. Assume that on January 1,
                1984, the monetary authorities increase the rate of monetary
                expansion from six percent to ten percent per year. Assume
                that within a year, the community completes its adjustment
                to the new policy and thus that the new rate of inflation is
                again fully anticipated.

            The following information is given:

                a. The (constant) percentage growth rate of output (y) is
                    four percent per year.

                b. The (constant) real rate of interest is three percent
                    per year.

                c. The elasticity of V — the income velocity of circulation
                    (the income-money ratio) — with respect to the nominal
                    rate of interest (i) is 0.5.

                d. On December 31, 1983, the nominal stock of money (M) was
                    $100, the real value of output was 400 units and the
                    price level (P) was 1.

            Using the above information, complete the following table:

	December 31, 1983	December 31, 1984
$\frac{\Delta M}{\Delta t}\frac{1}{M}$	6 percent	10 percent
$\frac{\Delta P}{\Delta t}\frac{1}{P}$		
i		
V		
M/P Annual inflation tax		
Change in the welfare cost of annual sub-optimal money holdings		

            Note: All the rates in the above table are per annum.

            Remark: Your score in this question will depend on your explanation
                     of each step.

                                    -21-

(10 minutes)   2.   "The current recession is due to the fact that there is not
enough money to pay for the inflation." Comment.
(Warning: This may be more subtle than it seems at first glance.)

(15 minutes)   3.   "In a fully employed economy, a reduction in the personal income
tax rate accompanied by a rise in the corporate income tax rate
which leaves total tax revenue unchanged, will lower the rate
of interest." Comment.

(20 minutes)   4.   Consider a money supply rule according to which the money supply
follows a sine function resulting in a time path of money characterized by a sine-wave (with no trend). Assume that this money
supply rule is known in advance to all economic agents who have
therefore perfect foresight. What will be the equilibrium path
of prices in that economy? In light of your answer, comment on
the following statement:

"In the absence of secular growth, the path of prices should
coincide with the path of money. If, however, economic agents
have less than perfect information concerning the monetary rule,
prices and money may (at least in the short run) follow different
paths."

Note: This is a complicated question. A full answer would
probably require more time than is allocated to it.
You are expected, however, to outline the major issues
that will have to be dealt with in a complete answer.

(5 minutes)   5.   "An economy's growth rate is higher the larger is the share of
income that is being saved." Comment.

(25 minutes)   6.   Use the simple IS-LM framework extended to an open economy under
fixed exchange rate to analyze the effects of (a tax financed)
rise in government spending on domestic goods and services.

A.   In your answer, specify the characteristics of:

(i)   the short run equilibrium (i.e., the situation where
goods and money markets clear but the balance of
payments need not be balanced),

(ii)   the long run equilibrium.

Analyze the effects of the degree of capital mobility on your
answers to (i) and (ii).

B.   Assume that the monetary authorities wish to sterilize
the effects of the balance of payments on the domestic
money supply. How does the degree of capital mobility
affect the action of the sterilization agency?

ECONOMICS 330

Jacob A. Frenkel
Autumn, 1976

Final Examination

Your time is 120 minutes; the weight of each question in total score is indicated at the margin.

(10) 1. Discuss the various factors which go into an individual's decision regarding how many traveler's checks to take on a vacation.

(15) 2. It has been argued that a large government debt is a burden in that each individual on average owes over $2,000 as her share of the debt. Others point out, however, that a large debt means that individuals hold and own large amounts of government securities and thus are wealthier. Who is right? Discuss briefly.

(10) 3. In the past ten years America's awareness of inflation has increased markedly. Suppose people now adjust their expectations more rapidly than earlier because of this experience. What are the implications in terms of the effects of policy?

(15) 4. Discuss the implications of using alternative monetary indicators as guides for monetary policy. What are the costs and benefits of having a monetary rule?

(30) 5. Use the framework developed in class to analyze the short run and long run effects of a transitory rise in the full employment deficit on the rates of inflation growth and unemployment. Characterize the adjustment process.

(15) 6. List the principal variables that have been used in the specification of the supply of money function. Survey the main empirical findings.

(10) 7. Present the key ideas you got from reading (choose one):

   (i) Tobin, J., "Banks as Creators of Money."
   (ii) Tobin, J. and W. C. Brainard, "Financial Intermediaries and the Effectiveness of Monetary Control."
   (iii) Brunner, K. and A. Meltzer, "Liquidity Traps for Money, Bank Credit, and Interest Rates."

(10) 8. While the monetary authority determines the nominal quantity of money, the private sector determines its real value. Comment.

J. A. Frenkel
Fall, 1976

Economics 330

Your time is 85 minutes; the weight of each question in total score is as indicated.

(20) 1. The accompanying exhibit shows "Cash Discount Coupon"--issued by a local gas station that also performs car-wash services. These certificates are issued to customers in proportion to their purchases of gasoline.

    1) Discuss the "moneyness" of these coupons in light of the various attributes of money.

    ii) Why might the gas station prefer to issue these certificates rather than to (a) lower prices? (b) join the "S & H Green Stamp" program?

HYDE PARK
CAR WASH, Inc.
1330 E. 53rd ST.   MI 3-1715

CASH DISCOUNT COUPON
Toward CAR WASH Only
Bottom Figure Shown is
Worth of This Coupon
Gas Up Today - Wash Any Day
25¢ Extra — Fri. Sat. Sun.

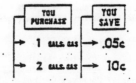

(20) 2. List the principal variables that have been used in the specification of demand for money functions. Comment briefly on the rationale underlying the inclusion of each of the variables. What are the main empirical findings concerning the demand for money? What does it mean to state that the demand for money is a "stable function"? Does the empirical record give any support to this assertion?

(10) 3. The demand for money depends on the differential between r, the rate
          of interest on "earning assets", and r_m, the rate of interest on money.
          Competition in the banking industry insures that (at least the implicit)
          interest rate on demand deposits would move along with r. Therefore,
          the interest elasticity of the demand for money would actually be much
          smaller than that suggested by the approach which neglects movements in
          r_m. Comment.

 (9) 4. Explain briefly how each of the following events would change the stock
          of money (currency plus demand deposits):

          a. Laws are changed so that all victimless crimes such as gambling are
              legalized.

          b. The Federal Reserve System begins charging banks a fee for
              transactions in the Federal Fund market.

          c. Banks are permitted to pay interest on demand deposits.

(21) 5. Comment briefly on the following statements:

          a. If there were only two commodities, there would be no reason for
              the existence of money.

          b. If there were only two persons in the world, there would be no
              reason for holding money since the "double coincidence" problem
              would not arise.

          c. In a world of perfect certainty, nobody will hold money.

          d. Risk does not affect the aggregate demand for money since one
              man's capital gains is another's capital loss.

          e. The rate of interest on 3-month treasury bills is 7 percent per
              year while the rate of inflation is 11 percent per year. It
              follows that the rate of interest is negative.

          f. The inventory theory of transactions demand for money predicts
              that the quantity of money demanded will increase less than in
              proportion to income, and therefore that the rate of inflation
              will exceed the rate of monetary expansion (ignoring growth of
              real output).

          g. The prohibition of the payment of interest on time as well as
              demand deposits would make the price level lower than it would
              otherwise have been, on the assumption that high-powered money
              is held constant and both prohibitions are effective.

FINAL EXAMINATION

Part I (30 minutes).   Answer the following.

1.   Postwar U. S. economic behavior has been characterized by business cycles in which real GNP remains above natural real GNP for several years, and then falls below for several years.   Describe how each of the following variables behaves over the business cycle, and why:

     a.   The "acceptance" or "reservation" wage in job search models.

     b.   The quit rate in job search models.

     c.   The actual quit rate.

     d.   Quarterly observations of inflation and unemployment plotted on a standard Phillips curve diagram (i.e., what do the "Phillips loops" look like and why).

2.   The relative size of the long-run growth rate of real GNP and the real rate of interest (q - r) was relevant for at least two issues in the course.   Identify the issues and explain what difference is made if q - r is positive or negative.

Part II (30 minutes)   Are the following questions true, false, or uncertain?   Explain your answer, using if possible the specific algebraic function or condition relevant to the question.

1.   Money is "super-neutral" when real balances appear in the consumption function, but not when real balances appear in the production function.

2.   A hyperinflation is made more likely, the larger is the absolute value of the interest-elasticity of the demand for real balances.

3.   "Portfolio crowding in" cannot occur if bonds and money are perfect substitutes.

4.   When the government budget constraint is taken into account, the multiplier for a fiscal stimulus financed by borrowing is greater than for a fiscal stimulus financed by money creation.

Part III (30 minutes)   Answer the following.

Consider the following rational expectations model of the labor and product markets.   (NOTE: Constants are eliminated by working with variables defined as deviations from their equilibrium values.   Hence equilibrium values for all variables used in the model are zero.)

$$(1) \quad Q_t^s = aN_t + e_t \qquad \text{(Production function)}$$

$$(2) \quad M_t - P_t = Q_t^d - v_t \qquad \text{(Quantity theory)}$$

$$(3) \quad Q_t^s = Q_t^d = Q_t \qquad \text{(Goods market clears)}$$

$$(4) \quad N_t^d = -b(W_t - P_t) \qquad \text{(Labor demand)}$$

$$(5) \quad N_t^s = c(W_t - {}_{t-1}EP_t) \qquad \text{(Labor supply, } {}_{t-1}EP_t \text{ is the}$$
$$\text{rational expectation of } P_t \text{ at t-1)}$$

$$(6) \quad N_t^d = N_t^s = N_t \qquad \text{(Labor market clears)}$$

1. Use these equations to show that the model includes a "Lucas supply function."

2. Use the whole model to show that only unanticipated money, not anticipated money, affects Q_t.

3. Now change equations (4) and (5) slightly to read:

$$(4') \quad N_t^d = -b(W_t - {}_{t-1}EP_t), \text{ and}$$

$$(5') \quad N_t^s = c(W_t - P_t).$$

4. Explain the difference between (4), (5) and (4'), (5') in words. What is at issue here? Which set is more plausible?

5. Use the new model to derive the effects of anticipated and unanticipated money on Q_t (assume c<1). Explain your conclusion.

Part IV (30 minutes) Write a beautifully coherent essay on one of the following:

1. "It is misleading to analyze the impact of supply shocks by taking nominal GNP growth to be exogenous. In fact there are numerous channels by which an increase in the price of OPEC oil can influence the growth rate of nominal GNP, holding constant the growth rate of domestic high-powered money and the natural employment Federal surplus."

2. Explain the relationships among the policy ineffectiveness debate and each of the following concepts:

    a. customer markets.

    b. idiosyncratic exchange.

    c. conjectural equilibrium.

University of California, Los Angeles
MONEY FIELD (2nd YEAR)

Econ 261—Graduate   Earl A. Thompson

ANSWER ANY FIVE.

1. (a) Derive Say's Law for a perfectly competitive monetary system.

    (b) Show that the classian's dichotomy between the real and monetary
         sectors of the economy holds in this perfectly competitive system.

    (c) Describe and debunk Patinkin's argument on the invalidity of such
         dichotomies.

2. (a) Under what conditions does an infinite horizon perfectly competitive
         economy without financial assets admit the Samuelson-Malinvaud
         dynamics inefficiency?

    (b) Why does the inefficiency disappear when privately, competitively
         supplied financial instruments are allowed?

    (c) Do these financial instruments have the property of money? How
         are they identified in the real world?

3. (a) What is the stock-flow fallacy in Keynesian thought?

    (b) Given that we do not want a short-run model with an equilibrating
         rate of inflation, how does the fallacy change the nature of the
         "commodity market" in the standard Keynesian model?

    (c) How is the bond market treated in the Keynesian model and how is
         it an incomplete representation of short term asset ownership?

    (d) Given the neoclassical production theory and one-commodity nature
         of the Keynesian production model, how should the completed bond
         market behave and how does this alter Keynesian conclusions?

4. (a) Why is the money supply in a modern, fixed, money-supply model
         statistically efficient?

    (b) What would happen if it were through deflation, attempted to be
         made statistically efficient?

5. Compare the statistical and dynamic efficiency of a modern, Keynesian
    money system, a competitive gold standard, and a competitive, fiat
    money system.

6. Present an FF-IM description of the major U.S. business fluctuations
    of the post World War II and explain why interest rates are now declining.

7. (a) Describe the basic rational expectations approach to macroeconomics.

    (b) How does the assumption of rational expectations, together with the
         ability of policy makers to <u>sometimes</u> acquire relevant information
         before the least informed laborers, lend support to interventionist
         policy?

University of California, Los Angeles

MONETARY THEORY

Ph.D. Qualifying Examination   Earl A. Thompson
Department of Economics, UCLA   Fall 1980

I. SAY'S LAW AND BUSINESS CYCLES

   Derive Say's Law for a perfectly competitive monetary system. Does the
   Law imply the absence of booms and recessions? How does the Law aid our
   understanding of business cycles in a gold-standard system?

II. THE NATURE OF EMPLOYMENT CYCLES

   A. Explain how inefficient aggregate employment fluctuations can occur in
      competitive economies with rational individuals and costless recontracting,
      identifying the appropriate source of market failure.

   B. What kind of "equilibrium" model can you use to derive this inefficient
      employment on an equilibrium outcome?

   C. How does the use of such an equilibrium model enable you to derive an
      optimal countercyclical policy?

III. NON-INTEREST BEARING, FIAT MONEY SYSTEMS

   A. Explain why a positive equilibrium price, of a non-interest bearing,
      always positively supplied, inconvertible paper money is impossible
      under perfect foresight and a finite horizon. What possibilities
      emerge under an infinite horizon?

   B. Suppose there is an infinite horizon, stationary economy with a constant
      supply of such money and a stationary equilibrium price path. Explain
      how an infinity of other, hyperinflationary price paths also equilibrate
      this system as long as the demand for money is not bounded away from zero.

   C. What characteristics of observed fiat money systems prevent the horrors
      suggested above? What has historically happened to monies that lose
      this characteristic?

ECON 202C—Graduate Macroeconomics
Final Exam

Earl A. Thompson
Spring 1980

I. Answer <u>Both</u> of the following questions.

1. <u>Classical Money Economies</u>

   (a) Outline a proof of Patinkin's proposition that real balances are indeterminate under a classical dichotomy between real and monetary sectors.

   (b) Why is the proof inappropriate in a classical money economy, one with competitive banking and convertibility of paper money into a real commodity?

   (c) How would you alter Patinkin's model to allow for these banking institutions and how would this alteration enable you to prove Say's Law, the classical dichotomy, and the determinancy of real cash balances in a perfectly competitive monetary system?

   (d) Finally, how does a classical dichotomy help you in analyzing the pre-1934 history of business cycles? Be Careful.

2. <u>The Keynesian Model</u>

   (a) Evaluate the logical underpinnings of the Keynesian commodity and bond markets, repairing any errors that you may find.

   (b) If you have made any substantial repairs, does the repaired model enable you to explain empirical regularities that contradict the standard Keynesian model? Explain.

II. Answer any three of the following five questions.

3. <u>Rational Expectations.</u> Does the assumption of "rational expectations" employed in recent macroeconomic models lead to an argument for or against the use of countercyclical economic policy? Explain fully.

4. <u>The Reason for Cyclical Unemployment</u>

   (a) Contrast the "confusion" theory of unemployment with the "contract" theory.

   (b) Outline a test of these theories.

   (c) How does the confusion theory enable you to represent Keynesian unemployment as equilibrium unemployment in a general, temporary equilibrium model?

5. (a) What is the short-run effect of a fall in the expected rate of inflation on the nominal rate of interest?

   (b) What is the recent drop in interest rates following the fall in expected inflation rates evidence for this result?

   (c) Why does the short-run effect differ from the long-run effect?

2

6. What is the effect of an increase in the propensity to save on the price level and nominal interest rate in a true savings-investment equilibrium?

7. Compare the efficiencies, both static and dynamic, of

   (a) A modern Keynesian system

   (b) A competitive gold standard, and

   (c) A competitive fiat money system.

Econ 102–Undergraduate   MACRO THEORY   Earl A. Thompson
Midterm Exam

Answer any FOUR.

1. What is the effect on equilibrium national income of a tax–financed
    increase in government expenditures of one billion dollars assuming
    that planned investment remains unaffected? Explain.

2. Say the IS curve shifts to the right by one billion dollars. What is the
    effect on equilibrium income assuming that the slop of the IS curve is
    the same as the slope of the LM curve and the slope of the aggregate
    demand curve is the same as the slope of the aggregate supply curve?

3. Rationalize Keynes' policy recommendation for an economy in a liquidity
    trap.

4. Suppose there is a shift out in the aggregate supply of labor as workers
    expect a lower price level. What is the effect of this shift on the
    equilibrium price level? Explain. What does the Keynesian theory imply?

5. What is the Gibson paradox and why is it a challenge to Keynesain theory?

Economics 262—Graduate   Earl A. Thompson
Monetary Economics (2nd Year)

I. Optimal Monetary Institutions

    A. The American Colonies relied on government produced, fiat money in
        the eighteenth century and, as a result, had much more price and
        employment stability than England, who relied on a metallic monetary
        standard and a competitive banking system.

        1. Briefly explain why this would occur.

        2. Why might it have been efficient for the U.S. to switch to
            an English—type system anyways?

        3. The U.S. missed the possibility of a competitive banking system
            backed by a fiat money. Why was this an error and why do you
            suppose it would have occurred?

II. Explain the following historical incidents:

    A. China, who was on the silver standard in the early 1930's, suffered
        no depression.

    B. "Greenbacks," the fiat currency issued by the Union in the U.S.
        Civil War, rose sharply in price at the end of the war while the
        Confederate issue fell to near zero.

    C. The U.S. stock market boomed just prior to the Great Depression.

III. What empirical regularities can you explain with a correct macro model
      that you cannot explain with a Keynesian model?

Claremont Graduate School

Ph.D. Qualifying Examination

Monetary Analysis

Mr. Willett and   Spring 1981
Mr. Bradford

Instructions:

Answer question 1, either 2 or 3, and either 4 or 5, for a total of three questions. Both readers will grade all questions.

1. A. Please briefly discuss the major factors influencing the costs of ending inflation and the costs of not ending inflation.

   B. In light of these and any other considerations which you wish to bring in, please recommend and critically analyze a strategy for determining the optimal (or at least a good) time path for the money supply in the United States over the next two decades.

2. Please discuss the major factors likely to influence the comparative inflationary effects of systems of pegged and flexible exchange rates.

3. Please critically analyze the following statement:

    "Those who argue that wage push is an important cause of inflation generally adopt a sociologically determined non-maximizing approach to economic behavior. In contrast both economic theory and the empirical evidence strongly suggest that wage push has not been a significant cause of inflation."

4. From the basic model of Barro and Grossman back to some of Patinkin's work in the 1940's and probably back to the early quantity theorists, there has been a tendency to construct monetary theory in abstraction from consideration of any alternative store of value. In contrast, James Tobin, Milton Friedman, and Patinkin in Money, Interest and Prices have emphasized asset portfolio substitution between money and alternatives (which bear at least implicit rates of return). Please write an essay which carefully assesses the issues which can validly be treated in terms of the simpler model(s), as opposed to those which require at least one asset for which money can be traded.

5. Derive the supply of money as a function of "the" market interest rate and monetary policy parameters. The basis of the model should be the asset choice behavior of banks and the private non-bank sector. Include borrowing of reserves from the central bank, and comment on how this is related to the federal funds rate. What difference does it make whether the monetary base is defined to include borrowed reserves? What is the effect in your model of a change in the interest ceiling on deposits?

Claremont Graduate School

Ph.D. Qualifying Examination

Monetary Analysis

Mr. Willett
Mr. Bradford

Three hour limit
Fall 1980

Instructions: Answer any three of the following four
questions, based on Economics 331, 332 and/or 274, or
general knowledge of the field. Both readers will
grade all questions.

1.   After several months of very low and sometimes
negative rates of U.S. monetary growth, a very rapid
increase was recently reported. In apparent response
interest rates rose. a) How would this be explained
from a monetarist perspective? b) from a Keynesian
perspective?

In the following period the rate of monetary
growth fell and following the reporting of these sta-
tistics so did interest rates. Again please offer
possible explanations from both (c) monetarist and
(d) Keynesian perspectives. (You may be interested
to know that a Keynesian variety of interpretation
was given in the L.A. Times financial page).

In your answer you should be sure to indicate
your particular meanings of monetarist and Keynesian
perspectives in this context. These meanings should
be reasonable in light of the literature, but you need
not attempt to cover all possible varieties of monetarist and Keynesian perspectives.

2.   Please critically discuss the following statement. "Monetary and macroeconomic analysis and
policy has been revolutionized over the past decade.
No longer can issues of inflation and unemployment
be reasonably discussed in terms of any particular
national economy alone. The major determinant today
of the macroeconomic developments in any particular
country is not national monetary and fiscal policies,
but the state of the world economy."

3.   Write an essay to explain in some detail exactly
what difference it makes, to macroeconomics and monetary theory, for each of the following to be regarded
as an exogenous policy parameter; consider at least one
important aspect of each separately, then inter-relate
them to whatever extent you can:

1. A representative rate of interest
2. Some well-defined stock of money
3. Some well-defined monetary base
4. (Not required for a passing answer, but an
   interesting extension) The level of some
   "reaction function" describing behavior of
   the monetary authority in response to the
   economic environment.

4.   Any conclusion we might reach about the interaction
between real and monetary phenomena will depend (at some
point in its development) on how we view the demand for
money. Compare and contrast the formal implications of
the following analyses:

1. Transactions costs involving the interest-
   bearing alternative to money
2. Uncertainty about capital gains or losses on
   the interest-bearing alternative to money
3. A model of a somewhat varied menu of interest-
   bearing alternatives to money.

Claremont Graduate School

Ph.D. Qualifying Examination in Monetary Analysis

Mr. Willett   Three hour limit
Mr. Bradford   Spring 1980

INSTRUCTIONS: Answer any three of the following four questions.
Both readers will grade all questions.

1.   While the original monetarist-Keynesian debate focused heavily
on the relative strength of monetary and fiscal policy, much of the
current policy debate between these groups focused on the desir-
ability of discretionary fine tuning versus steady as you go macro
policies and the nature of inflation-unemployment relationships.
Please briefly explain and critically evaluate these differences
in view and indicate to what extent the differences in policy recom-
mendations are due to differences in a) normative views about
values, and b) positive views about empirical relationships. Please
also indicate to what extent differences in the time horizon taken
for analysis may be important.

2.   Please discuss critically the following statement: "We can
analyze world inflation in terms of the demand and supply of
international liquidity (official reserves) in the same way that
we analyze national inflation in terms of the demand and supply of
money for that country."

3.   Banks and other financial intermediaries are often analyzed
more or less by analogy to firms which produce physical output.
Discuss this, both on the level of the individual entity as a profit maximizer and on the market level. Include the effects of
constraints such as required reserves and deposit interest ceilings,
to be contrasted to unrestricted competitiion. To what extent may
the supply of money as a function of the rate of interest be considered analogous to the supply of an ordinary output as a function
of its relative price? To what extent would static optimality
properties of pure competition be relevant to a hypothetical regime
of money(s) issued entirely by private agents, as opposed to the
actual "national monopoly" case?

4.   In monetary theory, use is often made of one or both of two
metaphors: money is an argument in the household's utility function
or money is an argument in the firm's production function. Discuss
In some detail the rationale for both of these approaches. At least
in passing, show the relevance to controversies in monetary growth
theory. Discuss the relevance (if any) of these metaphors to
(i) a utility function of present and future consumption, with
money the only instrument by which to defer consumption to the
future and (ii) a utility function of risk and expected return
associated with the whole portfolio.

-38-

Claremont Graduate School
Ph.D. Qualifying Examination in Monetary Analysis

Mr. Meigs   Fall 1979
Mr. Willett
Mr. Bradford

Instructions:

Answer either 1 or 2, and any two of 3, 4, and 5. The main
responsibility for grading questions 3, 4, and 5 will lie with
Bradford, Willett and Meigs respectively. To whatever extent
a question may seem too broad to be answered precisely, supply
specific assumptions which will improve precision.

1.   Within the time constraint, provide as much detail as possible
to show your understanding of the process(es) by which a change in
monetary policy makes itself felt (or tell why it doesn't) in terms
of employment, interest rates, and money prices and wages. A
strong answer will recognize the current problems which policy
makers face, not just construct a textbook model. Attention to the
international environment should not be forgotten. Always distinguish between a temporal sequence of events, based on your
explanation of lags in the structure of the economy, and a causal
relationship which your arguments can support.

2.   Please discuss the major strengths and weaknesses and difficulties in implementing the following four monetary strategies aimed
at holding relatively constant
        (a)   nominal interest rates
        (b)   real interest rates
        (c)   the rate of growth of the nominal money supply
        (d)   the rate of growth of the real money supply

3.   Sketch the classes of issues in monetary theory which depend
crucially on expectations (say held with unanimity and certainty)
about future prices and/or interest rates. Then compare and
contrast the refinements which make sense only (a) when the
(certain) expectations of different economic agents are not in
agreement, as opposed to (b) when there is a subjective probability distribution for each individual concerning possible future
states. This question is intended to stimulate your originality
in thinking of extensions from conventional theory, as much as to
see whether you can remember class lectures.

4. Some have claimed that oil price increases are inflationary while others have claimed that they are deflationary.
    (a) Please explain and attempt to reconcile these views.
    (b) To what extent will similar effects occur in the case of an exchange rate depreciation?
    (c) Please discuss the major factors which will influence the magnitude of the effects of commodity and import price increases on a country's price level and unemployment rate.

5. Monetarists assert that changes in growth rates of nominal money stock cause nominal incomes and prices to change in the same direction with various time lags. This implies that changes in money stock are a principal determinant of inflations and fluctuations in business activity in the United States and other countries. Critics of this view argue that the observed correlations between money stock changes and changes in incomes and prices reflect instead the influence of income changes on the money stock. Explain the channels of transmission through which income could influence the money stock in a country with a central bank and a money stock defined as bank deposits and currency held by the nonbank public. What could a central bank do to reduce the influence of income on money stock?

Claremont Graduate School
Ph.D. Qualifying Examinations

Spring 1979

Monetary Analysis

Answer each of the three questions. Both readers will grade all
questions, but Bradford will have the main responsibility for
question 1 and Willett for question 3. To whatever extent a question may seem too broad to be answered precisely, supply specific
assumptions which will improve precision.

1.   Any conclusion we might reach about the interaction between
real and monetary phenomena will depend (at some point in its development) on how we view the demand for money. Each of the following
has provided some path-breaking perspective on that:

    a) Keynes in the 1930's
    b) Baumol, Tobin and Patinkin in the 1950's
    c) Friedman, whose ideas are finally becoming prominent
        in the 1970's.

Compare and contrast these three perspectives in detail. Consider
not only substance, as it has been or will be incorporated in
textbooks, but also something of the historical interaction with
precursors, critics and imitators. In particular, how much is the
Monetarist Revolution like the Keynesian Revolution? To what extent do either or both displace, and to what extent make way for,
a "neoclassical synthesis?"

2.   In recent years there has been a resurgence of attention to
the effects of inflationary expectations in influencing inflation-
unemployment relationships and the effects of government policies.
Please pick three of the following cases and discuss in each of them
the differences it would make depending on which of two different
specifications of expectations formation were assumed to hold.
Please do not use the same two sets of assumptions in all three of
your answers (i.e, you should have considered at least three different specifications for expectations formation in total) and
please use the concept of rational expectations at least once.

(continued on next page)

a. The effects on IS-LM models or generalizations thereof, via interest rates;

b. The costs of using deflationary macroeconomic policies to reduce the current rate of inflation in the United States;

c. The effects of following more expansionary macroeconomic policies in a situation in which both the rates of inflation and of unemployment are high;

d. The incentives for governments to generate political business cycles in order to gain votes;

e. The full inflationary effects of an exchange-rate depreciation;

f. The case for retaining the discretionary use of monetary policy versus adopting a monetary rule.

3.   A. In what major ways may international monetary developments (for example, international financial flows, exchange rate and balance of payments changes and developments in the Eurodollar market) have effects on monetary conditions and inflation-unemployment relationships in the United States? To what extent do you think such open economy considerations have undercut the ability of the monetary authorities to control the economy over the past decade? To what extent have such considerations merely made good policy making more complicated? Can you think of circumstances in which open economy considerations would reduce domestic macroeconomic problems, at least in the short run?

B. To what extent, if any, would you need to revise your answers to part A if you had been asked to consider these questions from the standpoint of a small European country rather than the United States?

PhD Core Examination

THEORY OF INCOME

Winter 1981

Write in <u>black ink</u> and write on only <u>one side</u> of each page.

Write the following information on the <u>first page</u> of your examination paper:

> --name of examination
> --date of examination
> --your code number and <u>not</u> your name

Write the following information on <u>each page</u> of your examination paper:

> --upper left: code number
> --upper right: number of page

When you fold your paper at the end of the exam, write your code number on the back of the last page, and indicate total number of pages.

Results of the examination will be sent to you by letter.

ANSWER ALL QUESTIONS   TIME: THREE HOURS

I. (60 points--6 points each)
Indicate whether each of the following statements is TRUE, FALSE, or UNCERTAIN. Justify your answer briefly.

1. In measuring the quantity of "money" we aggregate (with appropriate weights) nickels and $100 bills. This is warranted because nickels and $100 bills are nearly perfect substitutes.

2. While the monetary authority determines the <u>nominal</u> quantity of money, the private sector determines its <u>real</u> value.

3. If the demand for money is semi-logarithmic (i.e., of the form used by P. Cagan), the revenue maximizing rates of monetary expansion and inflation are independent of the rate of growth of income.

4. Differences in international rates of interest on securities that are identical in all respects (except for the currency of denomination) indicate impediments to international capital movements.

5. The natural rate of unemployment is achieved whenever the expected and actual rates of inflation coincide.

I. (continued)

6. Since all banks now pay interest on both checking and savings accounts, the supply of money moves in the same direction as do interest rates.

7. Productivity growth in the U.S. in the 1970s was much lower than it was during the 1960s. This explains most of the difference in U.S. inflation rates between these two decades.

8. The removal of regulations mandating automobile safety devices (for example, seat belts) would increase both the level and rate of growth of measured, real GNP.

9. The existence of personal income tax implies that the equilibrium difference between the nominal and the real rates of interest exceeds the rate of inflation.

10. Since banks and automobile manufacturers are both simply private corporations, there is no more reason for government policy to be concerned with the liabiliti of banks (demand deposits) than with the liabilities of automobile manufacturers

II. (30 points)

Consider the following simple macroeconomic model.

$$y = c + i + g \qquad \text{[Income-expenditure identity]}$$

$$c = f(y(1 - t)) \qquad \text{[Consumption function]}$$

$$i = g(y,r) \qquad \text{[Investment function]}$$

$$\frac{M}{P} = L(y,r) \qquad \text{[Money demand function]}$$

$$y = F(n) \qquad \text{[Production function]}$$

$$\frac{W}{P} = F'(n) \qquad \text{[Labor demand]}$$

$$S(\frac{W}{P}) = n \qquad \text{[Labor supply]}$$

(i) In this model (with all variables given their usual interpretation) can an increase in the tax rate t increase tax revenues ty? Prove your answer.

(ii) Now replace the labor supply curve with the assumption that money wages are fixed at W_o. Answer question (i) under this alternative assumption.

III. (30 points)

As one of the means to reduce the welfare cost of inflation it has been
suggested that nominal balances should earn interest equal to the nominal
interest rate in the economy. Assume an economy that is growing along a
steady state growth path in which the government adopts the policy of
paying interest on money holdings and finances these payments by lump-sum
taxation. Assume that the utility function of individuals depends on the
rate of consumption and on the holdings of real cash balances, that the
subjective rate of discount and the rate of growth of population are constant
and that the production function is of constant returns to scale. Also assume
that individuals maximize the discounted stream of utility subject to a budget
constraint.

(i) What will be the effect of this policy on the elasticity of the demand
for real balances with respect to the rate of inflation?

(ii) Will the policy result in the (socially) optimal quantity of money?

Explain your answers in detail.

IV. (25 points)

Below is a chart of the yield curve on U.S. Government securities as measured
on various dates since January 15, 1980.

(i) Discuss the concept of the yield curve and the theories underlying the
determinants of its shape.

(ii) Analyze the changes in the shape of the yield curves which took place
between January 15, 1980 and January 15, 1981 and discuss in detail
the causes for these changes.

Yields on U.S. Government Securities

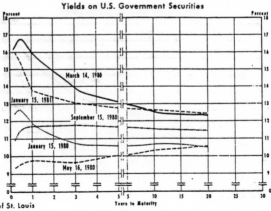

V. (15 points)

"It was the failure of government policies which should be held responsible
for the decline in real income which followed the rise in the price of imported oil. A full indexation of wages to the price index would have
prevented the fall in real income. Furthermore, interventions in the foreign
exchange markets made things worse: a free flexible exchange rate regime
would have insulated the economy from the foreign price shocks." Discuss.

VI. (20 points)

(i) Define the term "automatic (fiscal) stabilizer" and discuss the potential
role of automatic stabilizers in reducing real output variability over
the business cycle.

(ii) Specify what is meant by an "indexed" tax structure. What effect
would indexing the tax structure have on stability in the sense of
part (i)?

Ph.D. Core Examination

THEORY OF INCOME, EMPLOYMENT AND THE PRICE LEVEL

Summer 1980

Write in black ink and write on only one side of each page.

Write the following information on the first page of your exam paper:

- Name of Examination

- Date of Examination

- Your Code Number and NOT your name

Write the following information on each page of your examination paper:

- Upper left: Code Number

- Upper right: Number of the page

Do NOT fold your exam--paper clips will be provided. Write your code number on the back of the last page and indicate the total number of pages.

Results of the examination will be sent to you by letter.

Answer all questions.   Time: Three hours.   Maximum Score: 177 points.

I. TRUE-FALSE-UNCERTAIN (72 points - 6 points each)

1. If consumption is proportional to permanent income and expectations are posited to be rational, then the response of consumption to an unexpected change in income will be proportional to the amount by which the unexpected change in income alters expectations about permanent income.

2. While a temporary reduction in income taxes may not affect private consumption expenditures, a temporary investment tax credit will increase private investment outlays.

3. According to the permanent income theory of consumption, the multiplier for autonomous spending will be larger in an economy of civil servants with tenure than in an economy with only a spot market for labor.

4. A stationary economy with constant real income and constant real money supply has a flat yield curve if expectations are rational; that is, bonds of all maturities have the same interest rate.

5. If the commercial banks do not profit from inflationary finance, then the inflation tax on deposit money will be paid by borrowers from rather than lenders to the commercial banking system.

I. TRUE-FALSE-UNCERTAIN (continued)

6. Permitting banks to pay interest on demand deposits will reduce the rate of inflation (holding constant the rate of increase of central bank liabilities).

7. In an open economy with a fixed exchange rate, one expects that money and credit will be uncorrelated (at least in terms of deviations from their respective trends).

8. The demand for money cannot be elastic throughout the relevant range.

9. Suppose that interest elasticity of money demand is zero. In an IS-LM framework, a decrease in personal income taxes would lead to an increase in consumption which is matched by decreases in investment and private savings.

10. When the interest elasticity of money demand is zero, the central bank should peg the money supply rather than the interest rate, if it desires to minimize the variance of income.

11. The procyclical behavior of output-per-manhour or the tendency of time series production functions to display constant or slightly increasing returns to labor is inconsistent with diminishing returns to employment.

12. If a gift of domestic government bonds to domestic residents does not increase perceived net wealth (since individuals discount the implied tax liabilities), then by the same token a gift of domestic government bonds to foreign residents implies a decline in perceived net wealth by domestic residents.

II. (15 points)

Professor Arthur Laffer has recently argued that an increase in required commercial bank reserves is actually inflationary as it reduces the "quality" of money (i.e., the banks can provide fewer services to depositors) and hence the demand for real cash balances.

Analyze the above argument. Do you agree with it?

III. (20 points)

It is widely observed that the cyclical elasticity of output with respect to employment exceeds unity. The observation is also reflected in "Okun's Law".

(a) Indicate what reason(s) might account for the observation that the above elasticity exceeds labor's (distributive) share.

(b) How do you account for the related observation that unemployment and employment are not perfectly (and negatively) correlated?

IV. (20 points)

In 1980 American Express will announce a plan for selling dated 6-months travellers' checks at less than face value. Answer the following:

   (i) Present a theoretical analysis of the demand for such checks. What factors would determine the equilibrium price of such checks?

  (ii) How would the availability of these new American Express checks affect the amount of currency the public wants to hold?

 (iii) How would the availability of the checks affect the Treasury bill market?

V. (25 points)

Suppose that at the end of each period a person must make a cash payment of size x, where x is a random variable with density f(x). At the beginning of each period, the person decides to hold an amount of cash M, which can be used to make payments at the end of the period. If the required payment x is greater than M, the person must borrow x-M at interest rate i per period. Let r be the opportunity cost of holding a dollar of cash for one period. Assume that f(x) is symmetric and single-peaked so that the mean equals the median (for example, the normal distribution).

  (a) If r is greater than i, what is the optimal cash holding? Why?

  (b) Under what circumstances will the person set his cash balance M equal to the expected value of the cash payment x?

     - When will M exceed the expected value of x?

     - When will M be less than the expected value of x?

  (c) How does the optimal value of M respond to an increase in r? to an increase in i?

  (d) Suppose that r and i increase by the same absolute amount. What is the effect on the optimal value of M?

VI. (25 points)

In Great Britain there is serious policy debate concerning the appropriate policy response to the "problem" of the North Sea oil, which is not only substituting for Britain's normal oil imports, but also threatens to add significantly to Britain's exports over the next decade. The North Sea oil has led to a sharp rise in the value of the pound and is jeopardizing existing producers of tradeable goods.

  (a) What effect would you expect the North Sea oil to have on internal relative prices in Great Britain?

  (b) What, if any, monetary measures would you suggest that would affect the exchange rate in such a way as to "protect" existing industry?

  (c) Are there any fiscal measures that might be taken to weaken the effect of the North Sea oil on existing producers of tradeables? If so, what?

Ph.D. Core Examination

THEORY OF INCOME

Winter, 1980

Write in <u>black</u> <u>ink</u> and write on only <u>one</u> <u>side</u> of each page.

Write the following information on the <u>first</u> <u>page</u> of your exam paper:
- Name of Examination
- Date of Examination
- Your Code Number and <u>NOT</u> your name

Write the following information on <u>each</u> <u>page</u> of your examination paper:
- Upper left: Code Number
- Upper right: Number of the page

Do <u>NOT</u> fold your exam -- paper clips will be provided. Write your code number on the back of the last page and indicate the total number of pages.

Results of the examination will be sent to you by letter.

Answer <u>all</u> questions.   Time: Three hours.

I. True-False-Uncertain (60 points - 6 points each)

1. Since gold purchased for store-of-value purposes costs the same as gold purchased for dental or jewelry use, it must be the case that its price is dictated by real, not monetary considerations.

2. Assuming that changes in aggregate output depend only on <u>unexpected</u> changes in the money supply, then changes in the price level would depend only on <u>expected</u> changes in the money supply.

3. Assume that an increase in the real price of common stocks tends to increase real consumption. Then a rise in interest rates tends to increase savings.

4. The permanent income hypothesis indicates that a temporary reduction in sales taxes will have only a very small effect on consumption.

5. As more banks leave the Federal Reserve System, the System loses control over a corresponding portion of the money supply.

6. If the Fed would allow interest rates to fluctuate freely in response to supply and demand conditions in the money market, this would reduce the fluctuations in the price of the US dollar in terms of foreign currencies.

I. True-False-Uncertain (continued)

7. An increase in the Federal deficit accompanied by an equal increase in Federal Reserve holdings of government bonds does not increase the money supply.

8. If rational expectations are adaptive, then expectations cannot be rational.

9. Eurodollars refer to deposits denominated in US dollars that are held in European banks. An increase in the stock of Eurodollars tends to raise the dollar prices of internationally traded goods to the extent there is no offsetting decrease in the stock of dollars held in US banks.

10. An implication of rational expectations is that official announcements of policy changes are more important than the policies themselves.

II. (20 points)

Assume that the Federal Reserve Board announced that from now on they would maintain a constant stock of money in nominal terms. Discuss the consequences of this policy for the price level, interest rates, and the foreign trade balance. Would it make a difference if simultaneously there were a constitutional amendment that requires a balanced Federal budget for each fiscal year?

III. (20 points)

Discuss how both of the following policies would affect the cyclical behavior of the money supply.

(i) A Federal Reserve Board policy of attempting to maintain a Federal Funds rate target.

(ii) An international regime of fixed exchange rates.

IV. (35 points)

There are two securities A and B with positive expected returns r_A and r_B, respectively. Security A is a risk-free security with no possible capital gains or losses, while security B has an uncertain return with variance, σ^2. Assume a utility function which depends only on mean and variance to analyze the consumer's choice of portfolio where: A = proportion of the portfolio held in security A, $1 - A$ = proportion of the portfolio held in security B and $0 \leq A \leq 1$.

(i) Exhibit the optimal level of A on an indifference curve diagram.

(ii) Find the necessary conditions for diversification, i.e., $0 < A < 1$.

IV. (continued)

(iii) Assuming diversification, what will happen to the optimal level of A if r_A increases, with everything else unchanged?

(iv) What will happen to the optimal level of A if security A's return is untaxed and security B's return is taxed at a 50% rate with a full loss offset provision? (I.e., if there is a loss on holding security B, the government returns 50% of the loss.)

V. (45 points)

Consider a two-period, competitive economy with identical consumers, each of which values current and future consumption, c and c', and current and future labor supply, n, and n', according to the utility function

$$c + a^2 \ln(1 - n) + bc' + ba^2 \ln(1 - n')$$

where a and b are both between zero and one. The technology is such that n units of labor supplied produces n units of the (non-storable) consumption good.

There is a real government expenditure of x which must be met in the first period, so that society's first-period resource constraint is

$$c + x \le n .$$

In the second period, government expenditures are zero, so that the resource constraint is

$$c' \le n' .$$

The only financing possibilities are a flat rate income tax of t in the first period, with $tn = x$ or a tax of t in the first period, with a deficit of $y = x - tn > 0$ with a tax of t' in the second period to retire the debt, at the equilibrium interest rate r, or $t'n' = (1+r)y$. This question is concerned with the consequences of alternative financing methods.

(i) Find equilibrium labor supply (and output) in the first period as a function of the tax rate t in that period.

(ii) Find the maximum real revenues which can be raised by an income tax. (Assume in what follows that x is below this level).

(iii) If a positive debt y is incurred, what are the equilibrium interest rate r and future tax rate t' which are implied?

(iv) Given x, utility is maximized by a policy which equates t and t'. Explain why this is so.

(v) If this optimum policy is initiated in the current period, and if the future period legislature has the option of repudiating the debt, what is the utility-maximizing decision for this future legislature?

V. (continued)

   (vi) If the exercise of this option is correctly foreseen by the current
         period legislature and consumers, what financing policy will result?

   Hint: If you run into trouble with the specific example given, try to supply
         the best qualitative discussion of the issues raised in (i)-(vi) as you
         can.

Ph.D. Core Examination

THEORY OF INCOME

Summer, 1979

Write in black ink and write on only one side of each page.

Write the following information on the first page of your exam paper:

-Name of Examination

-Date of Examination

-Your Code Number and NOT your name

Write the following information on each page of your examination paper:

- Upper left: Code Number
- Upper right: Number of the page

Do NOT fold your exam-- paper clips will be provided. Write your code number on the back of the last page and indicate the total number of pages.

Results of the examination will be sent to you by letter.

_____

Answer all questions.   Time: Three hours.

I. True-False-Uncertain   (75 points)

1. If the interest elasticity of money demand is zero, the LM curve will be vertical and the income velocity of money will be constant.

2. The "natural" rate of unemployment is that rate which will prevail when the price level is stable and expected to remain stable.

3. Under a fixed exchange rate regime, the central bank cannot control the quantity of money, but it can control the magnitude of its own liabilities (i.e., the monetary base).

4. In an IS-LM framework in which money demand depends upon the nominal interest rate and investment depends on the real interest rate, an increase in the expected rate of inflation increases output.

5. Even though the stock demand for real cash balances presumably responds inversely to the rate of inflation, the real flow demand for those balances is positively related to that rate.

6. The "optimum" quantity of money will be achieved if the monetary authorities act to hold the nominal quantity of money constant.

7. In the absence of reserve requirements, the central bank could not control the money supply, even under flexible exchange rates.

8. An increase in the real rate of interest can cause either an increase or a decrease in saving as a fraction of national income.

9. An autonomous reduction in money demand (caused by an innovation in transactions technology, for example) will shift the aggregate domestic demand schedule for output to the left.

10. If expectations were rational, short-run movements in nominal and real cash balances would be uncorrelated.

11. The theory of monopoly indicates that if the central bank were to be privately owned (without regulation by the government), the managers of that bank would choose a rate of inflation at which the demand for money was elastic with respect to the rate of inflation.

12. The effect of an increase in the nominal rate of interest on production costs and hence the price level will be proportional to capital's distributive share of output.

II. (20 points)

The Republic of Panama has no monetary authority, and the U.S. dollar is the medium of exchange. Deposits and local loans are denominated in the Panamanian unit of account (the Balboa) but, apart from coins, the Balboa has no physical existence. The exchange rate between the Balboa and the U.S. dollar is fixed at unity.

   a) What determines the real and nominal quantities of money in Panama?

   b) Do you see any connection between the quantity of money and the supply of bank credit in Panama?

   c) What generalizations can you make about the behavior of the net foreign assets of such a banking system? Do they apply to all fixed exchange rate regimes?

III. (30 points)

Let: M_t be the nominal stock of money at time t;
        P_t be the aggregate price level at time t;
        $m_t = \frac{M}{P}$ be the real stock of money at time t; and
        m_t^* be the desired stock of real money at time t.

Suppose that the demand for real cash balances is given by:

$$\ln m_t^* = \alpha + \beta \ln y_t, \tag{1}$$

and that there is a lagged adjustment of real balances so that:

$$\ln m_t - \ln m_{t-1} = \gamma (\ln m_t^* - \ln m_{t-1}). \tag{2}$$

An estimated money demand equation is:

$$\ln m_t = 3.0 + 0.7 (\ln m_{t-1}) + 0.2 (\ln y_t).$$

a) What are the short-run and long-run income elasticities of money demand?

b) What is the speed of adjustment, γ ?

c) Suppose that we are in a steady-state growth economy (i.e., constant growth of real income, nominal money, and the price level). What rate of growth of the nominal money supply will hold inflation at zero?

d) Now suppose that instead of partial adjustment of <u>real</u> balances, there is partial adjustment of <u>nominal</u> balances, so that:

$$\ln M_t - \ln M_{t-1} = \lambda (\ln M_t^* - \ln M_{t-1}), \tag{3}$$

where M_t^* is determined from equation (1), taking P_t as given.

Show that:

$$\ln m_t = b_0 + b_1 \ln m_{t-1} + b_2 \ln y_t + b_3 \pi_t,$$

where $\pi_t = \ln P_t - \ln P_{t-1}.$

What are b_0, b_1, b_2, and b_3 in terms of α, β, and λ ?

e) Suppose now that the estimated equation is:

$$\ln m_t = 3.0 + 0.7 (\ln m_{t-1}) + 0.2 (\ln y_t) - 0.7 \pi_t .$$

What evidence does this equation provide about the elasticity of money demand with respect to the rate of inflation?

IV. (15 points)

In an open, fixed-exchange rate economy, the equilibrium price level
is proportional to the external prices of traded goods. Does it
follow that, for all countries pegging to the U.S. dollar, the recent
increase in the OPEC price of crude petroleum will lead to a permanent
increase in the price level?

V. (25 points)

Consider a small economy with a central bank. Assume that the monetary
system is such that there is a stable money multiplier. There are
three models of central bank policy that you should consider:

a) when international reserves increase, the central
bank should behave in such a way as to cause a corresponding increase in the domestic credit provided
by the banking system.

b) when international reserves increase, the central bank
should behave in such a way as to cause an exactly offsetting decrease in the domestic credit provided by the
banking system.

c) when international reserves increase, the central bank
should behave in such a way as to prevent any consequent change in domestic credit.

Give the rank ordering of these three rules for each of the following
institutional setups:

i) the country has traditionally maintained a fixed exchange
rate with the U.S. dollar, and expects to continue to do
so.

ii) the country has traditionally had inflation in excess of
that of the rest of the world, and has an exchange rate
that is indexed to its domestic price level.

iii) the country has a freely floating exchange rate.

Explain your ranking.

VI. (15 points)

A permanent rise in the ratio of saving to income can both increase the
rate of growth of consumption in the short run and reduce per capita
consumption in the long run. How do you resolve the apparent paradox?

Ph.D. Core Examination

THEORY OF INCOME

Winter 1979

Write in <u>black ink</u> and write on only <u>one side</u> of each page.

Write the following information on the <u>first page</u> of your exam paper:

- Name of Examination
- Date of Examination
- Your Code Number and <u>not</u> your name

Write the following information on <u>each page</u> of your examination paper:

- Upper left: Code Number
- Upper right: Number of page

When you fold your paper at the end of the examination, write your code number on the back of the last page, and indicate the total number of pages.

Results of the examination will be sent to you by letter.

Answer <u>all</u> questions.   Time: <u>Three Hours</u>.

I. [50 minutes]
Indicate whether each of the following statements is TRUE or FALSE. Briefly explain your answer.

1. In the quantity theory, the income elasticity of the demand for money is unity unless velocity depends on the rate of interest.

2. The inventory theory of transactions demand for money predicts that the quantity of money demanded will increase by less than the proportionate rise in income and therefore that the rate of inflation will exceed the rate of monetary expansion (ignoring growth of real output).

3. The stock market is a "leading indicator," which suggests that a cyclical downturn in stock prices discourages spending and helps produce a downturn in the economy.

4. The monetary rate of interest cannot be negative in a monetary economy.

5. The secular growth in the fraction of the labor force that is skilled is an automatic stabilizer of the business cycle because skilled labor has lower unemployment rates than unskilled labor.

6. A balanced budget increase in government spending does not contribute to inflationary pressures.

-58-

II. [20 minutes]
Consider an economy with externally imposed and stochastically fluctuating government expenditures (think of defense spending). What are the welfare issues involved in a comparison of two financing schemes:

a) a continuously balanced budget, with a flat rate income tax varying so that receipts equal expenditures;

b) a constant flat income tax rate, set so as to balance the budget on average, with government bonds issued (retired) to finance a deficit (surplus)?

III. [20 minutes]
Suppose banks could issue their own notes which could circulate and which they promise to exchange for Federal Reserve Notes on demand. How would this affect the velocity of Federal Reserve Notes?

IV. [25 minutes]
Consider a Cagan type demand for real money balances in log form:

(1) $$m_t - p_t = -\sigma\pi^*_t + u_t$$

where π^*_t is the expected rate of inflation between t and t+1 and u_t is a disturbance term that follows that process:

(2) $$u_t = au_{t-1} + \varepsilon_t; \quad |a| \leq 1$$

where ε_t is serially uncorrelated with zero mean.

Assume expectations about inflation are formed according to:

(3) $$\pi^*_t = \pi^*_{t-1} + b(\pi_{t-1} - \pi^*_{t-1})$$

where $\pi_t \equiv p_{t+1} - p_t$ is the actual rate of inflation between t and t+1.

Assume the money supply is constant at the level $m = \bar{m}$. You are asked to discuss whether and under what conditions the expectations formation process in (3) is rational.

V. [20 minutes]
Consider a "stabilization policy" which attempts to eliminate seasonal fluctuations in unemployment by expanding the money supply each year when schools close (summer) and contracting it in the fall. How would this policy affect the seasonal behavior of prices, interest rates, real output, unemployment and real balances?

VI. [15 minutes]
In either quarterly or annual U.S. time series, measured unemployment rates exhibit considerable positive serial correlation.

a) From what theoretical point of view does this observation
constitute a "puzzle"? Why?

b) How might this "puzzle" be resolved?

VII. [30 minutes]
Consider a two-commodity, three factor model of an economy with the
following properties: (i) there is a single mobile factor, labor,
which is used in the production of both commodities x and y, (ii) in
the short run, there are two specific factors, capital in x and
capital in y, which are used only in their respective industries,
and (iii) production functions are of constant returns to scale with
the usual properties and both goods are produced.

Assume that the economy is open to international trade and that the
relative price of x is exogenously raised. Analyze the effect of
this rise in price on

(i) the income of labor

(ii) the income of capital in x

(iii) the income of capital in y.

Ph. D. Core Examination

THEORY OF INCOME

Summer 1978

Write in <u>black ink</u> and write on only <u>one side</u> of each page.

Write the following information on the <u>first page</u> of your examination paper:

**Name of Examination   **Your code number and <u>not</u>
**Date of Examination   your name

Write the following information on <u>each page</u> of your examination paper.

** Upper left: Code Number   ** Upper right: Number of page

When you fold your paper at the end of the exam, write your code number on the back of the last page, and indicate the total number of pages.

Results of the examination will be sent to you by letter. Good luck.

ANSWER ALL QUESTIONS

Time: <u>THREE</u> HOURS

I.   (90 points)

Indicate whether each of the following statements is TRUE, FALSE or UNCERTAIN. Justify your answer briefly.

1. An implication of the permanent income hypothesis is that the 1974 increase in the world price of petroleum would have reduced the demand for complements of petroleum (e.g., automobiles) only if that price increase were expected to be permanent.

2. The Baumol-Tobin model of the demand for money implies that the (income) velocity of money is negatively related to income.

3. The Tobin mean-variance model cannot explain the speculative demand for M_1 because of the existence of savings accounts which have no risk yet pay a positive rate of interest.

4. If all government bonds were consols, there could be no burden of the public debt.

5. A once and for all rise in the price level increases the demand for nominal cash balances, but a continuous rise in the price level reduces the demand for real cash balances.

6. When banks are holding large amounts of excess reserves, an increase in the required reserve ratio would have little impact on the quantity of money.

7. Following neo-Classical growth theory, an increase in the rate of saving will only temporarily increase the rate of growth but may permanently reduce (per capital) consumption.

8. Under a 100 percent reserve requirement, the interest rate on demand deposits would be negative.

9. An implication of rational expectations in the bond market is that daily market price quotations would exhibit no serial correlation.

10. If banks were permitted to pay market-determined interest rates on all deposits, it would be impossible to use inflation as a tax because money holders could escape that tax by merely shifting from currency to deposits.

11. If an individual expects that a consol with a current yield of five percent will have a yield of 5 1/2 percent next month, then he should hold cash rather than consols.

12. Assuming that employers are risk neutral and employees risk averse, it follows that all labor contracts would be fixed in real terms.

13. If banks were permitted to pay interest on deposits at competitive rates, the demand for deposits would become a function of the real rather than the nominal rate of interest.

II. (20 points)

U.S. commercial banks with national charters (such as the First National Bank of Chicago) must be members of the Federal Reserve System and adhere to the regulations of that system (reserve requirements, etc.); commercial banks with state charters, however, are not compelled to be members of the Fed, and if they decline to be members, they are not subject to the Federal Reserve System regulations.

Recently an increasing number of state-chartered commercial banks have been withdrawing from the Federal Resreve System, which has caused the Federal Reserve to complain that the declining membership of the system makes it more difficult to accurately control the money stock.

1. Does their argument make sense? Explain.
2. Inflation has been blamed for leading to this decline in Federal membership and it has recently been proposed that the Fed pay interest on member bank reserves, the interest rate paid being tied to market interest rates. Would this help keep banks as members if the inflation rate continued to rise? If so, why?

III.   (20 points)

In a Keynesian world, monetary policy is supposed to influence economic activity by affecting the rate of interest and hence the willingness of the public to spend. Fiscal policy, on the other hand, is thought to affect aggregate demand directly, even though an expansionary fiscal policy is thought to affect interest rates in the same direction as does a contractionary monetary policy.

In a small open economy with a fixed exchange rate and without impediments to international capital movements, however, it is doubtful that domestic policy instruments can appreciably affect market interest rates.

1. Evaluate the effect of the openness of the economy on the cases for monetary and fiscal policy under Keynesian assumptions (assume a fixed exchange rate).

2. Evaluate the same effects under monetarist assumptions that changes in the quantity of money dominate (or even determine) changes in the level of economic activity in the short run and the price level in the long run (again, assume a fixed exchange rate).

IV.   (15 points)

Indicate the implications of the life-cycle hypothesis for the following:

1. The propensity to consume out of expected labor income for a young person versus an older person.

2. The aggregate level of consumption when there is an unfunded social security system (i.e., the present value of the benefits that the government will pay out to the public is more than the assets the government has set aside in order to make these payments].

3. The propensity to consume out of current income of bank clerks versus farmers.

V.   (20 points)

Discuss the reaction of a closed economy to a process of inflation initiated by a shift from a balanced budget to a persistent government deficit equal to four percent of GNP, financed by printing money at the Central Bank. In particular, indicate:
   a) the time path of the rate of change of money and of prices,
   b) the condition (s) determining the equilibrium rate (if it exists) of inflation in the new situation,
   c) the time path of real cash balances.

VI.   (15 points)

The residents of a particular country, Nedews, suddenly and inexplicably
develop a taste for the product lortep, which previously has been demanded
by only a few well known Nedewsian eccentrics. The only supply of lortep
in the world is produced in the kingdom of Capo under competitive conditions
and at constant cost (in foreign exchange).

Assuming no change in either monetary or fiscal policy in Nedews, analyze
the effects of this change in taste on Nedews' :

   a) balance of payments
   b) current account of the balance of payments
   c) level of employment
   d) price level (assuming a fixed exchange rate).

Indicate in each case whether or not there is any difference between the
short and long run effects (assuming that the change in taste is permanent).

Ph.D. Core Examination

THEORY OF INCOME

Winter 1978

Write in <u>black ink</u> and write on only <u>one side</u> of each page.

Write the following information on the <u>first page</u> of your examination paper:

     -----Name of Examination   ----- Your Code Number and <u>not</u>
     -----Date of Examination   your name

Write the following information on <u>each page</u> of your examination paper:

     -----Upper left: Code Number
     -----Upper right: Number of page

When you fold your paper at the end of the exam, write your code number on the
back of the last page, and indicate total number of pages.

Results of the examination will be sent to you by letter.

ANSWER ALL QUESTIONS

Time: THREE HOURS

I. (60 minutes -- 5 minutes each)

Indicate whether each of the following statements is TRUE, FALSE, or UNCERTAIN.
Justify your answer briefly.

1. Practically the whole Federal deficit in 1977 was financed by printing
money as witness the evidence which shows an increase of M2 of \$65 billion
in 1977 equal to the Federal deficit in that year.

2. It is impossible to have a situation where the price level is falling, interest
rates are rising, and the price of foreign currencies in terms of the U.S.
dollar is rising.

3. A minimum wage rate that remains the same in real terms cannot be a cause of
unemployment.

4. According to the theory of rational expectations with risk neutrality, the
variance of interest rates must vary inversely with their term to maturity.

5. The stimulating effect on output and prices of an increase in public
expenditure is greater when financed by issue of debt than by increased
taxes.

-65-

I. (continued)

6. A rise in the amount paid out in unemployment compensation to each unemployed person might increase the number employed as well as the number unemployed.

7. If all wage rates are fully indexed to the level of prices, real disturbances in an economy will distort the allocation of resources.

8. If inflation is fully anticipated, _relative_ prices will not be affected by inflation.

9. If both workers and firms are risk neutral, long term labor contracts would not affect the level of unemployment.

10. The more constant the money multiplier, the more tightly the monetary authority can control the level of economic activity.

11. Monetary policy will have no effect if interest rates do not change in response to the policy.

12. The U.S. dollar would appreciate relative to the West German Mark if short term interest rates in the U.S. rose relative to those in West Germany.

II. (30 minutes)

Evaluate:

As long as the marginal rate of time preference is constant, changes in the rate of monetary expansion will not affect the steady state (i) stock of capital (ii) consumption per head (iii) real balances per head (iv) income per head (including imputed services of real balances), and (v) welfare.

III. (18 minutes)

In his analysis of the determinants of the rate of interest, David Ricardo in his _Principles of Political Economy_ says: "Interest for money . . . is not regulated by the rate at which the bank will lend, whether it is 5, 4, or 3 percent, but by the rate of profits which can be made by the employment of capital, and which is totally independent of the quantity of the value of money. Whether a bank lent 1 million, 10 million, or a 100 million, they would alter only the value of money which they thus issued." Discuss and evaluate critically. In your analysis, refer to the concept of the neutrality of money in this context.

IV. (12 minutes)

"The accelerationist hypothesis that the long run Phillips curve is vertical is mainly of academic interest, since the fact remains that at any point in time unemployment can be reduced by monetary and fiscal expansion. The natural rate of unemployment is not a real constraint on practical policy." Discuss.

V. (15 minutes)

"A tax cut, by stimulating the economy and thereby expanding the tax base, can _increase_ tax revenues."

Outline the economic argument most favorable to this proposition. Is it favorable enough?

VI. (15 minutes)

The observation that interest rates are pro-cyclical is regarded by "monetarists" as a "paradox," but has received no special attention from "Keynesians." Why is this?

VII. (30 minutes)

Consider the simple Keynesian system (with variables expressed as deviations from means):

$$c_t = (.2) y_t$$
$$i_t = (.3)(y_t - y_{t-1}) + \varepsilon_t$$
$$y_t = c_t + i_t + g_t$$

$\{\varepsilon_t\}$ is a sequence of independent, normal variates, with mean 0 and variance 25.

(i) Explain the economic motivation for each of these three equations (c_t is consumption; i_t is investment; g_t is government expenditures; y_t is real GNP.)

(ii) With $g_t \equiv 0$, find the limiting (as $t \to \infty$) variance of y_t, i_t and c_t.

(iii) If $g_t = a y_{t-1}$, find the _a_ value which minimizes the limiting variance of y_t.

Ph.D. Core Examination

Theory of Income, Employment, and Price Level

Summer 1977

Write in black ink and write on only one side of each page.

On the first page of your exam paper, write:

- Name of examination
- Date of examination
- Your code number and not your name.

Write the following information on each page of your exam paper:

- Upper left: code number
- Upper right: number of page.

When you fold your paper at the end of the exam, write your code number on the back of the last page, and write the total number of pages.

Results of the examination will be sent to you by letter.

ANSWER ALL QUESTIONS. Time: 3 hours

Maximum possible score 180 points

I. [100 points]
Indicate whether each of the following statements is TRUE, FALSE, or UNCERTAIN. Justify your answer briefly.

1. The Central Bank can peg nominal interest rates (such as the Treasury Bill rate) in the short run but not in the long run.

2. Without reserve requirements on demand deposits and the prohibition of interest payments on those deposits, the Central Bank could not control the money supply.

3. The steady-state rate of inflation that maximizes government revenue from money creation is independent of the rate of real growth in the economy.

4. If no country had monopoly or monopsony power in international markets for goods, inflation could not be transmitted from one country to another.

5. The steady-state rate of inflation that maximizes government revenue from the inflation tax is independent of the rate of real growth in the economy.

-68-

6. In a world of fixed exchange rates and with a fixed nominal supply of money (but not necessarily a single currency), a country with a higher than average rate of growth of real output will have a higher than average rate of deflation.

7. In a world of perfect certainty, there would be no demand for money.

8. If banks were permitted to hold their reserves in the form of demand deposits in other banks, there would be no effective upper limit on the money supply.

9. In an open economy, the magnitude of the fiscal multiplier is determined by the marginal propensity to save, whereas in a closed economy it is the marginal propensity to hoard.

10. In a system of fixed exchange rates, a devaluation on the part of one country will permanently improve its balance of payments.

11. In a system of fixed exchange rates, a devaluation on the part of one country will permanently increase its holdings of foreign reserves.

12. A sale of securities by the Treasury will alter the money supply by the same amount if the Treasury keeps the proceeds in cash or if it deposits them at the Central Bank.

13. A sale of securities by the Treasury will alter the money supply by the same amount if the Treasury deposits the proceeds in commercial banks or if it uses the proceeds to buy goods and services.

14. If the demand for money is of the form: $\ln M^d = \ln P + \ln y - b \ln (1+C)$, where y is real income and C is the cost of holding money, and if it is known that the inflation tax can under no circumstances yield more than 50 percent of national income, then the elasticity "b" must be positive and greater than 0.5.

II. [20 points]
A prediction of the permanent income hypothesis is that windfalls tend to be saved, be they positive or negative. Discuss the implications of this prediction for:

(a) the cyclical behavior of the ratio of saving to income;
(b) the proposition that economic depression results from excessive saving;
(c) the apparent marginal propensity to consume of bank clerks versus farmers; and
(d) the procyclical movement in the demand for consumer durables.

III. [20 points]
Describe at least two approaches to the demand for money which are capable of explaining the apparent procyclical movements of velocity during the business cycle (i.e., velocity tends to fall during recession and rise during economic expansion).

IV. [20 points]
In the IS-LM model, if the money supply increases with the interest rate, what impact does this have on the strength of fiscal policy effects on aggregate demand? Why might there be a positive relationship between the supply of money and interest rates in (a) a closed economy and (b) an open economy?

V. [20 points]
Assume an economy in which:

$$y = \text{real national income} = A^t L^a K^{1-a},$$

where K = capital stock expressed in the same units as y,

L = labor input expressed in man-hours of constant quality,

A = positive constant greater than unity, and

a = a positive constant less than unity.

(a) Show that an equilibrium growth rate exists if the labor force grows at a constant rate and if saving is a constant fraction of income.

(b) How does the equilibrium growth rate in the above model depend upon the fraction of income that is saved (and invested)?

(c) Would your results change if all technical progress were labor augmenting [e.g., $y = (B^t L)^a K^{1-a}$, B > unity] or capital augmenting [e.g., $y = L^a (C^t K)^{1-a}$, C > unity]? Explain why or why not.

Ph.D. Core Examination

THEORY OF INCOME

Winter 1977

Write in <u>black ink</u> and write on only <u>one side</u> of each page.

On the <u>first page</u> of your exam paper, write:

- Name of Examination
- Date of Examination
- Your code number and <u>not</u> your name

Write the following information on <u>each page</u> of your exam paper:

- Upper left: code number
- Upper right: number of page

When you fold your paper at the end of the exam, write your code number on the back of the last page, and write the total number of pages.

Results of the examination will be sent to you by letter.

ANSWER ALL QUESTIONS.   Time: THREE HOURS

I. (60 minutes)
    Indicate whether each of the following statements is TRUE, FALSE, or UNCERTAIN. Justify your answer briefly.

1. In periods of rising prices, the real balance effect provides an automatic check against inflation.

2. A balanced budget insures that government spending does not contribute to the inflationary process.

3. The "permanent income" hypothesis is consistent with the fact that purchases of cars and other consumer durables rise with the transitory components of income.

4. An increase in the riskiness of bonds would not affect the speculative demand for money since one individual's capital loss is another individual's capital gain.

5. A rise in the marginal productivity of capital raises the desired rate of investment along with the rate of interest. Hence there is a positive cyclical association between the rate of investment and the rate of interest.

I. (Continued)

6. If the demand for money depends on permanent income, then measured velocity should exhibit pro-cyclical behavior.

7. The introduction of credit cards results in a higher velocity of money. Hence it raises the price level.

8. If cyclical fluctuations in output were entirely the result of fluctuations in the supply curve of labor, the real wage rate would fluctuate inversely with output.

9. Inventory models of the demand for cash balances imply that cyclical fluctuations in the velocity of money conform positivel to the business cycles.

10. If the risk aversion of employees greatly exceeded that of firms, wage rates of employed persons would be inflexible during a cyclical downturn in business.

ESSAY QUESTIONS

II. (10 minutes)
Consider an individual who earns $1,000 a month which is deposited into her savings account yielding 6 percent per year. Assume that she can withdraw part or all of her income at the beginning of the month free of charge but that any further withdrawal entails a payment of $1.50 per withdrawal. What will be her average cash holdings?

III. (30 minutes)
Consider an economy that is composed of two generations -- the "young" generation and the "retired" generation -- and assume that the economy is growing at the rate of population growth along the steady state growth path. The government considers the introduction of a new "social security" system by which each member of the young generation contributes 10 percent of his income to a fund that is distributed equally among members of the retired generation. The contribution carries with it the promise that when members of the young generation reach their retirement age they will receive 10 percent of the income of the new generation.

Under what conditions would the current young generation favor the introduction of the new system? Assume no bequest motive.

IV. (30 minutes)

Let M_t be the log of the nominal money supply in t, P_t the log of the price level, and y_t the log of real output (deviations from trend). Let ε_t and n_t be serially and mutually independent random variables with 0 means and variances σ_ε^2, σ_η^2.

Consider the following model:

(1) $M_t - P_t = y_t - k(E_t P_{t+1} - P_t)$, K > 0   Demand for money

(2) $M_t = M_{t-1} + \varepsilon_t$ Supply of money

(3) $y_t = \theta y_{t-1} + n_t$, $0 < \theta < 1$ Output equation

Here $E_t P_{t+1}$ denotes the expected value of P_{t+1} conditional on all variables up to and including period t.

Is this model consistent with observed aggregative behavior on real output, prices, and money?

V. (15 minutes)

Is it possible that a reduction in tax rates, by stimulating real output, can increase tax revenues and thus <u>reduce</u> the federal deficit? Answer, using a standard Keynesian model.

VI. (15 minutes)

Analyze the effects on the term structure of interest rates of an unexpected once and for all decrease in real national output. Suppose people expect that such an event is generally accompanied by a subsequent increase in the size of the Federal deficit. How does this affect the term structure?

VII. (20 minutes)

An earthquake in California causes very extensive property damage. Almost all of Los Angeles and San Francisco is destroyed and the western edge of California disappears into the Pacific Ocean.

  (i) Given <u>no</u> policy response on the part of the U.S. government, what is the immediate effect on total U.S. real output and prices? Why? On the rate of unemployment? Why?

  (ii) What policies <u>could</u> be pursued which would "smooth" the real effects?

  (iii) Do these policies lead to an increase in welfare? Why or why not?

Ph.D. CORE EXAMINATION

THEORY OF INCOME, EMPLOYMENT AND THE PRICE LEVEL

Winter, 1976

Write in <u>black ink</u> and write only on <u>one side</u> of each page.

Write the following information on the <u>first page</u> of your examination paper:

- Name of examination
- Date of examination   - Your code number and <u>not</u> your name

Write the following information on <u>each page</u> of your examination paper:

- Upper left: code number
- Upper right: number of page

When you fold your paper at the end of the exam, write your code number on the back of the last page, and indicate total number of pages.

Results of the examination will be sent to you by letter.

Answer all questions.   Time: 3 hours

I. (40 minutes) Indicate whether each of the following statements is True (T), False (F), or Uncertain (U), and state <u>briefly</u> your reason.

1. Required reserves held by a bank are a liability of the bank.

2. An expansion of investments and an expansion of loans by commercial banks have identical effects on the quantity of money.

3. and 4. Recently, corporations have for the first time been permitted to hold time deposits at commercial banks. The resulting transfer from demand to time deposits

    3. tended to increase M_1 (currency plus demand deposits).

    4. tended to increase M_2 (M_1 plus commercial bank time deposit)

5. Inflation in the United States has contributed to the recent depreciation in the value of the British pound.

6. The accelerator refers to the effect of a change in the rate of change of consumption on the desired stock of capital.

7. The real balance effect is absent if all money is "inside" money.

8. The real interest rate equals the nominal interest rate divided by a price index.

-74-

9. The more rapidly the quantity of money grows, the lower will be the quantity of real money balances.

10. The higher the rate of interest, the lower will be the Keynesian multiplier.

11. The larger the share of foreign trade in a country's economy, the lower will tend to be the Keynesian multiplier.

12. and 13. In the simple Keynesian model with fixed prices,

    12. A constant positive rate of growth of the quantity of money implies a constant interest rate.

    13. A constant rate of government deficit spending with a fixed stock of money implies a constant interest rate.

14. If the change in the money supply is always anticipated, fluctuations in the money supply could not cause fluctuations in aggregate real output.

15. In a period of high unemployment, an increase in government expenditures, even if financed by an equal increase in taxes, will raise aggregate output at least by the amount of the increase in expenditures.

16. Over long periods of time, the true rate of inflation will tend to lie between the rate given by the Paasche Price Index (given period weights) and the Laspeyre Price Index (base period weights). Note: the Consumer Price Index is an approximation to a Laspeyre Price Index.

17. Any attempt of the monetary authority to maintain a constant level of real money balances by means of adjustment of M_1 would ultimately destroy the monetary standard.

18. A gold standard tends to maintain a constant real value of money balances.

19. According to the multiplier accelerator model of business cycles an increase in real income due to good weather has the same effect on aggregate investment as an increase due to technical progress.

20. In an economy in which utility of each consumer depends on his consumption of goods and his stock of real balances, an increase in the endowment of goods for identical consumers leads to the same level of utility as an increase in nominal balances of the same value but the two sources of wealth increases lead to a different equilibrium price level.

II. (40 minutes) Indicate whether each of the following statements
is True (T), False (F), or Uncertain (U), and state briefly your
reason.

1. The recent development by savings and loan and other thrift
institutions of substitutes for demand deposits has simultaneously tended to reduce M_1 and raise the price level.

2. "To the extent that the strengthened program (of price control
does help to check the upward tendency of wages and prices,
it might also help to dampen the public's demand for money."
-- Andrew Brimmer

3. The "Phillips Curve" slopes negatively in the long run if
and only if there is money illusion.

4. If an increase in stock prices tends to increase real
consumption, then a rise in the interest rate tends to increase
savings.

5. and 6. In a simple Keynesian model with fixed prices:

5. A shift from taxes to a deficit financed by issuing
bonds implies a rise in the interest rate.

6. A treasury policy of substituting long-term obligations
for short-term obligations in the federal debt outstanding
will produce deflationary effects if and only if the
expectations hypothesis about term structure of interest
rates is false or incomplete.

7. A household investor has a choice between two kinds of
one-year Treasury Bills. The first pays a 2 per cent annual
return plus the percentage increase in the CPI (Consumer
Price Index) over the term to maturity of the bond while
the second pays a nominal return of 7 per cent. If the
consumer expects the CPI to rise by 5 per cent during the
term to maturity then he should prefer the Treasury Bill
which pays the fixed nominal return of 7 per cent.

8. A government that is trying to maximize its real revenue
from inflation will continue to accelerate the rate of growth
in the money supply.

9. If the savings function of each person is $S = a + by$, where
y is his total current income, $0 < b < 1$, and $a > 0$, and if the
rate of return on savings was the same for everyone, then income
inequality will decline over time, and tend to vanish
eventually.

10. Reserves over time for Eurodollars are held in the form of demand deposits at U.S. banks. Therefore, to calculate the effect of changes in the stock of money on various variables such as nominal U.S. income, one should subtract these deposits from M_1 or M_2.

III. (20 minutes) Assume an open economy whose imports and exports constitute a small part of the total world market in these goods so that it can regard the demand for its exports as infinitely elastic and the supply of its imports as also infinitely elastic, subject to range restrictions. Let the monetary authorities increase the nominal stock of money at a constant annual rate.

a. Using the quantity theory describe the effects on wage rates, the price level of consumer goods, and the prices of imports and exports if the exchange rates are allowed to float.

b. Under what circumstances, if any, would this monetary policy be consistent with fixed exchange rates?

IV. (20 minutes) "The expansive monetary policy in the U.S. today won't have very different effects than it would have had in 1932 or 1933, after the Great Contraction. Then, it would not only have promoted employment and a growth in output but would have removed distortions in the price and wage structure. Today, it would still promote employment and output growth but only at the cost of increasing distortions in the price and wage structure and laying the groundwork for further trouble."

Analyze, with special reference to the differences in circumstances between 1932 and today that would justify the predicted difference in results.

V. (30 minutes) It has been argued by Ben Klein that during the period when the U.S. was on a specie standard, the public at large took for granted that there was a "normal" level of prices and formed its expectations of future price movements on the basis of the relation between current prices and this "normal" level.

(a) Discuss why this might have been a sensible basis for forming expectations.

(b) Specify a particular hypothesis about how the public estimated the "normal" price level. If your hypothesis were correct, what relation would it imply between (1) the level of prices and the nominal rate of interest? (2) The rate of price change in the nominal rate of interest?

VI. (30 minutes) "Crowding-out" has been used to refer to a supposed reduction in private investment as a result of an increase in borrowing by the Federal government to finance a deficit.

 (a) Give a theoretical interpretation of "crowding-out" in Keynesian terms. Indicate the behavioral parameters that will determine the extent of crowding-out.

 (b) Are there different effects in the short-run and long-run?

 (c) Translate the analysis in (a) into quantity-theory terms.

Write in <u>black ink</u>   and write on only <u>one side</u> of each page.

On the <u>first page</u> of your exam paper, write :
- Name of examination
- Date of examination
- Your code number and <u>not</u> your name.

Write the following information on <u>each page</u> of your exam paper
- Upper left :   code number
- Upper right: number of page

When you fold your paper at the end of the exam, write your code number on the back of the last page, and write the total number of pages.

Results of the examination will be sent to you by letter.

ANSWER ALL QUESTIONS. <u>Time:</u> THREE HOURS

I. (78 minutes - 6 minutes each)
Indicate whether each of the following statements is TRUE, FALSE, or UNCERTAIN. Justify your answer briefly.

1. In real terms, the inflation tax as seen by holders of real cash balances is exactly the amount of their (voluntary) additions to nominal cash balances divided by the price level.

2. A balanced-budget multiplier of unity implies that there is a "burden" associated with public debt.

3. The observation that during episodes of very high rates of inflation (25% per month or higher), money contracts tend to be made in terms of foreign currency constitutes a refutation of Gresham's Law.

4. The natural rate of unemployment is achieved whenever the expected and actual rate of inflation coincide.

5. The "natural rate of unemployment" is the rate of unemployment that would tend to emerge if the central bank kept the quantity of base money(high-powered money) absolutely constant.

6. The distinction between money and other means of payment rests ultimately on the ability of the state to insist on payment of taxes in legal tender.

7. As no tax can exceed the tax base, the proceeds of the inflation tax, as a fraction of national income, can never exceed the inverse of the income velocity of money.

8."If we wish to increase the rate of growth of our economy, we must increase the saving rate."

9.An increase in the domestically-held money supply that is matched by an equal increase in officially-held international reserves will leave the domestic price level unaffected.

10.If the government finances a deficit by printing money, the multiplier for an increase in government spending will depend in no way on the community's marginal propensity to save.

11.The collection cost of the "inflation tax" will be greater, the more of the cost of check clearance is borne by the central bank.

12.If the financial community expects that a period of deflation and decelerating inflation will be succeeded by a period of inflation and accelerating inflation, the yield curve should be U-shaped.

13.In a growing economy with a constant money supply, nominal income will be falling.

II.Discussion question (30 minutes)
Neglecting all real capital held by the banking system, consolidation of the accounts of all commercial banks with those of the central bank reveals that the nominal money supply (M) is equal to reserves of foreign currency(R) plus domestic credit(both public and private) extended by the banking system (C):

$$M = R + C$$

As reserves must be denominated in the domestic unit of account, R must be thought of as the direct contribution to the money supply of all past operations by the central bank in the foreign exchange market.

1. What will be the effect on the money supply of an open market sale of government bonds by the central bank? Does it make any difference if those bonds are purchased by residents or by foreigners?

2. Assuming fixed exchange rates, describe the short and long run effects on the money supply and the price level of:

   a. efforts by the central bank to fix domestic interest rates, via expansion of domestic credit, at a level below that prevailing in the international capital market in which the country in question participates;

   b. a central bank policy aimed at a rate of expansion of the money supply greater than is consistent with the rate of real growth and the (world) rate of inflation;

   c. a fiscal surplus the proceeds of which are used to retire outstanding government bonds.

Theory of Income   Summer 1976

II. (cont.):
     3. Assume that the central bank devalues the currency by 20%. What,
        if any, will be the immediate effect on R? What will be the final
        effect on the nominal money supply?

III. (25 minutes)

     In an article published in 1946, Colin Clark forecasted with remarkable
     insight a coming period of secular inflation. He based himself on the
     argument that when the government share of national income rises above a
     certain critical level, the normal pressures to avoid inflation would be
     replaced by government and public willingness to tolerate inflation.

     1. Outline Clark's argument in modern terms.

     2. Discuss possible circumstances in which Clark's assumption that the
        government gains from inflation does not hold.

     3. Discuss the likelihood that despite the circumstances of part (2),
        governments would still follow an inflationary policy.

     4. In the light of your answers to (2) and (3), discuss the argument that
        "indexing would take the profit out of inflation."

IV. (15 minutes)
     Discuss the following statement, indicating in each case the assumption
     required to make the proposition referred to correct: "According to
     'Keynesian' theory, the fourfold rise in oil prices at the end of 1973
     was a deflationary shock to the world economy ; according to the 'mone-
     tarist' view, it was neither inflationary nor deflationary; according to
     the 'sociological' view of labour markets, it was inflationary."

V.   (20 minutes)
     1. Should outstanding travellers' checks be included in M_1?

     2. If so, should the total of borrowing power on credit cards, charge
        accounts, etc. be included in M_1?

     3. If U.S. banks are required to clear checks on the U.S. banks at par,
        why are they not legally obliged to sell travellers' checks to their
        customers at their face value (i.e., without charging a small percentage
        of the face value of the checks, the standard charge being one per cent)?

     4. In May, some Chicago banks advertised their willingness to sell tra-
        vellers' checks to people preparing for their vacations, for a fixed
        fee of 75¢ for any amount of checks up to $1500(these figures are
        approximate). How do you account for this sale of money at a discount
        from the usual price?

VI. (12 minutes)
    It has been proposed in various countries that the government should provide
    government employment for unemployed workers for whom no suitable jobs are
    currently available. Discuss this proposal (a) with reference to its
    macroeconomic policy implications, (b) with reference to its implications
    for the labor market.

Ph.D Core Examination
THEORY OF INCOME
Summer 1975

INSTRUCTIONS

Write in <u>black ink</u>; write on only <u>one side</u> of each page

Write the following information on the first page of your exam paper;
-- Name of examination
-- Date of examination
-- Your code number and <u>not</u> your name

Write the following information on <u>each</u>' page of your examination paper.
-- Upper left: code number
-- Upper right: number of page

When you fold your paper at the end of the exam, write your code number on the back of the last page, and indicate total number of pages.

Results of the examination will be sent to you by letter.

ANSWER ALL QUESTIONS. TIME: 3 HOURS.

I. (one hour - 4 minutes per question)
Indicate whether each of the following statements is TRUE, FALSE, or UNCERTAIN. In each case write a few sentences explaining your answer. Your grade will be determined by your explanation.

1. The "golden rule" is a guide to policy only in uninteresting cases.

2. Of the various ways in which the budget can be used to influence aggregate demand for stabilization purposes, orthodox balanced budgeting will involve the largest reliance on government spending in time of depression.

3. Ruritania has a law fixing the maximum interest rate on bank loans at 2 per cent above the central bank's rediscount rate. Removal of the ceiling would raise the cost of bank credit to the borrower.

4. The "permanent income" hypothesis of the consumption function implies that the per capita aggregate savings ratio is determined by the rate of technical progress.

5. There is no necessary inconsistency between a finding that the demand for money in a country is not significantly influenced by the rates of interest on bills and bonds, and the theory of "the inflation tax."

2.(cont.)

6. If the payment of interest on hand-to-hand currency is impractical, then welfare considerations would still dictate the payment of interest on commercial bank reserves held at the Federal Reserve.

7. If the money stock is held constant, the price level will fall at just the right rate to obtain the optimum quantity of money.

8. The empirical observation that money is a luxury good is inconsistent with the inventory approach to the demand for money.

9. If the monetary authority raises the money supply at a faster rate than usual when unemployment is high, and vice versa, the average rate of unemployment over the cycle will be reduced.

10. If commercial banks were allowed to pay (explicit) interest on demand deposits and the quantity of high-powered money is held fixed, the price level will rise.

11. If the monetary authority raises the money supply at a faster rate than usual when unemployment is high, the average rate of unemployment over the cycle will be unaffected, but the amplitude of fluctuations will be reduced.

12. A general expectation that the rate of inflation will move to a higher "plateau" should produce a uniform upward shift in the yield curve.

13. The negative real rates of return on financial assets observed in many countries during the past year or two indicate an explosive inflationary situation that cannot last.

14. An experience since February 1973 has conclusively shown, floating exchange rates are more inflationary than fixed exchange rates.

15. Short-term real investment such as inventory accumulation should be less interest-elastic than long-term real investment such as housing, because the discounting required in evaluating future expected earnings must have a relatively smaller effect on present value the shorter-term the investment.

II. (15 minutes)
In order to bail itself out of financial difficulties, the City of New York has decided to secede and issue its own currency (the bills will carry a picture of John Lindsay). The mayor of New York knows that the demand for real balances of New York City currency would take the form

$$m_{NY} = Ae^{-\gamma(\mu_n - \mu_{us})} \quad ,$$

where μ_n is the (constant) rate of increase of New York City currency and μ_{us} is the (constant and exogenously given) rate of increase of the United States money supply.   A   and γ are constants.

(a) What value of μ_n should be chosen in order to maximize the present value of revenue from New York City money issue, assuming that μ_n is constrained to be constant over time?

(b) What considerations might suggest that New York City would choose a variable, rather than a constant, rate of monetary expansion?

III. (20 minutes)
The existence of a social security system implies that individuals have less of an incentive to acquire a stock of assets to finance consumption during their retirement years. Hence, the stock of privately-held capital will be smaller than otherwise. Analyze this conclusion, assuming that:

(a) Social Security operates on a "pay-as-you-go" basis -- that is current payments to old people are financed solely by current taxes on young people, and

(b) all people over 65 are eligible for Social Security payments, with the amount of payment independent of previous or current amounts of work or income.

IV. (25 minutes)

(a) (15 minutes)
Suppose that every contract contains an escalator clause so that the nominal price moves up or down in accordance with the movement of a price index mutually acceptable to the parties concerned. Would it still be possible for the monetary authorities to tax money balances by using inflationary monetary policies? If so, why?

(b) (10 minutes)
What difference, if any, would it make to your answer if such escalator clauses were compulsory in every contract but contractors could waive the clause for a small fee paid to the government?

(cont.)

V.(30 Minutes)

1. (20 minutes)
Consider an "expansionary" fiscal operation that involves a cut in (lump-sum) taxes financed by issue of government debit. It has been argued that this operation would have a positive effect on nominal income if and only if the interest elasticity of money demand is negative.

   (a) Construct a simple model in which this argument is valid.

   (b) Discuss the limitations of this model-- in particular, what other considerations would affect the issue of whether the fiscal operation alters nominal income?

2. (10 minutes)
Suppose that in fact the central bank stabilizes the level of interest rates, while tax rate brackets remain fixed in nominal terms. What if anything will limit the expansion of nominal income?

VI.(30 minutes)

1.(15 minutes)
"Since a monopolistic producer will always produce on the elastic range of his demand curve, prevalence of monopolistic competition will mean that devaluation will always improve a country's balance of payments."

   (a) Consider this statement on the assumption that the "elasticities approach" is valid.

   (b) Criticize the theory of the effect of devaluation implied.

2.(15 minutes)
Consider the view that, in an open economy, monetary policy should be used for " full employment," and fiscal policy should be used to balance the balance of payments. Discuss the assumptions required for this proposition to hold. Would it make a significant difference whether the monetary authority automatically financed government deficits or not?

Theory of Income

Winter, 1975

Write in <u>black ink</u> and write only on <u>one side</u> of each page.

Write the following information on the <u>first page</u> of your examination paper:

   ---Name of examination
   ---Date of examination   ---Your code number and <u>not</u> your name

Write the following information on <u>each page</u> of your examination paper:

   ---Upper left: code number
   ---Upper right: number of page

When you fold your paper at the end of the exam, write your code number on the back of the last page, and indicate total number of pages.

Results of the examination will be sent to you by letter.

     ANSWER ALL QUESTIONS.   Time: 3 hours.

I. (40 Minutes) Consider a hypothetical stationary state (i.e., a state with fixed output) with the following initial conditions:

Population   1,000

Money supply $200,000

Income before tax $1,000,000

Taxes:
     Poll tax of $10 per person
     Income tax of 5% of total income

Government spending = $60,000

Price level = 1

Demand for money: $M = \frac{1}{5}Y(1 - \frac{1}{P}\frac{dP}{dt})$,

   where Y = aggregate nominal income ($ per year)

           M = nominal quantity of money ($)

           P = price level

           $\frac{1}{P}\frac{dP}{dt}$ = rate of change of price level in ratio terms (e.g., 5% per year = .05)

(a) The government raises spending to $100,000 per annum and keeps it fixed in nominal terms, financing any deficit by printing money.

    (i) The ultimate equilibrium level of nominal income is $ ____

    (ii) The ultimate equilibrium level of the nominal stock of money $ ____

    (iii) The equilibrium <u>real</u> level of government spending is ____ times the initial level.

(b) The government increases its spending to $100,000 per annum and keeps it fixed thereafter at 10% of total income.

    (i) Explain <u>briefly</u> why there is no new equilibrium level of nominal income.

    (ii) The new equilibrium value of $\frac{1}{P}\frac{dP}{dt}$ is _____

    (iii) It will be attained at t (time) = _____

(c) With the assumed taxes, the <u>maximum</u> fraction of the income of the community that the government can spend in equilibrium is _____. (<u>Prove</u> that your answer is correct.)

II. (30 Minutes) Indicate whether each of the following statements is True (T), False (F) or Uncertain (U), and justify your answer <u>briefly</u>.

1. During an accelerating inflation, employees tend to economize on cash balances. Accordingly, payment in kind will be a partial substitute for cash, measured real wages tend to fall, and wages "lag" prices.

2. According to the "natural rate" hypothesis, an expansion of the quantity of money that increases the employment of labor, and increases the job experience of the work force, and hence its human capital, will not affect real output of the economy in the long run.

3. For a given amount of high-powered money, the effective prohibition of the payment of interest on time as well as demand deposits would make the price level lower than it would otherwise have been.

4. The inventory theory of transactions demand for money predicts that the quantity of money demanded will increase less than in proportion to income, and therefore that, if output is constant, the rate of inflation will exceed the rate of monetary expansion.

5. If there were only two commodities, there would be no reason for the existence of money.

6. If there were only two persons in the world there would be no reason for holding money since the "double coincidence" problem would not arise.

7. In a world of perfect certainty, nobody will hold money.

8. A rise in the price of oil is inflationary.

9. A rise in the price of money is deflationary.

10. With a progressive tax system, the elasticity of tax revenue with respect to the price level exceeds unity.

III. (35 Minutes) Assume that a rebate of 10% of income taxes due on 1974 income is made effective in early 1975. Give a formal analysis in IS-LM terms of the effect of the rebate on income, employment, and prices, indicating the conditions that will determine its effect, and distinguishing between the impact effect and longer-term effect.

    An alternative to the rebate of 10% of income taxes due on 1974 income would be a cut of 10% on tax liabilities for 1975 income. What differences are there in the effects that the two proposals would have on output, employment, and prices?

IV. (20 Minutes) Franconia has a pegged exchange rate, high unemployment, and a large deficit in its balance of payments.

    Two economists are invited to submit recommendations for raising employment and reducing the deficit.

First Economist: "To solve the deficit problem, the government should reduce expenditures. Since part of governmental expenditures is for imports, the reduction will improve the trade balance. The unemployment problem should in turn be solved by monetary expansion."

Second Economist: "The government should increase its expenditures to solve the unemployment problem; to correct the deficit, the authorities should conduct contractionary monetary policies.

Evalute critically the two opposing views.

V. (20 Minutes) It is commonly maintained that (a) internationally traded goods must have the same prices in all countries when expressed in a common currency; (b) the relative prices of non-traded and traded goods are fixed by relative costs of production. It would seem to follow that (c) the rate of inflation must be the same for any countries that have fixed exchange rates between their currencies.

    In experience, rates of inflation are not the same even when exchange rates are fixed. How can you account for the differences?

VI. (15 Minutes) The failure to detect a countercyclical movement of real wages is evidence against the Keynesian approach in which output movements are determined solely by movements in aggregate demand. Comment.

VII. (10 Minutes) The demand for money depends on the differential between r, the interest rate on "earning assets," and r_m, the interest rate on money. Competition in the banking industry insures that the (at least implicit) interest rate on demand deposits moves along with r. Therefore, the interest elasticity of money demand must actually be much smaller than that suggested by the approach which neglects movements in r_m. Comment.

CORE EXAMINATION

Theory of Income, Employment, and Price Level

Summer 1974

(WRITE IN BLACK INK)

WRITE THE FOLLOWING INFORMATION ON THE FIRST PAGE OF YOUR EXAMINATION
PAPER:

- Your code number and not your name
- Name of examination
- Date of examination

Write only on one side of each page

Write the following information on each following page of your exam
paper:

- Top left: code number
- Top right: number of page

When you fold your paper at the end of the exam, write your code
number on the back, and indicate total number of pages.

Results of the Examination will be sent to you by letter.

Answer all questions.   Time: 3 Hours

I.   (90 points) (13 questions)

Indicate whether each of the following statements is TRUE (T),
FALSE (F), or UNCERTAIN (U), and indicate briefly your reason:

1. In a pure inside money system, either zero interest-elasticity
    of spending or perfect interest-elasticity of demand for
    money at positive interest rates is sufficient to make
    monetary policy unable to insure full employment even with
    flexibility of wages and prices.

2. If the interest rate is expected never to rise at a rate
    faster than itself, and transactions are costless, no
    consumers would ever hold stocks of inventories.

3. In a system of universally floating exchange rates, the
    prices of commodities would become infinite in terms of
    international money because under a floating exchange rate
    system there is no need whatsoever for international reserves.

4. A switch of asset preferences from commercial bank time deposits to savings and loan association deposits would decrease the money supply and hence be anti-inflationary.

5. The interest rate parity theorem says that if country A's exchange rate is expected to appreciate in terms of country B's, and country B's exchange rate is fixed in terms of country C's, country A's interest rate must lie below C's interest rate by the expected rate of appreciation of B's currency minus twice the permitted range of variation of C's market exchange rate with B from its parity value.

6. The schedule of the marginal efficiency of capital in conjunction with the market rate of interest determines the rate of output of new capital goods.

7. The life cycle theory of savings would be disproved by the observation that fathers of young children suddenly informed that they will die of cancer within six months typically do not quit work and embark on a spending spree.

8. In a closed economy with 100 percent reserve requirements, ex post expenditure on goods and services must equal output but income will exceed output if the rate of inflation is increasing.

9. Assuming that each one point increase in the expected rate of inflation causes a 5 percent decline in the demand for real cash balances, then in the long run the government can capture, via money creation, up to 20 percent of the stock of real cash balances each year.

10. The effect of an increase in the money rate of interest on production costs will be less inflationary the smaller is capital's distributive share of output.

11. An increase in saving reduces the consumer demand for goods which in turn tends to reduce the price level.

12. Say's Law holds in an economy where there is no durable good of any kind.

13. A country which has no comparative advantage in any good incurs a balance of trade deficit.

II. (25 minutes) (1 question)

Country X has

Potential growth in aggregate real income	5% per year
Population growth	1% per year
Real interest rate	3% per year
Demand curve for money	$M = \dfrac{Ay^{3/2}PN}{1+r}$

where M = total quantity of money demanded
P = Price level (= 100 at time $t = t_o$)
y = per capita real income
r = nominal interest rate (expressed as ratio per year; e.g., 3% = .03)
N = population

a. What annual rate of monetary growth will be consistent with stable prices, once long-run equilibrium is attained?

b. As of time t_o, prices have been rising at the rate of 8% per year for many years past. What has been the rate of growth of the quantity of money?

c. At time t_o, the rate of monetary growth is changed to the rate given in your answer to (a) above. What is the long-run equilibrium price level?

III. (30 minutes) (1 question)

A recent earthquake in Nicaragua destroyed a sizable fraction of the physical capital of the country but caused relatively few deaths or injuries. Analyze the effect you would expect this to have on

a. Each of the main Keynesian functions,

b. Short-term equilibrium level of income and employment,

c. Long-term equilibrium position (or path).

IV. (20 minutes)   (1 question)

Suppose that a change in the demand curve for labor by any firm
sometimes reflects forces unique to that firm, sometimes those
unique to the industry it is a member of, and sometimes those
applicable to the economy as a whole. When a change in demand
occurs, workers and employers are unaware of whether it is
unique to their firm or industry, but on the basis of past
experience, assume a probability p that it is unique to their
firm or industry. They can acquire some precise information
by spending additional resources, including time, equal to $ c
per period. Assume that no rigidities prevent money wage rates
from fully adjusting to any changes in demand or supply of labor.

Could there be cyclical fluctuations in unemployment in
such an economy? If so, why or why not? Would the
values of p and c be relevant?

V. (20 minutes)   (1 question)

Suppose that the aggregate production function is $y = A \cdot F(\ell)$,
where A measures the amount of "energy" input and where ℓ
is the amount of labor input. Suppose that the supply of
energy is exogenously reduced.

a. What would be the effect on the general market clearing
values of real money balances, real wage, output, and
employment?

b. Suppose that the rate of change of nominal wages and prices
is held fixed in the short run. What then would be the
effects on output and employment?

VI. (10 minutes)   (1 question)

Discuss the following:

An increase in reserve requirements at commercial banks may not
be contractionary since it may lower the demand for money by
more than the supply.

VII. (15 minutes)   (1 question)

Consider an "expansionary" fiscal operation involving an increase
in the amount of debt finance and a reduction in the amount of
tax finance for a given amount of government expenditure. Under
what circumstances would this operation lead to

a. a short-run increase in nominal income?

b. a long-run increase in nominal income?

c. a continued growth of nominal income?

CORE EXAMINATION

Theory of Income, Employment, and Price Level

Winter, 1974

(WRITE IN BLACK INK)

WRITE THE FOLLOWING INFORMATION ON THE FIRST PAGE OF YOUR EXAMINATION
PAPER:

- Your code number and not your name
- Name of examination
- Date of examination

Write only on one side of each page

Write the following information on each following page of your exam
paper:

- Top left: code number
- Top right: number of page

When you fold your paper at the end of the exam, write your code
number on the back, and indicate total number of pages.

Results of the Examination will be sent to you by letter.

Answer all questions.   Time: 3 hours

I.   (60 minutes) Indicate whether each of the following statements
     is TRUE (T), FALSE (F), or UNCERTAIN (U), and indicate briefly
     your reason:

     1. and 2. An excise tax is replaced by a direct tax on corporate
        income yielding the same revenue. From the point of view of
        national income accounting,

        1. Net national product in nominal terms is unchanged.

        2. National income in nominal terms is unchanged.

     3. A balanced budget multiplier of unity implicitly assumes that
        additional government expenditures provide services to neither
        consumers nor producers.

     4. A rise in a tariff will, according to Keynesian analysis, lead
        to an increase in both the interest rate and the level of
        consumption.

5. Under a fractional reserve system, the banking system can expand loans by a multiple of any increase in its reserves; under a 100% reserve system only by the amount of the increase in reserves.

6. A lowering of the maximum rate that commercial banks may pay on time deposits will, all other things the same, tend to raise M_1, i.e., currency plus demand deposits.

7. The short-run impact of monetary expansion on nominal income will be smaller the slower the adjustment of actual to desired real money balances.

8. A monetary expansion will reduce interest rates in the short-run but will inevitably raise interest rates in the long-run.

9. The real value of cash balances M/P is found by dividing the nominal stock (M) by the price level (P). Likewise, the real rate of interest (r) is found by dividing the nominal rate of interest (i) by the price level.

10. Risk does not affect the aggregate demand for money since one man's capital gain is another's capital loss.

11. If a country's central bank confines itself to pegging the exchange rate, economic growth of that country relative to the rest of the world will generate a surplus in the balance of payments.

12. The real effects of a continuous and anticipated rise in the quantity of money by 1000% per year are identical to the effect of allowing each individual to add an extra zero a year to the denominations of his notes (so that, for example, a $10 bill becomes a $100 bill, etc.).

13. If the observed term structure of interest rates on government bonds first falls and then rises with increasing maturity, this implies that future short term interest rates are expected to first fall and then rise.

14. The usual price index for goods will understate the rise in a price index that measures the change in total real income, including the income from "leisure" when real wage rates (i.e., money wage rates divided by the price level of goods) are rising, and overstate the rise when real wage rates are falling.

II. (5 questions)

1. (20 points)

Some central banks fix the ratio of cash plus short-term securities to total commercial bank liabilities ("the liquidity ratio") rather than the cash reserve ratio, variation of the liquidity ratios in place of open market operations, and direct central bank purchases of securities from government rather than open market purchases. Examine the view that these methods (a) raise less the cost of the public debt, (b) contribute less to generating inflation, than the traditional method of a fixed cash reserve ratio combined with open market operations.

2. (20 points)

How do you account for the facts that (i) in spite of the very sharp appreciation of the German mark since early 1973, the German trade surplus has remained very substantial, (ii) in spite of a fairly large depreciation of the pound relative to the major European currencies, Britain continues to run a large current account deficit, (iii) in spite of Canada's substantial oil resources, the Canadian dollar has remained only slightly above par with the U.S. dollar?

3. (15 points - Discussion question)

The charter of the Federal Reserve System, along with those of many other central bankers, endorses the principle that credit should be provided for production purposes and not for speculation. Write a critical analysis of this proposition under the alternative assumptions of:

    a) a fractional reserve banking system
    b) a system requiring 100 percent reserves
    c) "free" banking (no reserve requirements) in an
        open economy with a fixed exchange rate (e.g.,
        the case of Panama)

4. (20 points)

Adaptive expectations with respect to the price level means that the expected rate of change of prices is proportional to the differences between the actual and the expected price levels. Assume the demand for money varies inversely with the expected rate of change of prices. If the monetary authorities increase the nominal money supply at a constant rate, and if there are adaptive expectations, can the desired stock of money ever equal the actual stock of money? What would happen if price level expectations were "rational"

II. 4.(Continued)

in the sense that the actual and expected price levels
were the same? Would it be possible to predict price
levels accurately if the monetary authorities attempt
to maintain a constant real stock of money by their
manipulation of the nominal stock of money?

5. (15 points)

A prominent economist argues that too much emphasis is
given to monetary factors in explaining the levels of
employment and prices. Thus, automobile sales account for
about 3 percent of U.S. National Income. A doubling of the
relative price of gasoline causes a large reduction in the
demand for automobiles and in prices actually paid for
new and used cars. This in turn results in general
unemployment. There is little that monetary policy can do
to restore full employment. Hence certain changes in
relative prices can cause unemployment. Appraise.

Ph.D. Core Examination
Theory of Income, Employment, and the Price Level

Write the following information on the <u>first page</u> of your examination paper:

    -----Your CODE NUMBER and not your name
    -----Name of examination
    -----Date of examination

Write the following on each <u>following page</u> of your exam paper:

    -----Top left: code number
    -----Top right: number of page

WRITE ONLY ON ONE SIDE OF EACH PAGE. WRITE IN BLACK INK.

When you fold your paper at the end of the exam, write your code number on the back, and indicate the total number of pages.

I. (60 points) Indicate whether you believe each of the following statements to be TRUE, FALSE, or UNCERTAIN. In each case write a few sentences explaining your answer. Your grade will be determined by your explanation.

1. The equilibrium interest rate on government bonds is higher, the higher is the equilibrium price-earnings ratio for shares of common stock.

2. A spontaneous rise in the expected rate of inflation will increase all interest rates by the same amount.

3. A balanced-budget multiplier in excess of unity implies that the marginal value of public-sector output exceeds its marginal cost.

4. The turnover of bank deposits in the Province of Quebec (ratio of checks drawn to deposit balances) is substantially lower than that in the rest of Canada. This means that if the federal government spends money on public works in Quebec, the multiplier effect on Quebec incomes is small, because the money rapidly drains out of the Province.

5. If the services of money are an input to the production process and if money has no direct utility yield, then the long-run behavior of the capital-output ratio and per capita income is independent of monetary policy.

6. One test of the "permanent income" hypothesis versus the "life-cycle saving" hypothesis about the consumption function would be to determine whether younger people save a higher proportion of their permanent income than older people.

7. Females can now receive social security retirement benefits beginning at the age of 62. It would reduce inflationary pressure if the law were changed so that benefits would begin at age 65.

8. If demanders and suppliers of labor always correctly perceive the rate of inflation, then the Phillips curve is vertical in both the long and the short run.

9. The marginal efficiency of investment must always be lower than the marginal product of capital, even in a recession.

10. An increase in the public's desire to hold savings and loan association deposits should decrease M_1 and increase M_2.

11. If the demand for money is interest-elastic, the balanced-budget multiplier must be greater than unity.

12. An excess stock supply of money is not necessarily inflationary as that excess supply is quite consistent with equilibrium in the flow markets.

II. (20 points).

A small number of countries do not have a central bank (or similar institution) and hence money created in some other country (call it country A) is used domestically as the circulating medium. In this situation:

a) what are the determinants of the money supply?

b) what is the relevance, if any, of the concept of high-powered money?

c) what determines the internal price level?

d) how would inflation in country A influence the price level in the country in question? Is your answer the same whether the rest of the world uses fixed or flexible exchange rates?

III. (20 points).

Discuss the welfare costs of inflation and in so doing be certain to cover the following points:

a) costs of an anticipated vs. an unanticipated inflation;

b) true social costs vs. those costs that would appear as a reduction in measured GNP;

c) the relation between the inflation tax revenue and the welfare cost (cost of collection);

d) the probable distribution of the welfare costs of a fully anticipated inflation between labor and capital.

IV. (10 points).

How would you explain a simultaneous rise in the real wage rate and in the rate of "unemployment" assuming a stable price level?

V. (20 points).

Assume a simple economy with a government, a central bank, and a commercial banking system, but no other financial intermediaries. The currency/deposit ratio is .3, the commercial banks' cash reserve ratio is .2, the central bank holds a ratio of .25 of gold to government debt, the gold reserve is $10 billion, total government debt is $120 billion, total real capital is $160 billion, and the public finances a quarter of its holdings of real capital by personal loans from commercial banks.

   (i) Draw up a two-way table or a diagram showing the amounts of assets and liabilities of various kinds held or owned by the central bank, the commercial banks, and the public.

   (ii) Assuming that the interest rate on government debt is determined by the equation $i = \frac{G}{2M}$, where M is the money supply and G is public debt held by the public, what is the rate of interest?

   (iii) What would be the effect on the money supply and the interest rate of a doubling of the price of gold?

   (iv) What would be the effect on the money supply and the interest rate of a doubling of the currency/deposit ratio?

VI. (20 points).

   (a) Why are government deposits usually excluded from the definition of the money supply?

   (b) Should the same rule be applied to deposits owned by non-residents?

   (c) Should certificates of deposit be included in the money supply?

VII (30 points).

If the price level changes at a constant rate, the nominal and real interest rates adjust so that there is equilibrium in the public's holdings of real and nominal assets. Suppose that the rate of change of the price level changes in an unpredictable fashion over time. What changes, if any, would this require in the theory of portfolio balance? What empirical effects would this have? Would variable rates of change in the price level increase the social cost of inflation?

CORE EXAMINATION

Theory of Income, Employment, and Price Level

Winter, 1973

Preliminary Examination for the Ph.D. Degree

WRITE THE FOLLOWING INFORMATION ON YOUR EXAMINATION PAPER:

> Write the examination in dark ink pen
> Put your code number on every page
> Number your pages consecutively
> Put the name and date of the examination on the first page

Results of the examination will be sent to you by letter.

Answer all questions. Time: 3 hours; total points 180 (one point per minute). Allocate your time optimally !

Problems (7€ points)

1. Answer the following questions true, false, or uncertain. Briefly defend your answer.

    1. If interest payments on demand deposits were permitted, M_1 would increase and M_2 would decrease.

    2. In 1972 GNP was 9% higher than in 1971; If the income elasticity of demand for money is 1.8, then a budget deficit of 16.2% of GNP could have been financed by printing money without producing inflationary pressures.

    3. Monetary policy cannot affect the price level or the level of output if the economy is in a liquidity trap.

4. There will still be a tradeoff between inflation and unemployment if employers and workers have the same expectations, regardless of whether expectations are correct or incorrect.

5. Individuals in a closed growing economy will hold the optimal level of real balances if the stock of currency is constant. (Assume all money is currency.)

6. Money will not be neutral in an economy where the government debt is positive.

7. The longer the average life of a nation's capital goods, the more interest elastic will be the demand for newly produced capital.

8. In a static, full-employment model with markets for commodities, labor, and money, an increased rate of government expenditures financed completely by increased taxes will lead to a higher price level.

9. If the expected real rate of return is constant over time, then an upward, sloping term structure of interest rates must reflect expectations of a rising rate of inflation.

10. An economy that imports less than it exports is accumulating either capital or international reserves.

11. If the cost of searching for a better job were reduced, the natural or equilibrium level of unemployment would be reduced.

II. (30 points)

Suppose that everyone in the United States currently expects prices to rise in the indefinite future at 4% per year. Suppose that President Nixon then announces that prices will henceforth rise at 2% per year, and everyone believes him, at least as long as his statement is not falsified for an extended period. What is the short-run impact (i.e., while price change expectations are fixed at 2% per year) of this shift in expectations on interest rates, the rate of inflation, real income and capital accumulation?

What policy actions would have to be taken to produce this rate of inflation in the long run? Analyze the long-run impact of the change in the rate of inflation on the variables mentioned above.

III. (25 points)

Keynes wrote: "...with a given organization, equipment and technique, real wages and the volume of output (and hence of employment) are uniquely correlated, so that, in general, an increase in employment can only occur to the accompaniment of a decline in the rate of real wages. Thus, I am not disputing this vital fact which the classical economists have (rightly) asserted...The real wage earned by a unit of labor has a unique inverse correlation with the volume of employment."

Reconcile Keynes' argument with the empirical observation that real wages typically move procyclically.

IV. (15 points)

How closely would you expect the Fed to be able to attain any desired growth rate of M_1? Trace the links between Federal Reserve actions and M_1, indicating which are least predictable.

V (15 points)

"A comparison of movements in the money stock and consumer price level over the past five years shows that if any relation exists between them, it is negative. In 1967-68, money grew at the rapid rate of 10.3% per year, while inflation averaged a little over 3%. In 1969, money

(cont'd)

actually declined by -.7%, while prices rose at a rate of almost 6%. Since 1970, monetary growth has averaged about 12% per year, while prices have decelerated to the current low rate of inflation of about 3%. Clearly, if we are to finally beat the inflation, we should maintain the current high rate of monetary expansion, and perhaps even increase it."

Analyze this statement, keeping in mind that the numbers presented are correct.

VI   (25 points)

The emerging international payments mechanism will apparently require each nation to hold a target amount of international reserves, say some fraction of its imports. If a nation's reserve holdings deviate significantly from the target amount, the offending nation will be required to adjust its exchange rate (devalue if reserves are too low, appreciate if reserves are too high).

   a.   What policy actions may government officials take to encourage or discourage international reserve flows, while remaining on a fixed exchange rate standard?

   b.   If the purchasing power parity theory holds continuously over time, what effect would you expect an exchange rate adjustment to have on reserve flows in the long-run, and in the short-run?

CORE EXAMINATION

Theory of Income, Employment, and Price Level

Summer, 1972

(WRITE IN BLACK INK)

Preliminary Examination for the Ph. D.

WRITE THE FOLLOWING INFORMATION ON YOUR EXAMINATION PAPER:

> Your Code Number and NOT Your Name
>
> Name of Examination
>
> Date of Examination

Results of the Examination will be sent to you by letter.

Answer all questions. Time: 3 hours

I. 72 points. Answer the following questions True, False or Uncertain and briefly explain your answer. (12 questions)

1. If the demand for money is completely interest-inelastic, fiscal policy cannot alter employment unless the central bank simultaneously changes the stock of base money.

2. In an open economy, an increase in the value of exports must be accompanied by an increase in national income.

3. If money is non-interest-bearing and the income from the holding of money balances is properly imputed, and if the demand for money is interest-inelastic, monetary inflation must raise the long-run equilibrium level of output per head.

4. To control the money supply, the central bank needs control of two of the following three policy instruments: the rediscount rate, the required reserves to deposit ratio at commercial banks, the cash base.

5. The unit balanced-budget multiplier theorem implies that if government is committed to maintaining full employment by fiscal policy, under conditions of chronic economic stagnation, its role in the economy as measured by its expenditure must be higher if it maintains a balanced budget than if it operates by increasing its expenditure only.

-104-

6. The prohibition of interest payments on demand deposits is necessary to the achievement of a second-best optimum in money-holding, because there is no practical way of paying interest on notes and coins, and these are very close substitutes for deposits.

7. A household will add a relatively low yield asset to its portfolio only if the new asset reduces the overall variability of the value of the portfolio over time.

8. In a two sector economy, monetary and fiscal policies that permanently raise the price of capital goods relative to consumption goods will permanently raise the economy's per capita consumption.

9. If bonds and real capital (in the form of common stocks) are perfect substitutes in the portfolios of households, then movements in the interest rate should be highly correlated with fluctuations in investment expenditures.

10. A tax on the velocity of each bank account, the rate of tax being positively related to the rate of inflation, would reduce the inflationary consequences of an increase in the growth rate of the money supply.

11. Government policies attempting to ensure correct expectations of inflation are not in the public interest, since they would tend to make the economy unstable.

12. Government policies attempting to change the natural rate of unemployment would lead to ever-accelerating inflation or deflation.

II. 18 points (1 question)

In the theory of economic policy in a small open economy, it is usually assumed that the domestic price level is determined by the world price level, and domestic interest rates by world interest rates.

(a) If these assumptions are broadly correct for most European countries, Canada, and Japan, why should such countries occasionally feel obliged to devalue or revalue their currencies?

(b) Why are such exchange rate changes typically followed, at least for a time, by changes in the relative prices of exports and imports in the direction predicted by the "elasticity approach" to devaluation?

III. 20 points (1 question)

A "sophisticated" Keynesian view of inflation is that the government's commit-
ment to maintain full employment by appropriate monetary and fiscal policies
permits unions and firms in concentrated industries to push up wages and
prices respectively, in the knowledge that the adverse effects of such wage
and price increases on demand will be offset by fiscal and monetary expansion,
this process diffusing itself to increases in wages and prices in the competitive
markets for labour and commodities; and that therefore inflation can be stopped
by breaking the monopoly power of unions and firms. Discuss the hypothesis
and the likely effectiveness of the proposed remedy.

IV. 20 points (1 question)

Assume the following simple Keynesian model

$$C = C(T, i, Y); \frac{\partial C}{\partial T} < 0, \quad \frac{\partial C}{\partial i} < 0, \quad \frac{\partial C}{\partial Y} > 0$$

$$I = I(i) \qquad \frac{\partial I}{\partial i} < 0$$

$$\bar{M} = L(i, Y)$$

$$Y = C + I + G,$$

where T represents tax revenues and G government expenditure, and the other symbols have their conventional meanings. Let r be the average output-to-capital ratio,
and r' be the marginal output-to-capital ratio. Assuming that government policy
next period ensures that both the capital actually employed this period and the
capital created by investment this period are fully employed, develop the conditions under which (a) monetary expansion by itself (b) a reduction in taxes
this period financed by an equal amount of money creation (G construct), will increase the observed rate of growth of output

$$\frac{Y_{t+1} - Y_t}{Y_t} .$$

IV. 30 points (1 question)

How would you expect the following events taken one at a time to affect the
rate of unemployment in the short-run and in the long-run?

(a) Consumer preferences over the mix of available goods changes continuously and in unexpected ways over time.

(b) The average age of workers entering the labour force rises to 40, and
the average retirement age falls to 50.

(question continues)

4

(c) The real interest rate rises.

(d) The government agrees to hire any unemployed worker at the same wage as he earned at his most recent job.

(e) The government moves from a monetary policy of a steady 4 per cent rate of increase in money to one of a steady 15 per cent rate of increase in money.

. 20 points (1 question)

iscuss the view that the wage-and price-controls imposed on August 15, 1971 ave done nothing to reduce the rate of inflation and/ or the rate of unemployment at the monetary policy followed since then would not have done anyway.

CORE EXAMINATION

Theory of Income, Employment, and Price Level

Winter, 1972

(WRITE IN BLACK INK)

Preliminary Examination for the Ph.D.

WRITE THE FOLLOWING INFORMATION ON YOUR EXAMINATION PAPER:

Your Code Number and NOT Your Name
Name of Examination
Date of Examination

Results of the Examination will be sent to you by letter.

Answer all questions.   Time: 3 hours

I.   90 points. Answer the following questions True, False or Uncertai
     and briefly explain your answer.   (13 questions)

1.   According to the inventory approach to the demand for money,
     a 10% rise in an individual's money income due to a 10% rise
     in the wage rate would increase his demand for money holdings
     by the same percentage.

2.   Inflation has been a widely used means of obtaining government
     revenue because the interest elasticity of the demand for
     money is less than unity.

3.   Fluctuations in long term interest rates would have a smaller
     amplitude and would lag those in short term rates if people's
     expectations about interest rates are fully realized.

4.   If the interest elasticity of the demand for real money
     balances were a constant for all values of real balances,
     then there would not exist an optimal stock of money.

5.   The difference between the nominal and the real interest rate
     equals the expected percentage change of prices in equilibrium
     only if interest rates are expected to remain constant.

6.   A system in which commercial banks are willing to lend to
     business firms on good security at competitive interest rates
     while the central bank maintains a constant rediscount rate,
     is inherently unstable.

7.   In the IS-LM framework an increase in the excess of imports
     over exports tends to reduce the price level at full employmen
     with a given stock of money.

8. If tax revenues, government bonds held by the public, and high powered money are all unchanged, then government expenditures cannot change.

9. For any given ceiling of interest rates on deposits, a $1 open-market purchase expands the money supply by a greater amount when the market interest rate is high than when the latter is low.

10. An increase in the interest-rate ceiling on time deposits causes no change in the ratio of currency to demand deposits, as long as no interest is paid on either currency or on demand deposits.

11. If the demand for investment depends only on the interest rate, the IS curve is downward sloping, but if investment demand depends on both the interest rate and income, the IS curve is upward sloping.

12. The Treasury can minimize the cost of a given national debt by selling short-term bills in a recession, when short-term bill rates are low relative to long-term bond rates.

13. In a model with perfect foresight and with interest paid on currency, reserves, and deposits, a tax cut financed by money creation has no effect on national income.

II. 20 points (1 question)

In a closed economy with full employment a government decreases its rate of expenditures on final goods and services, and buys back from the public an amount of government bonds equal to the reduction in the rate of expenditures. Describe the behavioral assumptions under which these policies would lead to

(a) a decrease in the interest rate and fall in the price level

(b) a decrease in the interest rate and a rise in the price level

(c) no change in the interest rate and no change in the price level.

III. 30 points (3 questions)

1. Dividends and earnings per share of common stock are $1 and the current price of a share is $40. The interest rate of government bonds of all maturities are 6 percent. The real rate of return on capital is expected to remain constant. Assuming this represents a long run equilibrium, what is the expected rate of change of prices?

2. An open market purchase of 3-6 month Treasury Bills lowers the amount outstanding by 1.1 percent while raising demand deposits by 0.6 percent. The Treasury Bill rate falls from

6 to 4.3 percent and the price level rises by 0.1 percent.
Real income remains constant. Assume no interest is paid on
demand deposits, and there is no currency in the system.

(a) What is the interest elasticity of velocity?

(b) What is the interest elasticity of the demand for Treasury
   Bills in real terms?

3. Let y = real income and y* = permanent real income. Let
   m = real money balances and assume actual and desired real
   money balances are always equal. Let the demand for money
   be given by the function as follows:

   i. $\log m = c + \beta \log y*$.

   Assume there are adaptive expectations so that

   ii. $d \log y*/dt = c (\log y - \log y*)$.

   a. If real income has been growing at a constant rate of r,
   what must be the time path of the nominal stock of money that
   would maintain a constant price level?

   b. If as a result, $d \log y*/dt = r + c(\log y - \log y*)$, what
   time path of the nominal stock of money would maintain a
   constant price level?

IV. 40 points

Consider a monetary policy society with the following parameters:

Government debt outstanding = $200 billion

Fraction of debt owned by central bank = .25 (remainder owned by
public)

Bank reserve requirements = .5

Public's currency/deposit ratio = .5

Bank borrowing from central bank = $10 billion

Balanced budget

No interest paid on currency, reserves, or deposits

No initial central bank holdings of gold or foreign exchange.

(a) Given the above information, what is the initial money supply
   (currency + deposits)?

(b) The following is a list of alternative methods of expanding
   the money supply. In each case, calculate the new values of
   the appropriate parameters in the above list necessary to
   achieve a 10 percent increase in the money supply.

   (i) An inflow of gold from abroad purchased only by the
      Central Bank.

CORE EXAMINATION

Theory of Income, Employment and Price Level

Summer 1971

Preliminary Examination for the Ph.D. and A.M. Degree

WRITE THE FOLLOWING INFORMATION ON YOUR EXAMINATION PAPER

- Your code number and not your name
- Name of examination
- Date of examination
- Number each page

Results of the examination will be sent to you by letter.

WRITE IN BLACK INK

Answer all questions. Time: three hours (180 minutes or approximately one minute per point).

I. Answer the following questions true, false, or uncertain. Briefly defend your answer. (6 points each)

T F U 1. If a satisfactory demand for money function can be fitted without using the interest rate as an argument, velocity must be insensitive to the expected rate of inflation.

T F U 2. The long run Phillips curve must be vertical; otherwise steady inflation would reduce labor's share in national income over time.

T F U 3. If long-term interest rates exceed short-term interest rates, the market must be expecting that short-term rates will rise in future.

T F U 4. In an open economy, an increase in saving with no change in investment will require that exports also increase.

T F U 5. As the multiplier of national income with respect to the money supply can be expressed as a factor multiplied by the abstract exogenous spending multiplier, it follows that the effectiveness of monetary policy will be in direct proportion to the effectiveness of fiscal policy.

T F U 6. If the public increases its demand deposit holdings by switching its deposits from savings and loan associations to commercial banks, the quantity of money (defined as currency plus demand deposits) will be unchanged.

T F U 7. A policy of accelerating monetary growth if interest rate are above 4 per cent, and decelerating monetary growth i interest rates are below 4 per cent would result in the price level approaching either infinity or zero.

T F U 8. The inflationary impact of a government deficit depends on how it is financed. Borrowing from the central bank is the most inflationary, borrowing from commercial banks is the next most inflationary, and borrowing from the public is least inflationary.

T F U 9. If the nominal money supply is growing at 12 per cent per annum, nominal income at 10 per cent per annum, and the elasticity of velocity with respect to real income is -0.5, the rate of inflation will be 6 per cent.

T F U 10. If a country's actual output falls short of its full empl ment potential by $1 billion, and it has a current accour deficit of $1 billion, it can restore both external and internal balance simply by devaluing.

T F U 11. The classical dichotomy is valid only if the demand for money is not a function of the rate of interest.

T F U 12. The real balance effect depends on the fraction of the total money supply that is an obligation of the govern- ment.

II. (15 points)

In recent testimony before the Joint Economic Committee of the U.S. Congress, the Chairman of the Council of Economic Advisors to the President argued that, despite the growing rate of unemployment, additional fiscal stimulation of the economy was not justified because estimates of the government deficit had already been increased from 5 to 20 billion dollars in total.

(a) As there has been no increase in government expendi- tures since the time at which the $3 billion estimate of the deficit was made, what factors would account for the increase in the deficit?

(b) Does the increase in the deficit constitute an expansionary force? Explain your answer.

III. (20 points)

The rate of change of prices in an economy can be expressed as a function of the rate of change of real income, perhaps certain exogenous factors such as changes in the exchange rate, and assuming the existence of lags, current and lagged rates of change in the nominal money stock. Estimates of this function for a number of countries have revealed two key characteristics:

(a) the sum of the coefficients of the rate-of-change-of-money variables sum to an amount not statistically significantly different from unity.

(b) one or more of the coefficients of the rate-of-change-of-money variables is negative.

On the basis of conventional economic theory, rationalize both of these results.

IV. (20 points)

Analyse the effects of the following policies on the U.S. balances of payments in the short run and in the long run. Explain your answers carefully.

(a) an additional tax on income from foreign bonds held by Americans that reduced the after-tax yield on foreign bonds to one-half the after-tax yield available on comparable American bonds.

(b) a permanent decrease in nominal government expenditures, with any resulting budget surplus being used to retire government debt.

(c) an across-the-board 50 per cent increase in tariffs on American imports.

V. (30 points)

"From the point of view of government, inflation often constitutes an appealing way of raising tax revenue."

(a) Discuss this statement.

(b) What factors determine the maximum-yield rate of inflation (i) in a static economy (ii) in a growing economy? Could price stability ever be more profitable than inflation?

(c) What modifications would you make in your analysis to discuss the effects on U.S. welfare of inflation in the U.S. given the role of the dollar as an international reserve currency?

VI. (20 points)

How would you account for the fact that in many advanced industrial countries, including the U.S. and the U.K., unusually rapid inflation has been accompanied by abnormally high unemployment?
Present explanations in terms of (a) Keynesian theory (b) quantity theory (c) your own ideas, using the last to criticize the other two.
In the light of your analysis discuss the choice between fiscal and monetary methods of economic stabilization.

Note: You are encouraged to be speculative in part (c).

CORE EXAMINATION

Theory of Income, Employment, and Price Level

Winter 1971

(WRITE IN BLACK INK)

Preliminary Examination for the Ph.D.

WRITE THE FOLLOWING INFORMATION ON YOUR EXAMINATION PAPER:

- Your Code Number and NOT Your Name
- Name of Examination
- Date of Examination

Results of the examination will be sent to you by letter.

Answer all questions.   Time: 3 Hours

I. Answer the following questions, True, False, or Uncertain and
   briefly explain your answer.
   Time: 60 minutes

1-5.   According to the inventory theory of the demand for money:

1.   Positive transactions costs for the purchase and sale of bonds
     are a necessary condition for an individual to hold a positive
     real stock of money.

2.   Uncertainty with respect to the timing and amount of receipts
     and expenditures is a sufficient condition for individuals to
     hold a positive real stock of money.

3.   A belief that current rates of interest will rise is neither
     necessary nor sufficient.

4.   The income elasticity of the demand for real balances with
     respect to real income is equal to 1/2.

5.   The interest elasticity of the demand for real balances is
     equal to -1/2.

6.   People would hold the optimal amount of real balances if
     competitive interest were paid on all bank deposits and there
     were no currency.

7.   Seasonal movements in the nominal stock of money accompanied by
     inverse seasonal movements in the prime commercial rate of
     interest imply a seasonally shifting supply of money.

8.   The yield on common stocks is expected to be independent of
     the rate of inflation.

-115-

9. Even if the monetary authority accomodates the public's demand for currency, they can still maintain a constant nominal stock of money.

10. The neutrality of money does not depend on the proposition that velocity is independent of the interest rate.

11. To maintain a balance of trade in the long run a country on a gold standard requires flexible wage rates.

12. Short term interest rates tend to be below long term interest rates at troughs of business activity and above long term interest rates at peaks of business activity because of regressive expectations about the price level.

13. A decline in aggregate demand is accompanied by a stable price level only to the extent that there is an increase in unanticipated investment.

14. An increase in the rate of monetary expansion will raise the equilibrium physical capital stock of the stationary state.

15. An equal increase in the money supply effected by a purchase of securities in the open market will lower the interest rate by more than an increase in the money supply accomplished through lump sum transfers.

16. An acceleration of the rate of inflation increases the rate of growth of output.

17. The balanced budget multiplier is equal to unity.

18. A budget surplus at full employment is deflationary.

19. The money supply is an endogenously determined variable in an open economy.

20. The credit card industry is likely to reduce the profits of banks from their depository activities.

21. The accelerator refers to the effect of a change in the rate of change of consumption on the desired stock of capital.

22. The greater the durability of the goods involved, the larger the accelerator effect.

23. The "Phillips curve" slopes negatively in the long run if and only if there is money illusion.

24. An increase in U.S. barriers to imports would, on strict Keynesian lines, tend to reduce the level of unemployment, provided other countries did not retaliate.

25. The multiplier in its simplest form is equal to an infinite sum of powers of the marginal propensity to save.

26. Suppose the high employment budget of the federal government shows a deficit of $2 billion; the actual budget, a deficit of $6 billion. This means that the unemployment is abnormally high.

27. The IS curve should be expressed in terms of real interest rates; the LM curve in terms of nominal interest rates; hence the intersection of the two is meaningless.

28. The higher the rate of interest, the lower will be the Keynesian multiplier.

29. Substitution of taxes on property for taxes on earnings (to yield the same revenue at the same national income) will tend to lower national income.

30-32. In the simple income-expenditure model with rigid prices:

30. A constant positive rate of growth of the quantity of money implies a constant interest rate.

31. A constant rate of government deficit spending with a fixed stock of money implies a constant interest rate.

32. A rising stock of capital is inconsistent with a constant interest rate.

II. Essay Questions
   Time: 30 minutes each

1. In calculating taxable income, a corporation that makes a capital investment is entitled to subtract the cost of the capital item from its income, provided it spreads the cost over a period of years corresponding to its estimated economic life. President Nixon recently announced a liberalization of depreciation allowances in the form of lower permissible economic lives for capital items.
   (a) Since the same total amount will be deducted in any case, how does this benefit the taxpayer?

   (b) The measure raises the yield on depreciable investment. What effect could this be expected to have on:
      (i) Investment spending on depreciable items
      (ii) Total investment spending
      (iii) Interest rates
      (iv) National income
      Analyze on both income-expenditure and quantity theory lines.

   (c) Even if it does not affect the amount of investment, it will have other effects on aggregate income. Explain why and how.

2. The annual rates of change of two U.S. monetary aggregates for various periods are as follows:

	Annual Rates of Change (percent per yr M_1	M_2
January 1967 to January 1969	7.6	9.7
January 1969 to July 1969	5.1	3.5
July 1969 to February 1970	1.6	0.1
February 1970 to December 1970	6.0	9.8

M_1 = currency plus demand deposits adjusted.

M_2 = M_1 plus commercial bank time deposits other than large negotiable CD's.

The monetary growth from January 1967 to January 1969 was follow by spiraling inflation. Yet the monetary growth from February 1970 to December 1970, though almost the same in magnitude, is expected by many to be followed by moderating inflation. Suppose this did in fact happen. How would you explain it theoretically In your answer, do not give any weight to the difference between 6.0 and 7.6 (if you wish, for purposes of the answer, assume the 6.0 replaced by 7.6), or to changes in the tastes and preference of the members of the community.

3. Using some principles of monetary theory, how would you explain the following observations:
   (a) Gas and electric utilities hold lower average money balances relative to their volume of sales than do manufacturing firm
   (b) The ratio of demand deposits to savings deposits at commerci banks falls during business expansions and rises during business recessions.
   (c) During rapid inflations, interest rates tend to rise in nominal terms, but to fall in real terms.

4. In the context of a world economy in which the U.S. has a preponderant influence, answer the following questions:
   (a) Analyze the consequences of devaluation of a major currency on the balance of payments.
   (b) What special considerations, if any, would be involved in devaluation of the dollar?
   (c) How would you expect the introduction of SDRs to help solve:
      i)   the liquidity problem
      ii) the adjustment problem
      iii) the confidence problem

CORE EXAMINATION

Theory of Income, Employment and Price Level

Summer, 1970

Preliminary Examination for the Ph.D.

WRITE THE FOLLOWING INFORMATION ON YOUR EXAMINATION PAPER:

- Your Code Number and NOT your name
- Name of Examination
- Date of Examination

Results of the examination will be sent to you by letter.

Answer all questions.   Time: 3 hours.

I.   (60 points)
      Indicate whether each of the following statements is True (T),
      False (F), or Uncertain (U) and state briefly your reason.

_____ 1. If money is a Giffen good, the real balance effect will
           guarantee the stability of monetary equilibrium.

_____ 2. The recent change in Regulation D, by which required
           reserves are computed against deposits of two weeks ago
           instead of current deposits, increases by two weeks the
           length of time it takes the Federal Reserve to change the
           money stock.

_____ 3. Changes in stock market prices have no effect on the
           investment decisions of those firms which finance expansion
           from retained earnings.

_____ 4. The prohibition of the payment of interest on time as well
           as demand deposits would make the price level lower than
           it would otherwise have been, on the assumptions that high-
           powered money is held constant and both prohibitions are
           effective.

_____ 5. Discussions of the optimal rate of savings can have
           relevance only to disequilibrium situations since the
           equilibrium growth rate is independent of the savings
           ratio (so long as the rate of population growth is constant).

_____ 6. The excess of investment over saving (including the public
           sector) must equal the excess of imports over exports.

_____ 7. The balanced budget multiplier cannot, theoretically, exceed unity.

_____ 8. If the nominal cost of holding cash balances were to fall to zero, then it would also be true that the value of money must be zero.

_____ 9. Because the marginal propensity to consume with respect to wealth is estimated to be much lower than with respect to income, a shift from an income to a wealth tax-keeping total revenue constant -- will have a positive multiplier effect.

_____ 10. Once people become accustomed to inflation, the Phillips Curve reduces to a single point.

_____ 11. The permanent income hypothesis predicts that gamblers will consume less of their income than will bank clerks.

_____ 12. National income will fall if resources are shifted to the prevention of pollution.

II. Discussion Questions

1. (15 points)
The tax surcharge of 1968 (i) was temporary and (ii) exempted certain individuals with low tax liabilities. (a) Provide an analysis using any theory of the consumption function which explains why these features would weaken the effects of an income tax surcharge. (b) Under what conditions would temporary increases in the rate of investment tax credit suffer from the same or similar weaknesses in reducing current aggregate demand?

2. (15 points)
The Gibson Paradox asserts a correlation between the rate of interest and the level of prices. Is it a paradox?

3. (25 points)
A popular policy prescription of those favoring growth as a policy objective is for tight fiscal policy and easy monetary policy.

4. (20 points)
What effects on international financial arrangements and the domestic economy would follow from

(a) a refusal of the U.S. to purchase gold at a fixed price

(b) an increase in the price at which the U.S. buys gold from and sells gold to foreign central banks (but no other change in the two-price system).

5. (10 points)
In prisoner-of-war camps in the second world war each
prisoner received an identical parcel of goods each month.
Trade soon began, and cigarettes became the currency of
the camps. Would a cigarette smoker have been better off
had another good, of which he had an excess supply at
cigarette equilibrium prices, been used as currency?

6. (20 points)
An economy with a fixed exchange rate is experiencing a
persistent loss of reserves of foreign exchange, a loss
that cannot be attributed to capital movements.

   (a) Describe and defend the set of policy measures you
   would recommend to eliminate this loss of reserves
   assuming that expenditure equals income despite the
   loss in reserves.

   (b) Same as (a) but assume that expenditure exceeds income
   by the rate at which reserves are declining.

7. (15 points)
The rate of inflation in Panama is currently one-third
that of the rate of inflation in the U.S., despite the fact
that Panama has no Central Bank and consequently uses the
U.S. dollar as its medium of exchange.

   (a) For what reasons would you expect Panama and the U.S.
   to have highly similar rates of inflation?

   (b) What hypotheses can you suggest to explain the marked
   difference in the current rates of inflation in the
   two countries.

Theory of Income, Employment, and Price Level

Winter, 1970

(WRITE IN BLACK INK)

Preliminary Examination for the Ph.D.

WRITE THE FOLLOWING INFORMATION ON YOUR EXAMINATION PAPER:

> Your Code Number and NOT Your Name
> Name of Examination
> Date of Examination

Results of the examination will be sent to you by letter.

Answer all questions. Time: 3 hours.

(40) I. Indicate true, false, or uncertain and provide a brief
         explanation.

1. Between 1946 and 1965 the price level increased substantially.
   During this same period the nominal money stock increased
   almost every year, but by an average rate well below 4 per
   cent per annum. It follows, therefore, that if the 4 per
   cent money stock rule had been used in this period, inflation
   would have been much worse than it actually was.

2. The term structure of interest rates slopes downward when
   there are excess supplies of short term securities and
   excess demands for longer term securities.

3. We know that everyone holds money, and that real balances
   can be manipulated by monetary policy. It follows that the
   appropriate monetary policy would increase the wealth and
   hence welfare of each individual separately.

4. When the stock of capital is growing, the marginal efficiency
   of investment exceeds the marginal product of capital. Explain.

5. The instability of the equilibrium path in Harrod-Domar growth
   models can be attributed entirely to the particular assumption
   made about the aggregate production function. Explain.

6. A recession in which prices and wages continue to rise
   provides evidence of a cost push inflation. Explain.

7. A government deficit financed by borrowing money from the
   commercial banks is more inflationary than the same deficit
   financed by borrowing money from the general public.

8. A change in the rate of monetary expansion from a steady rate of zero per cent (generating, say, zero per cent inflation) to a steady rate of 10 per cent will end up by producing inflation at a steady rate of 10 per cent (assuming no real growth) but in the process of adjustment the rate of price rise must for some period exceed the rate of expansion of the money supply.

20) II. Interpret, and if you can, reconcile the following three quotations from Keynes.

(a) "It is for this reason, amongst others, that a high bank rate should be associated with a period of rising prices, and a low bank rate with a period of falling prices." (J.M. Keynes, Monetary Reform, 1923, p. 25).

(b) "We have, therefore, . . . a simple and direct explanation why a rise in the Bank rate tends . . . to depress price levels." (J.M. Keynes, A Treatise on Money, 1930, Vol. I, p. 155).

(c) "An increase in the quantity of money may be expected, cet. par., to reduce the rate of interest . . .; a decline in the rate of interest may be expected, cet. par., to increase the volume of investment . . .; an increase in the volume of investment may be expected . . . to increase employment . . . Finally, if employment increases, prices will rise. . . And when output has increased and prices have risen, the effect of this will be to increase the quantity of money necessary to maintain a given rate of interest." (J.M. Keynes, General Theory, 1935, pp. 142-43).

40) III. Vast oil fields were recently discovered on the North Slope of Alaska. The rights to develop the fields were auctioned off in a mammoth auction involving the payment of large sums of money to the State of Alaska for the rights. These oil fields will yield little or no oil for some years, but in the meantime large sums will be spent to develop the fields and to build pipelines or other means to transport the oil.

(a) What effect, if any, would you expect the auction itself and the transfer of funds to have on the economy?

(b) Analyze the effect of the discovery and the early years of development on nominal and real income using

(i) Income-expenditure theoretical framework.

(ii) Quantity-Theory framework.

(25) IV. What is the Phillips curve? How can you explain the empirical results that show a satisfactory Phillips curve relationship for a country like Britain, but a more confused pattern for the United States? What sort of empirical relationship would you expect to find for Brazil or other countries that have a long history of inflation?

(30) V. Beginning in 1962, the Kennedy Administration introduced a series of measures designed to stimulate private investment in plant and equipment, the principal ones being (1) an investment tax credit equal to 7 per cent of the amount spent on eligible plant and equipment, and (2) a shortening of the length of time over which business firms could depreciate their assets.

On the assumptions that in the years from 1962 to 1966 where still remained some "slack" in the economy and that savings behavior is described by the equation $S = KY$, describe the effects of the tax stimuli on

(a) Saving, interest rates, residential construction, money supply and the balance of payments assuming that the monetary policy actually pursued in 1962-66 successfully kept national income on the same time path as it would have followed in the absence of the tax measures.

(b) Saving, national income, residential construction, money supply and the balance of payments, assuming that the monetary policy actually pursued in 1962-66 successfully kept interest rates on the same time path as they would have followed in the absence of the tax measures.

(25) VI. The Federal Reserve System has authority to buy Federal National Mortgage Association obligations (FNMA obligations channel funds into mortgage granting intermediaries) for its open market portfolio. This authority was granted with the hope that these operations would subsidize the home building industry, particularly in tight money periods. Analyze this policy in terms of

(a) the factors which are likely to make it more or less effective in subsidizing the home building industry, and

(b) the effects the policy might have on other types of economic activity.

CORE EXAMINATION

Theory of Income, Employment, and Price Level

Summer, 1969

Preliminary Examination for the Ph.D.

WRITE THE FOLLOWING INFORMATION ON YOUR EXAMINATION PAPER:

> Your Code Number and NOT your name
> Name of Examination
> Date of Examination

Results of the examination will be sent to you by letter.

Answer all questions.   Time: 3 hours

Part I.   (60 minutes)   Indicate whether each of the following statements is True (T), False (F) or Uncertain (U) and state briefly your reason.

1. A shift on the part of the public out of demand deposits and into savings deposits will generally increase the supply of inside money but leave the supply of outside money unchanged.

2. The inventory theory of transactions demand for money predicts that the quantity of money demanded will increase less than in proportion to income, and therefore that the rate of inflation will exceed the rate of monetary expansion (ignoring growth of real output).

3. An inflation is described as a reduction in the value of money; hence a devaluation is inflationary because it reduces the value of our money in terms of other currencies.

4. To optimize the quantity of money holdings, it is necessary to allow banks to pay interest on demand deposits.

5. The fact that short-term interest rates currently exceed long-term rates suggests that the short-term market is being flooded with high-risk securities.

6. As the LM function describes those combinations of interest rates and incomes such that the money market is in equilibrium, it follows from the portfolio approach to the demand for money that the bond market is also in equilibrium along the LM function.

7. From the point of view of monetary policy, the crucial difference between commercial banks and non-bank financial intermediaries is that banks hold their cash reserves on deposit with the central bank, whereas the intermediaries hold their cash reserves on deposit with commercial banks.

8. A long-run marginal propensity to consume of unity (or higher) is inconsistent with sustained saving and hence investment.

9. A tax surcharge cannot reduce inflationary pressure unless there is a "liquidity trap" in the demand for money.

10. The most that the government can add to the growth rate (in percentage points) by inflationary financing is $100 \, \dfrac{\overline{\Pi}}{vk}$, where $\overline{\Pi}$ is the rate of inflation, v the velocity of circulation, k the capital-output ratio.

11. Empirical studies in the United Kingdom suggest that incomes policy has been able to reduce the rate of wage increase by about one percentage point at any level of unemployment. This finding implies that incomes policy is a useful component of balance-of-payments policy.

12. The international monetary system would be unable to cope with greater flexibility of exchange rates, because the large forward discounts and premia that would develop in times of currency crises would make international trade unprofitable.

13. If the demand for goods were a function of real income only, and the demand for money were a function of interest rates only, then the demand for securities (bonds) must be a function of both real income and interest rates.

14. The immediate effect of an increase in social security payments would be to increase national income relative to personal income.

15. The simplest Keynesian multiplier for an increase in government expenditure is the reciprocal of the marginal propensity to save; the simplest money multiplier is the reciprocal of the marginal propensity to hold money. Therefore the Keynesian and quantity theories will make exactly the same prediction about the effect of an increase in government expenditure financed by printing money, provided that the public holds all its marginal savings in the form of money.

Part II

1.   (30 minutes)
     The Phillips curve, as interpreted by Phelps and others,
     postulates an inverse relationship between the percentage rate
     of unemployment and the rate of change of money wages, of the
     form

$$\frac{\dot{w}}{w} = f(u)$$

where w is the money wage rate, $\dot{w}$ its rate of change, and u is
the unemployment percentage, with $f'(u) < 0$.

   (a) How would you modify the Phillips curve to provide a trade-off
       relationship between the rate of inflation and the
       percentage rate of unemployment?

   (b) Assuming that a stable Phillips curve has been estimated for
       a given economy, what sort of position on it would you expect
       a rational government to choose as a policy target, and
       why?

   (c) What would you expect to happen over time in an economy
       that adopted a policy target of the kind described?

   (d) In the light of your answer to (c), how would you write the
       equation for the Phillips curve? What would you expect the
       results of statistical testing to show about it, and why?

2.   (30 minutes)
     The celebrated balanced-budget theorem in its general form
     states that aggregate demand is not neutral with respect to the
     size of the government budget.

   (a) In the context of a simple Keynesian model, demonstrate
       sufficient conditions for the balanced-budget multiplier
       to be positive.

   (b) Same as (a), but demonstrate sufficient conditions for
       that multiplier to be negative. How do you interpret this
       result?

   (c) As the budget is always, in a certain sense, balanced, why
       is it usually asserted that balancing it with bond sales to
       the public is more expansionary than balancing it with taxes?
       If you demonstrate this proposition mathematically, be sure
       to give a verbal interpretation of that proof.

3. (30 minutes)
The government of a certain country, tired of the expense of policing its currency against the illegal counterfeiting of small bills, decides to license the private production of such bills, subject to a royalty payment to the government. Specifically, the government licenses anyone to print one-dollar bills in any quantity and guarantees these bills the attribute of legal tender, provided that (a) the issuer pays one dollar to the government for every dollar he prints for private use (b) the issuer guarantees to replace every dollar bill he has issued in the past on request and free of charge. This policy is effective in turning all forgers into legitimate businessmen and removing the need for a forgery squad of policemen.

(i) Assuming a closed economy:

(a) What is the effect on the price level?
(b) What is the effect on (measured) real rational income?
(c) What is the effect on the economic welfare of the country?

(ii) Assuming an open economy, what will be the effects of this policy

(a) if the country has a fixed exchange rate
(b) if it has a floating exchange rate.

4. (30 minutes)
"The Keynesian Theory lacks a theory of the determination of prices in the long run. The Quantity Theory lacks a theory of the determination of output and the interest rate in the short run."

(a) In what sense if any is this generalization true?

(b) Discuss the line of analysis that each theory would suggest as a remedy for the defect attributed to it.

(c) How would you develop your answer to (b) into a synthesis of the two theories?

CORE EXAMINATION

Theory of Income, Employment and Price Level

Winter, 1969

Preliminary Examination for the Ph.D.

WRITE THE FOLLOWING INFORMATION ON YOUR EXAMINATION PAPER:

- Your Code Number and NOT your name
- Name of Examination
- Date of Examination

Results of the Examination will be sent to you by letter.

Answer all questions.   Time: 3 hours.

I. A. Indicate whether each of the following statements is True (T),
       False (F), or Uncertain (U), and state briefly your reasons:

_____ 1. If the capital stock is growing, then the marginal efficiency
         of investment is greater than the marginal product of capital.

_____ 2. In an economy growing at a rate of 4 percent per year in which
         the income elasticity of demand for money is 2.0, a budget
         deficit of up to 3 percent of government expenditures can be
         financed by money creation without producing inflation.

_____ 3. In a simple income determination model, the elasticity of
         income with respect to changes in the marginal propensity to
         consume is given by mpc/(1-mpc).

_____ 4. The instability of the growth equilibrium in Harrod-Domar models
         can validly be attributed to the particular assumptions made
         about the production function.

_____ 5. A decline in prices raises real balances for a fixed quantity
         of money. This is known as the real balance effect.

_____ 6. A real balance effect is compatible with a liquidity trap.

_____ 7. A decrease in rental rates on cars which led to no change in
         the total number of cars in operation would raise recorded
         national income.

Ph.D. Core Theory of Income...Winter, 1969

B. Fill in the missing numbers and briefly describe how you obtained them. Neglect any effects of the corporation or personal income taxes. Assume all rates are on an annual basis.

Annual interest rate on government consols =	6.5	perc‑
Annual dividends as a percent of earnings =	25	perc‑
Dividend yield of common stock =	3	perc‑
Rate of return on real estate =	5	perc‑
Annual percentage rate of change of a price index of goods and services =		
Percentage rate of change in the price per share of common stock =		

II. Assume that in a closed economy tax revenue is proportionate to income, that the government fixes the level of its spending, and that the government finances all budget deficits by money creation. Analyze the consequences of this policy for the equilibrium level or rate of change of nominal income and show the effect of an increase in the level of government spending from an initial position of equilibrium. Discuss separately two cases: (a) the government fixes the nominal level of its spending; (b) the government fixes the real level of its spending.

III. "It is of no manner of consequence with regard to the domestic happiness of a state whether money be in a greater or less quantity. The good policy of the magistrate consists only in keeping it, if possible, still increasing" (David Hume, 1742). What is the verdict of two centuries of further writing on money on this proposition?

IV. "Many commentators have written as if commercial banks were losing deposits to their non-banking competitors." A closer look, however, shows that this notion is misleading.

"If a commercial bank depositor writes a check in favor of his mutual savings bank, the savings bank will either re-deposit the check in its own commercial bank account or extend mortgage credit to an individual. The individual, in turn, will either deposit the check in his bank account or turn it over to the seller of the house he is buying. And the seller will either put the check in his bank account or turn it over to his creditors who will put it in theirs....

"The crucial point is that commercial banks compare for deposits only with other commercial banks. They cannot lose deposits to other financial institutions or financial instruments."

Discuss.

Ph.D. Core Theory of Income...Winter, 1969

V. Consider the following neo-keynesian system in which C_t is real consumption, I_t is real investment, Y_t is real income and X_t is real autonomous expenditures.

$$C_t - \gamma \, C_{t-1} = k(1-\gamma)Y_t$$

$$I_t - \delta \, I_{t-1} = m(1-\delta)Y_t + X_t - \delta \, X_{t-1}$$

$$Y_t = C_t + I_t$$

What are the necessary conditions for stability? If these are satisfied, can the model generate cycles?

VI. Panama has no central bank but uses U.S. currency (plus some coin of its own), relabelling a dollar as a Balboa.

Netherlands has a central bank, which uses a national currency denominated in guilders.

The U.S. has a central bank which issues a national currency denominated in dollars.

The U.S. and Netherlands have fixed exchange rates with other major currencies. Assume that none of the countries has any extensive exchange control.

The monetary authorities of all three countries proclaim that they cannot control the quantity of money.

Discuss.

CORE EXAMINATION

Theory of Income, Employment, and Price Level
Summer, 1968

Preliminary Examination for the Ph. D.

WRITE THE FOLLOWING INFORMATION ON YOUR EXAMINATION PAPER:

Your Code Number and NOT your name
Name of Examination
Date of Examination

Results of the examination will be sent to you by letter.

Answer all questions. Time: 3 hours.

Part I: (60 points) Indicate whether each of the following
statements is True (T), False (F) or Uncertain (U),
and state briefly your reason.

1. If the balanced budget multiplier is unity, the unbalanced
    budget multiplier must be above unity.

2. A shift on the part of the public from time to demand
    deposits will reduce the money supply.

3. If the velocity of circulation is constant, a tax increase
    that is used to repay government debt will reduce
    inflationary pressure on the economy by the amount of the
    increased tax revenue collected.

4. The demand for money is less elastic with respect to
    market interest rates than with respect to the expected
    rate of inflation or deflation.

5. The immediate effect of a shift on the part of corporations
    from internal to debt finance of new investment would
    be to reduce disposable personal income and to increase
    net national product.

6. Since the state and not the public bears the cost of
    printing notes and minting coins, there will be a tendency
    towards excessive use of currency in making payments.

7. A "truth in lending law" requiring firms that sell goods
    on credit to state clearly the rate of interest they
    charge their customers, would reduce interest rates and
    hence be inflationary.

8. Inflation causes economic waste by reducing the value of old age pensions and thus obliging society to provide supplementary income to old people.

9. A rise in interest rates is inflationary because it raises the costs of production.

10. A country on a floating exchange rate will have to hold more international reserves than a country on a fixed exchange rate, because speculation against the currency is more likely under the former system.

11. Inflation would stop if average wage increases could be confined to equality with the average rate of increase of productivity in the economy.

12. The inventory theory of transactions demand for money predicts that transactions demand will have an income elasticity of +1/2 and an interest elasticity of -1/2.

Part II: (30 points) Identify briefly each of the following concepts.

1. The marginal efficiency of capital

2. Wicksell's "natural" rate of interest

3. The Pigou effect

4. The Ricardo effect

5. The accelerator

6. "Own" rates of interest

7. The purchasing power parity doctrine

8. The Phillips curve

9. The optional quantity of money

10. Fiscal drag

Part III: (80 points)

A. What inferences can be drawn about the distinction
    between real and monetary disturbances from the
    observation that interest rates are high during booms
    and low during recessions?

B. An Englishman holidaying on a small Mediteranean island
    paid all his expenses with checks on his English bank.
    The inhabitants were so impressed by his gentlemanly
    bearing that instead of cashing his checks they used
    them thereafter as money. Who paid for the Englishman's
    holiday?
    Answer in terms of (i) the quantity theory (ii) the
    Keynesian theory, assuming (a) a fixed (b) a floating
    exchange rate.

C. Debt finance of public (consumption) expenditure is said
    to pose a burden for future generations as it induces
    the current generation to consume more than it otherwise
    would. (a) What conditions must be fulfilled for this
    burden to exist? (b) Does debt finance of public
    investment pose a similar burden? If so, why; if not,
    why not?

D. Analyze and forecast the quantitive implications of the
    current 10% income tax surcharge on GNP, money supply,
    interest rates, and the rate of change in prices.
    State clearly the model you are using and the assumptions
    you are making about the other major economic variables.

Income, Employment, and the Price Level

Preliminary Examination for the Ph.D. and the A.M. Degree
Winter Quarter, 1968

WRITE THE FOLLOWING INFORMATION ON YOUR EXAMINATION PAPER:

    Your Code Number NOT your name
    Name of Examination
    Date of Examination

Results of the examination will be sent to you by letter.

Answer all questions. Time: 3 hours.

I. (35 points) Indicate whether each of the following
    statements is True (T), or False (F) and briefly explain
    your answer.

    1. In the classical quantity theory, the income elasticity
        of demand for money is one unless velocity depends on the
        rate of interest.

    2. The optimum quantity of money is that amount of outside
        money that makes the nominal interest rate zero.

    3. Consider an economy which consists of two industries,
        one a monopoly and the other perfectly competitive, and
        in which the quantity of money has been stable.
        A change to a steady rise in the money supply will raise
        real income in the short run.

    4. In the Keynesian system, a rise in the expected price
        relative to the current price will produce a rise in
        real income because this will increase the marginal
        efficiency of investment.

    5. National income would increase if a given amount of
        indirect taxes were replaced by the same amount of direct
        taxes.

    6. A devaluation intended to eliminate a balance of payment
        deficit will certainly be successful if the country has
        a monopoly in the goods it exports because this implies
        a high elasticity of the demand for exports.

7. If the prices of internationally traded goods in terms of the home currency eventually rise by the same amount as the devaluation, this will defeat the purpose of devaluation.

8. A rise in the price of gold without charging any exchange rates would be inflationary for the U.S. at present.

9. According to Say's Law the aggregate supply of goods and services equals aggregate demand regardless of the absolute price level and regardless of the interest elasticity of demand for real balances.

10. The multiplier in its simplest form is equal to both the inverse of the marginal propensity to save and to an infinite sum of powers of the marginal propensity to consume.

11. Even if the economy is not in a liquidity trap, an increase in the money supply may have no effect on the level of investment.

12. In the absence of costs of servicing bank deposits and restrictions on interest payments on deposits, the rate of interest on deposits should tend to be equal to the interest rate on loans made by the bank.

II. (20 points) The quantity of money is increased by a given amount, say, $10 billion.

a. By a reduction in bank reserve requirements that induces banks to expand loans by an amount that produces as its final effect a $10 billion increase.

b. By the declaration and distribution of a veteran's bonus amounting to $10 billion financed by printing money (assume any secondary expansion by banks is prevented by appropriate changes in reserve requirements).

c. By an expansion in government expenditures of $10 billion financed by printing money (again assume any secondary expansion by banks is prevented).

Analyze the differential effects to be expected from these three measures in terms of (a) the quantity theory, (b) the income-expenditure theory.

III. (15 points) President Johnson has proposed that the
      present requirement for a gold reserve be removed and
      Congress will probably enact a bill to this effect shortly.

   a. What is the present requirement?

   b. What is the history of such a requirement under the
       Federal Reserve System?

   c. What are the arguments in favor of keeping the require-
       ment?

   d. What are the arguments in favor of removing the
       requirement?

IV. (10 points) "It is ... of utmost importance ... to
     remember that the direction in which the interest rate
     apparently moves is generally precisely the opposite of
     that in which it really moves, "(Irving Fisher, The Theory
     of Interest, p. 494). Explain or attack this statement.

V.   (10 points) Consider a very simple multiplier-accelerator
     model:

$$C_t = \alpha Y_{t-1}$$
$$I_t = \beta (Y_{t-1} - Y_{t-2})$$
$$Y_t = C_t + I_t$$

   1. Under what restrictions on the parameters is the resulting
       path of income (Y) stable?

   2. Under what conditions will a change in I result in a
       cyclical path in Y?

VI. (10 points) The Federal Reserve conducts its open market
operations with short term government securities.
According to some authorities, the impact of a given purchase
or sale of government bonds is greater the longer the term to
maturity of the bonds. Ideally, they argue, all government
bonds ought to be perpetuities ("consols"). What effect would
you expect if the Treasury converted all government bonds held
by the Federal Reserve System to consols and if the Fed. thereafter used these consols in its open market operations?

CORE EXAMINATION

Theory of Income, Employment and Price Level
Summer, 1967

Preliminary Examination for the Ph.D.

WRITE THE FOLLOWING INFORMATION ON YOUR EXAMINATION PAPER:

Your Code Number and NOT your name
Name of Examination
Date of Examination

Results of the examination will be sent to you by letter.

Answer all questions. Time: 3 hours.

Part I. Indicate whether each of the following statements is True (T) or False(F) and state briefly your reason. (One hour).

_____1. Free reserves are the difference between total reserves and required reserves.

_____2. Member banks may count both currency in vault and deposits at their Federal Reserve Bank as satisfying reserve requirements.

_____3. All banks in the U.S. that are members of the Federal Reserve System are required to be members of the Federal Deposit Insurance Corporation, but the reverse is not true.

_____4. The Federal Funds rate is the rate at which member banks may borrow from the Federal Reserve System.

5-8:   A depositor in a commercial bank transfers funds from a demand deposit to a time deposit at that bank.

_____5. The bank's total reserves are thereby increased.

_____6. The bank's excess reserves are thereby increased.

_____7. The amount of currency plus demand deposits that can be outstanding in the System is increased.

_____8. The amount of currency plus demand deposits plus commercial bank time deposits that can be outstanding in the System is increased.

____9. If income velocity of circulation of money is not affected by an increase in real income per capita, then the income elasticity of demand for real balances is zero.

____10. A rise in interest rates can be expected to raise the income velocity of circulation of money.

____11. The real balance effect is absent if all money is "inside" money.

____12. In order for a real balance effect to exist, wealth must be one of the variables entering the consumption function.

____13. The real interest rate can be obtained from the nominal interest rate by dividing by a price index.

____14. The more rapidly the quantity of money grows, the lower will be the quantity of real money balances.

____15. The higher the rate of interest, the lower will be the Keynesian multiplier.

____16. A tariff reduction involves a shift in the IS (or EE) curve associating a lower real income with each interest rate.

____17. A substitution of taxes on property for taxes on earnings (to yield the same revenue at the same national income) will tend to lower national income.

18 to 20. In the simple income-expenditure model with rigid prices:

        ____18. A constant positive rate of growth of the quantity of money implies a constant interest rate.

        ____19. A constant rate of government deficit spending with a fixed stock of money implies a constant interest rate.

        ____20. A rising stock of capital is inconsistent with a constant interest rate.

Part II.   Each of the following statements is true.
            Prove it.   (1/2 hour).

1.   The slope of the LM (or LL) curve is flatter, the more
elastic the demand for money with respect to the interest rate
and the less elastic with respect to income.

2.   Monetary velocity can be expected to be uncorrelated with
the level of prices but to be sensitive to the rate of change
of prices.

3.   Treasury policy of substituting long term obligations for
short-term obligations in the federal debt outstanding will
produce deflationary pressure on the economy if and only if
the expectations hypothesis about the term structure of interest
rates is false or incomplete.

4.   For a given quantity of money, an increase in the government
deficit will produce inflationary pressure on the economy, if
and only if the elasticity of demand for real money balances
with respect to the rate of interest is less than zero.

5.   The usual balanced budget multiplier is unity if and only
if liquidity preference is either absolute or depends on
income excluding government expenditures.

Part III.   Consider the following two proposed fiscal policies.
             (1/2 hour).

        (a)   Balance continuously the high-employment budget.

        (b)   Keep tax rates constant.

     In considering (a), assume that it can be followed (i.e., that
it is possible with at most a brief lag to change taxes in response
to changes in government expenditures so that, at high employment,
the proceeds of all taxes would equal the amount of expenditure
at that level of employment).   Assume also all other conditions,
including monetary policy, the same for (a) and (b).
     Aside from the effect on the average level of income, which
policy do you believe would produce greater <u>stability</u> of income?
Justify your answer as rigorously as you can.

Part IV.   Analyze the likely short and long run effects on
            interest rates, prices, employment and income velocity
            of an increase in the rate of monetary expansion from,
            say, a non-inflationary full employment rate to a
            higher rate.   (1/2 hour).

Part V.   In a closed economy the central bank can determine
            the nominal quantity of money, while the public
            determines its real value, whereas in an open economy
            the nominal quantity of money is determined by the
            balance of payments.

            Discuss the validity of this statement under alternative
            assumptions of fixed and flexible exchange rates.
            (1/2 hour).

CORE EXAMINATION

Theory of Income, Employment and Price Level

Summer, 1966

Answer all questions. Time: 3 hours.

MAXIMUM SCORE = 180 Points.

Part I: 90 Points - Indicate whether you believe the following
statements to be true, false, or uncertain. In each case write
a few sentences explaining your answer.

1. Monetary and fiscal policies can increase employment only
    insofar as they lower the real wage rate.

2. Monetary and fiscal policies differ, in a closed economy,
    primarily in their differential effects on the interest rate.

3. The economic cost of inflation is less than the economic cost
    of unemployment.

4. Rapid monetary expansion lowers the rate of interest in the
    short run but raises it in the long run.

5. A tax on the production of capital goods generally lowers the
    marginal effeciency of investment.

6. Unemployment and GNP velocity are inversely correlated over
    the business cycle because the demand for cash is inversely
    associated with the rate of interest.

7. An increase in govt. spending generally lowers the real wage
    rate and raises the interest rate if the money supply and
    money wage rates are constant.

8. Repressed inflation is less likely to distort the efficiency
    of resource allocation than open inflation.

9. A monetary rule based on a constant percentage yearly increase
    in the money supply would not work in an open economy if the
    exchange rate is fixed.

10. A fiscal deficit financed by borrowing from the commercial
    bank is more inflationary than a deficit of the same size
    financed by borrowing from the general public.

11. A rise in the money supply will normally cause a sufficient
    reduction in the rate of interest, so that the demand for cash
    balances will increase to absorb the increased money supply.

12. A rise in the rate of price inflation in one period will itself
    tend to increase the rate of inflation in subsequent periods.

13. The elimination of import restrictions will tend to increase the degree of "built in" stability of the economy.

14. It is possible that a reduction in income tax rates will by itself so stimulate production that income tax yields will rise.

15. The effects of open-market operations on the demand for goods and services operates exclusively through the interest rate.

Part II: 30 Points - Within the last couple of years there have been discoveries of very large bodies of minerals in Canada, not previously known. As a matter of pure theory, (A) under condition of wage rigidity and underemployment, how would you expect these discoveries, other things being the same, to effect the following variables in Canada, assuming the nominal money stock is constant.

1) Interest Rate. 2) Employment. 3) Consumption.
4) The Real Money Stock.

In each case, indicate whether you expect an increase, decrease, or no change in designated variable, and justify briefly your answer.

B) Answer the same question under conditions of flexible wages and full employment.

Part III: 60 Points - "The Fed. gave signs of tightening its monetary policy another notch... In the week ended Wednesday, the net borrowed or 'minus' reserve position of member banks, a rough indicator of monetary policy, rose to the highest level since Feb. 17, 1960 (an average of $456 million a day). Providing another indication of tight money, total borrowings by member banks from the Fed. in the latest period averaged $827 million a day, a 6½ year high.
      "Other figures...showed that commercial and industrial loans at major New York City banks continued to move upward...up $2,121 million since the start of the year... In the like week last year, business loans at the 13 reporting banks in New York fell $96 million and the cumulative advance from the start of 1965 was $1,804 million." (Wall Street Journal, July 8, 1966).

      "Commercial banks from coast to coast boosted their prime rate... from 5 1/2 per cent to 5 3/4 per cent... The prime-rate hike caused speculation that the Fed. would any day now increase its 4 1/2 per cent discount rate. (Time, July 8, 1966).

a. Explain briefly the following technical terms from these excerpts:
   1. Net borrowed or "minus" reserve positions (also called "free reserves" or "minus free reserves").
   2. Prime Rate.
   3. Borrowings by member banks from the Reserve System.
   4. Discount Rate.

b. Why is net borrowed reserves regarded as an indicator of monetary policy? Why"rough" indicator?

c. How can the Federal Reserve System affect or control net borrowed reserves?

d. How do you explain the fact that despite the allegation of tight money in the first paragraph there was a more rapid expansion of bank loans in 1966 than in prior years (assume as is correct, that this is true for all banks in the U.S. and not merely New York banks.

e. Does your answer to d. raise any questions about the validity of "net borrowed reserves" as an indicator of tightness of money?

f. Explain the relation between the rise in member bank borrowings from the Federal Reserve and the facts cited in the last paragraph.

g. If banks can lend at 5 3/4 per cent and borrow at 4 1/2 per cent why are borrowings so moderate? (Note that commercial bank loans are around $200 million).

h. What alternative indicators of tightness of money would you suggest?

Theory of Income, Employment and Price Level
Winter, 1967

Answer all questions. Time: 3 hours.

MAXIMUM SCORE - 192 Points.

1. (30 points)
   Indicate in the following table the immediate effect (+,-,0)
   on the items listed in the columns of changes in the items
   listed in the rows. Assume no other changes occur except
   those explicitly mentioned. If necessary you may briefly
   state your assumptions.

	GNP	NNP	Nat. Income	Personal Income	Personal Disposable Income
a) Increase in social security taxes.					
b) Removal of special tax credit for accelerated depreciation.					
c) Decrease in Fed. taxes.					
d) Increase in corporation income tax.					
e) Increase in import tariffs.					
f) Sale of TVA to private companies.					

Part II: Answer the following questions.

1. (30 points).
   a) The reason that bank deposits are also included in the
   stock of money is not far to seek. When a person has $10 in
   his pocket and $100 in the bank he is in a position to spend
   $110 at any time. These two kinds of money represent his
   cash resources because currency and bank deposits are
   convertible into each other at a bank at any time.
   Hence currency and bank deposits are close substitutes for
   each other.

b) The relative prices of two commodities are more nearly constant, the more closely substitutable the two items are for each other. Hence for nearly perfect substitutes we expect to observe nearly constant price ratios and (possibly) erratic fluctuations in relative quantities. In contrast, for complementary goods it is the relative quantities that remain nearly constant while the relative prices are subject to wider fluctuations. Since the proportions between currency, demand deposits and time deposits remain nearly constant over time this suggests they are more nearly complements than substitutes.

I) Reconcile these two statements if you can. State whether you agree or disagree with them and remedy their deficiencies.

II) How would you apply the criteria they suggest to determine whether Treasury Bills or Savings and Loan deposits should be included as part of the stock of money.

2. (30 points)
The U.S.A. is currently experiencing a substantial balance of payments deficit that is being financed by sales of gold to foreigners. Devaluation of the dollar would, it is argued, reduce or eliminate that deficit by increasing the world demand for U.S. output and by reducing the U.S. demand for foreign output. In a Keynesian framework the implied shifts in demand are clearly expansionary from the viewpoint of the U.S., and hence this proposal has received little support from those Keynesians concerned with the past and current inflation. It has also been pointed out that devaluation would directly aggravate current inflation because prices of many import and export goods would increase immediately as a result of the increase in the dollar price of foreign exchange.

I) In the event of devaluation are there any forces that would cause the prices of goods and services not entering international trade to rise? Are there any forces causing the prices of these goods to fall?

II) In a number of cases, countries with balance of payments deficits have found that a devaluation has been immediately followed by both inflation and unemployment. How might one explain this?

3. (30 points)
a) Use the LS-LM framework to analyze the effect of a "tight-money" policy on interest rates, the price level, and real wages. Describe the conditions under which such a policy will be associated with falling interest rates.

b) Use the Quantity Theory framework to analyze the consequences of an increase in social security taxes with an equal increase in social security payments.

Answer the following questions true, false or uncertain, and briefly explain your answer. (6 points each).

1. With a constant amount of high powered money an increase in loanable funds can result from a decrease in the public's holding of currency.

2. Even with zero transactions costs, uncertainty in the timing and amount of receipts and expenditures would explain the public's willingness to hold money.

3. Rising real wages tend to reduce the velocity of money.

4. One of the real costs of settling international obligations in gold is the interest foregone on the gold reserves.

5. If an increase in stock prices tends to increase real consumption then a rise in the interest rate tends to increase savings.

6. Under flexible exchange rates, the prices of domestically produced goods will be independent of the balance of trade.

7. From a position of less than full employment, a move to full employment will require a fall in real wages, and vice versa.

8. An open market purchase of Govt. bonds by the Fed. Res. will have an expansionary effect only if it is true that an excess supply of real cash balances implies excess demand for bonds and securities.

9. For a given level of Govt. expenditures a shift from tax to bond finance is expansionary because of the implied deficit.

10. If, in the long run, the marginal propensity to consume is 1, sustained growth is not possible as saving will approach zero.

11. If the demand for money is a function of the short-term rate of interest, and if the level of investment spending is a function of the long term rate, monetary policy will be unable to influence investment and hence the level of real output.

12. The marginal propensity to spend out of real income is necessarily less than unity if the elasticity of demand for real cash balances with respect to real income is positive.

CORE EXAMINATION

Theory of Income, Employment and Price Level
Winter, 1966

Preliminary Examination for the Ph.D.

Answer all questions.   Time: 3 hours.

PART I.
  Indicate by inserting in each box 0, +, or -, the direction
  of effect of each operation on each magnitude.
  Consider only initial effect of operation not subsequent
  reactions of banks or others.   Assume that M (quantity of
  money) is defined as equal to currency plus demand deposits
  of commercial banks.

Effect of	Total Bank Reserves	Fed. Res. Credit outstanding	Free Reserves	Excess Reserves	M
1. Fed. Res. Sale of Govt. Bond to.. a) Commercial Bank					
b) Public					
c) U.S. Treasury					
2. Rise in Reserve requirements imposed by Fed. Res. on Commercial Banks.					
3. Rediscounting of bill by member bank at Fed. Res. Bank.					
4. Transfer of deposit by U.S. Treasury from member bank to Fed.					

PART 2

Circle the letter corresponding to the correct answer.
Defend your choice briefly.

1.   In the Keynesian system an increase in the money supply
       will tend to...

       a)   increase output and raise the marginal physical
            product of labor.
       b)   raise the price level and lower investment.
       c)   raise the interest rate and lower investment.
       d)   lower the marginal physical product of labor and
            raise real income.
       e)   raise consumption and decrease the price of capital
            goods.

2.   The marginal efficiency of capital falls as investment
       increases because...

       a)   the interest rate is low when investment is high.
       b)   effective demand is high when investment is high.
       c)   of diminishing returns in the capital goods industries
       d)   as the capital stock increases the return on capital f
       e)   an increase in investment must be accompanied by an
            increase in the money supply.

3.   In an economy with goods, money and securities an excess
       demand for money is consistent with: (I) an excess demand
       for goods and an excess demand for securities; (II)   an
       excess demand for goods and an excess supply of securities
       (III) an excess supply of goods and an excess supply of
       securities; (IV) an excess supply of goods and an excess
       demand for securities...

       a)   only I and II.
       b)   only III and IV.
       c)   only II and IV.
       d)   only II, III and IV.
       e)   only I, II and III.

4.   "Equilibrium" with rising prices implies that...

       a)   the stock of money is constant.
       b)   the nominal interest rate is higher than the real
            interest rate.
       c)   the income velocity of money is equal to the interest
       d)   the rate of growth of monetary expansion is equal to
            the rate of growth of output.
       e)   the short term interest rate is lower than the long
            term interest rate.

5.   Suppose that from a position of internal balance (full
     employment, stable prices) and balance of payments deficit
     the authorities want to correct the deficit while retaining
     internal balance. To this end they may recommend...

a) a more restrictive fiscal policy to correct the external balance and a more expansive monetary policy to offset its deflationary effects.
b) an increase in the interest rates to correct the external balance and an increase in wage rates to offset its deflationary effects.
c) a reduction in wage rates to improve the trade balance and lower income taxes to prevent inflation.
d) sales of foreign currencies in the forward exchange markets to improve the balance of payments and a reduction in wages to expand employment.
e) depreciation of the exchange rate to improve the balance of payments, and tighter monetary policy to prevent inflation.

PART 3.

1. Analyze the effects of a Federal Reserve open market operation using the Keynesian framework.

2. Analyze the effect of a Federal tax cut using the Quantity Theory framework.

In each case make explicit any special assumptions you find necessary or convenient.

PART 4.

Derive the LS-LM diagram. Under the assumption of rigid prices, use it to show the effects of an increase in the rate of govt. expenditure to a new level maintained indefinitely, with no increase in tax rates - any deficit being financed by printing money. Distinguish the initial and ultimate effects on real income, interest rates, the money supply, and govt. budget.

PART 5.

Suppose banks were not legally required to hold reserves and could borrow freely from the Fed. at the quoted rediscount rate. How would this effect the operation and effects of monetary policy?

PART 6.

"The depreciation of paper money is apt to arise not so much from an extension of its quantity as from want of sufficient confidence in it. The great object of a bank should therefore be to maintain the public confidence to which it contributes by furnishing in return for bills confessedly good a species of paper money still better." Discuss.

MONEY AND BANKING

Preliminary Examination for the PhD and the A.M. Degree

Winter Quarter 1981

WRITE THE FOLLOWING INFORMATION ON YOUR EXAMINATION PAPER:

Your code number at the top left-hand corner of each page.
Number the pages at the top right-hand corner.
The name of the examination at the top of each page.
Write only on one side of the paper.
Write in black ink.

Results of the examination will be sent to you by letter.

Answer all questions.   Time: 4 hours

I.   (20 minutes)

A money market fund is a mutual fund which holds as assets short-term government securities and commercial paper. Its liabilities are demand deposits, which may be withdrawn by check. Originally, money market funds were unregulated by the Federal Reserve system.

  (i)   Would a legitimate public interest be served by the imposition of
        reserve requirements on these funds? Explain.

  (ii) What are the general principles which are appropriate for determining
        whether a corporation's liabilities should be classed as "money" and
        regulated as such?

II.   (25 minutes)

"It makes no difference whether government expenditures are financed with taxes or with bonds." Describe a scenario where the statement is true, and two (independent) reasons for which it would not be so.

III.   (30 minutes)

An interesting feature of the Diamond overlapping generations model is that one can find examples where per capita capital accumulates even when each generation plans to consume its entire wealth (no altruism). In such a context, is it possible to find cases where future generations derive higher utility than present ones? Does that require that future capital (in per capita terms) be higher than at present? Write down the model and at the very least clearly indicate how you would go about answering these questions.

-152-

IV. (30 minutes)

Some economists argue that with flexible exchange rates, a country would succeed in appreciating its currency if the Central Bank were to peg the interest rate at a higher level. Analyze this issue using a model with rational expectations and perfect wage/price flexibility.

V. (40 minutes)

Consider a closed economy with income Y, government expenditures on goods and services G, government debt B, and a supply of base or high-powered money M (all variables in current dollars). Then if the tax rate is t and the nominal rate of interest is r, the government budget constraint is

$$(1) \qquad rB + G - tY = \frac{dM}{dt} + \frac{dB}{dt} \quad .$$

Let real income be y and the price level P, so that $Y = Py$. Assume that y grows at a given percentage rate λ. Let money and income be related by the crude quantity-theoretic $kY = M$, k constant. Let the real interest rate be the constant ρ and assume the Fisherian equation $r = \rho + \frac{1}{P}\frac{dP}{dt}$.

Next, consider a policy regime in which the ratio $g = G/Y$ is fixed, in which the tax rate t is constant, and in which the rate of growth $\pi = \frac{1}{M}\frac{dM}{dt}$ is constant.

(i) Derive, given these assumptions, the differential equation giving the motion $\frac{db}{dt}$ of the debt-income ratio $b = B/Y$ as a function of ρ, π, λ, t, k and b.

(ii) Use this equation to discuss the long-run consequences of operating monetary and fiscal policies with fixed rules.

VI. (30 minutes)

A consumer observes n prices $p_1,\ldots,p_n$ in a given period. These prices (logarithmic deviations from means) are related by the model

$$p_i = \alpha_i x + \varepsilon_t \quad , \quad i=1,\ldots,n$$

VI. (continued)

or, in vector notation:

$$p = \alpha x + \varepsilon .$$

The random variables x, $\varepsilon_1, \ldots, \varepsilon_n$ are unobservable, mutually uncorrelated normally distributed, with 0 means and variances σ^2, $\lambda_1, \ldots, \lambda_n$. Find the expected value of x conditional on $(p_1, \ldots, p_n)$.

VII. (60 minutes)

Assume that consumption is described by the following permanent income model:

$$c_t = \beta y_{pt} + \varepsilon_t$$

where

y_{pt} = permanent income at time t = $(1 - \delta) \sum_{i=0}^{\infty} \delta^i E_t y_{t+i}$ $0 < \delta < 1$

y_t = real disposable income at time t

E_t = the expectation conditioned on information available at time t

c_t = consumption at time t

β = propensity to consume out of permanent income

ε_t = error term at time t.

In macroeconometric models, this relationship is estimated by assuming that expected future income is forecast with data on current and past income which leads to permanent income being described by a distributed lag on current and past income. I.e.,

$$y_{pt} = \sum_{i=0}^{\infty} \theta_i y_{t-i}$$

and the resulting consumption function estimated is:

(*) $$c_t = \sum_{i=0}^{\infty} \alpha_i y_{t-i} + \varepsilon_t$$

where

$$\alpha_i = \beta \theta_i$$

VII. (continued)

It is often argued that the $\sum_{i=0}^{\infty} \theta_i = 1$ because if y permanently rose by \$1,

permanent income would match this rise only if $\sum_{i=0}^{\infty} \theta_i = 1$. Therefore, many

econometricians assume that the estimated $\sum_{i=0}^{\infty} \alpha_i$ equal β, the propensity to

consume out of permanent income.

(a) Do you agree that the estimated value of the $\sum_{i=0}^{\infty} \alpha_i$ is a good estimate

of β? Why or why not? Be specific and use examples to illustrate
your answer.

(b) In a simultaneous equation system, (*) is identified by the exclusion
restriction that no other variables besides current and past income
appear on the right-hand side of (*). Can you explain why these exclusion restrictions should not be generally valid? (For example, is
there a plausible story why money growth might appear in the right-
hand side of (*)?)

(c) According to (*), if a permanent income tax cut were set to be implemented one year in the future, consumers would only respond to it
when the tax cut actually was implemented. Do you think that this is
reasonable? Why or why not? What issue does your answer raise for
the use of tax cuts as a tool for stabilization policy?

(d) Given that expectations are rational, what relationship would you expect
to find between consumption and income using Granger or Sims causality
tests? Explain your answer. What kind of relationship between consumption and money growth would you expect to find?

(e) How would you interpret the above results in terms of our usual
concept of causality?

May 14, 1974
1:00-5:00 P.M.

Write in black ink and write only on one side of each page.

Write the following information on the first page of your examination paper.

YOUR CODE NUMBER AND NOT YOUR NAME
NAME OF EXAMINATION
DATE OF EXAMINATION

Write the following information on each page of your examination paper:

UPPER LEFT: CODE NUMBER
UPPER RIGHT: NUMBER OF PAGE

When you fold your paper at the end of the exam, write your code number on the back of the last page, and indicate total number of pages.

Results of the examination will be sent to you by letter.

Answer all questions. Time: 4 hours*

*NOTE: The exam is only 200 minutes. You have 40 minutes at the beginning on which you can think but not write.

I. (72 minutes) True, False, or Uncertain (briefly defend your answer--6 minutes each).

A. The Baumol model implies that, over calendar time, an economy will experience a rising velocity.

B. If the government pushes passed the revenue-maximizing rate of inflation, the economy is unstable.

C. Under flexible exchange rates, if one country suffers higher inflation than the rest of the world, a capital outflow from that country is likely to result.

D. The adaptive expectations model for the rate of price change is inconsistent with the rational formation of expectations.

E. In the long run the stock of capital is determined by the equation of the marginal product of capital to the rate of time preference. Since the rate of time preference is fixed, changes in the monetary growth rate cannot affect the long-run capital-labor ratio.

F. The interest rate-sensitivity of money demand in Baumol/Tobin-type models depends on an individual moving in and out of an interest-bearing asset over the receipt period. Since most households would not find it worthwhile to make two trips to the asset market between each income payment, the actual sensitivity of household money demand to the interest rate must be quite small.

G. The optimum rate of deflation will be below the marginal product of capital if there are dead-weight costs associated with raising government revenue by other forms of taxation.

H. Speculative demand for money slows down the impact of a change in the money supply on aggregate demand.

I. If gold were revalued to the market price, rather than the official price, open market sales would have to be made in order to stabilize the monetary base.

J. After a "long" period of a stable rate of inflation, a sudden reduction in the rate of monetary expansion will produce a reduction in real cash balances, at least in the short run, in a closed economy.

K. If, other things equal, inflation accelerates when output exceeds its equilibrium level and vice versa, then the estimated Phillips curve will tend to be negatively sloped.

L. A balance of payments deficit in excess of a simultaneous fiscal deficit by the Central Bank cannot contract the domestic money supply if the former is financed by gold sales or foreign currency.

II. (13 minutes)

According to Mundell, "The optimum level of public debt is that which equates the marginal social cost of public capitalization of income streams with the marginal social benefits of capitalization. The social benefits of public capitalization will exceed costs if the private market is undercapitalized, as it probably is due to the imperfect capitalization of human income." Explain this statement.

III. (15 minutes)

The Federal Reserve-MIT-Penn model consists of a set of structural equations which describe the behavior of key economic variables. Suppose that one has available for these equations estimated parameter values and estimates of the moments of the stochastic terms, which are based on post-World War II experience. Suppose then that one compares the performance of different monetary rules by working out the (distribution of the) time paths of employment, prices, etc., predicted by the model for each monetary rule (and for a given time path of exogenous variables).

Evaluate this procedure in the light of the rational expectations hypothesis. Can the procedure be modified to take account of rational expectations? Do you think that such modification is important?

IV. (35 minutes)

Consider a bank whose assets consist of securities (S) and reserves (T). Its liabilities are all in the form of demand deposits (D). Suppose that the rate of return on the three assets are $r_s > 0$, $r_R > 0$, and $r_D \gtrless 0$, with r_s the largest of the three rates. Suppose that required reserves are $\ldots$ by λD, where λ is a constant between 0 and 1, and that banks hold neither excess nor borrowed reserves. Finally, suppose that there are real maintenance costs associated with maintaining the level of deposits as expressed b $\ldots$

function, $z(D)$, where $z(0) > 0$, $z' > 0$, $z'' > 0$--that is, maintenance costs increase with D at an increasing rate. Ignore any other element of bank costs or revenues.

1) Derive the bank supply of demand deposits function in terms of r_s, r_R, r_D and λ for a competitive bank.

2) Suppose that the demand for demand deposits is solely an inverse function of r_s-r_D, and that r_s, r_R and λ are determined exogenously:

   a) Discuss the determination of r_D.

   b) What is the effect of an increase in λ on r_D?

   c) What is the effect of an increase in r_R on r_D?

   d) Does the system have a sensible equilibrium under 100% reserve requirements, $\lambda = 1$?

   e) Discuss some implications of imposing a ceiling value on r_D (say, zero) which is below the equilibrium value of r_D.

V. (25 minutes)

Discuss how the following situations would affect the traditionally defined money stock (currency plus demand deposits).

A. Decriminalization of victimless crime.
B. U.S. international support for the dollar.
C. Severe winter storms over the Northeast.
D. Shift of foreigners to Eurodollar deposits.
E. General prohibition of branch banking.
F. Recent court ruling allowing discounts for cash customers over credit card price.

VI. (25 minutes)

Consider the U.S. economy which is initially in full international equilibrium. Employing international IS-LM analysis (Y and r are variable) discuss the macroeconomic consequences of the following actions and situations. Assume the balance of payments is less sensitive than the demand for money to the interest rate.

A. Arabs form a cartel to increase the price of oil, which is inelastically demanded in the U.S.
   1. Under fixed rates,
   2. Under floating rates.
B. Assume Arabs invest all the increased oil proceeds in U.S. securities. Describe the new equilibrium under floating rates.

VII. (15 minutes)

According to Lucas, the slope of the Phillips' curve (which relates output to the amount of unanticipated price change) will be smaller for countries in which the variance over time of the absolute price level is larger. Explain the origin of this hypothesis.

Money & Banking Prelim

Summer 1973
July 31
1:00-4:30 p.m.

WRITE THE FOLLOWING ON YOUR EXAMINATION PAPER:

Your code number and NOT your name in left corner of each page
Name of the examination
Date of the examination

Number the pages of your examination in right corner of each page

PLEASE NOTE THAT THE EXAM IS 3 1/2 HOURS LONG AND THE QUESTIONS ARE ONLY
3 HOURS AND 20 MINUTES. YOU HAVE TEN EXTRA MINUTES FOR THOUGHT -- NOT
WRITING!!

I. TFU (6 minutes each)

(1) As the average length of time between wage and other payments increases, the demand for money increases.

(2) If the term structure of interest rates rises out to maturities of three years, then falls, investors are irrational.

(3) An increase in the ratio of required bank reserves to demand deposits will not be contractionary if it reduces the demand for money more than it reduces the supply of money.

(4) An effective ceiling restriction on the interest charged on loans by banks is expansionary since it lowers the cost of funds to borrowers.

(5) The effect of a change in the quantity of money on aggregate demand will operate with a lag because the demand for money depends on "permanent" values of income, interest rate, etc., (e.g., distributed lags of past values of these variables), and not just on current values.

(6) In the long run a higher rate of inflation will raise the nominal rate of interest and may either raise or lower the real rate of interest.

(7) Commercial banks make a profit on the spread between the rates on their loans and deposits. If the reserve requirement for deposits at commercial banks were 100%, it would not be possible for banks to make a profit and they would be unwilling to accept any deposits.

(8) If the interest elasticity of the demand for money is non-zero, then an increase in government spending financed through an equal increase in taxes will increase nominal income.

(9) If the elasticity of demand for real balances with respect to the rate of inflation was minus one in a stationary economy, then there would be no government revenue from inflation.

(10) Flexible exchange rates permit countries to pursue independent monetary and fiscal policies.

(11) Borrowed reserves have increased from an average of about $400 million during last year to over $1 billion since May. This indicates that the Federal Reserve is pursuing a contractionary monetary policy.

(12) General equilibrium growth theories imply that a more rapid rate of monetary expansion will result in a lower level of per capita income and the same rate of growth in per capita income.

(28 minutes)

Suppose that the government reduces taxes and, in one case, finances the added deficit through issue of new money and, in another case, finances it through issue of new interest-bearing debt. What theoretical arguments suggest that the expansionary impact of the finance through money will be (a) greater, (b) of longer duration?

(30 minutes)

"If the demand for money is unstable but the demand for goods is stable, then the Fed should control interest rates in order to stabilize nominal income. If the demand for money is stable but the demand for goods is unstable, then the Fed should control the money stock."

(a) Analyze the above statement using a simple IS-LM model, in which wages and prices are flexible and continuous full employment is maintained. Treat an unstable demand for money as an LM curve which shifts randomly and an unstable demand for goods as an IS curve which shifts randomly. Assume

        (i)   that the Fed can achieve either the interest rate or the money supply it is aiming at instantaneously;

        (ii)   that the expected rate of inflation is zero;

        (iii) that "controlling interest rates" means choosing a constant interest rate, and "controlling the money supply" means choosing a constant money stock.

(b) Discuss the question of interest rate versus the money stock as the variable the Fed should control in a more general context, in which you do not necessarily make assumptions (i) and (ii) of part (a).

(30 minutes)

[a] "a substantial amount of the unemployment compatible with zero inflation is involuntary and nonoptimal,...., whether or not the inflations associated with lower rates of unemployment are steady or ever-accelerating. [b] Neither macro-economic policy makers, nor the elected officials and electorates to whom they are responsible, can avoid weighing the costs of unemployment against those of inflation." (James Tobin)

Discuss parts [a] and [b] of the above quotation. In particular

        (i)   (5 minutes) discuss the optimality properties of the zero inflation rate;

        (ii)   (15 minutes) discuss whether inflations associated with lower rates of unemployment are steady or ever-accelerating;

and (iii) (10 minutes) explain the costs of inflation and unemployment.

V. (20 minutes)

Briefly explain how each of the following events would change the stock
of money (currency plus demand deposits).

a. Laws are changed so that all victimless crimes such as gambling and
    prostitution are legalized.

b. The Federal Reserve System begins charging banks a fee for transactio
    in the federal funds market (the federal funds market involves banks
    loaning reserves to other banks for very short periods).

c. Banks are permitted to pay interest on demand deposits.

d. The Federal Reserve System sells the entire U.S. monetary gold stock
    American dollars at $120 per ounce.

VI. (20 minutes)

The current low price of the dollar in foreign exchange markets reflects
a shift in the tastes of foreigners for the outstanding stock of dollars
held abroad, leading to a desire by foreigners to reduce their holding
of dollars. The outstanding stock can be reduced only by U.S. surpluses
over the next few years. The exchange rate would thereafter tend to
appreciate. Alternatively, the U.S. Treasury could borrow foreign
currency from foreign central banks and buy back dollars, raising the
exchange rate immediately, and paying back the foreign currency over the
years. Discuss the relative merits of these two arrangements.

MONEY AND BANKING

Preliminary Examination for the Ph. D. and the A. M. Degree Autumn Quarter 1972

WRITE THE FOLLOWING ON YOUR EXAMINATION PAPER:

Your code number and NOT your name
Name of Examination
Date of Examination

The results of the examination will be sent to you by letter.

Answer all questions. Time: 4 hours

Part I. (75 minutes) Indicate whether the following statements are true, false,
or uncertain and give a brief justification of your answer.

1. "An excess of money will . . . show itself in two ways--partly through a
rise in all prices, partly through a fall in the rate of interest. But the
latter . . . can only be a temporary phenomenon . . . " (Wicksell, Interest
and Prices, xxiv, discussing Ricardo's views. Underlining in original).

2. In 1952 countries A and B have identical economies (tastes, technology,
factor endowments) and identical histories. In country A the continuously
compounded growth rate of the money supply is 0 per cent from 1953 to 1962
and 10 per cent from 1963 to 1972. In country B the money supply grows at
a constant rate of 5 per cent so that by December 31st the nominal money
supplies in the two countries are the same. The price level will be higher
in country A than in B on December 31, 1972.

3. When the U. S. Treasury receives tax payments the money supply falls,
but when State governments receive tax payments the money supply is unaffected.

4. Increases in Federal spending with taxes unchanged are bound to be inflationary since the demand for money is interest elastic.

5. The current excess of long-term over short-term interest rates on
government securities means that the rate of inflation expected in the
near future is less than that expected for several years from now.

6. An economy in which the creation of all money is a private monopoly with
a limit on total nominal issues, will not have any automatic tendency to
full employment.

7. A vertical long-run Phillips curve need not concern policymakers since
their horizon is only about four years at most--and in the short run there
certainly is a trade-off between inflation and unemployment.

8. The creation of a single European currency and a single European monetary authority will tend to widen the dispersion of the growth rates of the different European countries.

9. If the banking system holds 20 cents in highpowered money for every dollar of deposit liabilities, and the required reserve ratio is raised from .12 to .16, the banking system will begin holding more than 20 cents but less than 24 cents per dollar of deposit liabilities.

10. A secular trend in income velocity of money is inconsistent with a demand for money function that is unit elastic with respect to income.

11. The commercial banking system earns monopoly profits in its time deposit business during periods when they would be able and willing to pay higher rates of interest on time deposits, but are prevented from doing so by Regulation Q interest ceilings.

12. A country that experiences rising unemployment and rapid inflation in non-election years, and falling unemployment and declining rates of inflation in election years, is likely to be a country where monetary authorities understand monetary theory.

13. If the Europeans are successful in establishing a European currency, the U.S. should experience a large--if temporary--balance of payments surplus.

14. In a fixed exchange rate system of international payments, a small country that depreciates its currency must then undergo a period of increases in domestic prices.

15. If workers base their anticipations of inflation on past rates of inflation, then we expect an increase in the rate of actual inflation to be associated with an increase in the unemployment rate, and a decrease in the rate of inflation to be associated with a decrease in unemployment.

Part II. (20 minutes)

The market rate of interest on Canadian government bonds was lower than the rate on comparable American bonds throughout 1972.

(a) What explanations would you offer for this differential?

(b) What evidence would you need to support or reject your hypothesis?

(c) If the Canadian rate had been lower throughout the past 20 years, would you change your explanation? How?

rt III. (20 minutes)

der a system of fractional reserve requirements, the accounting and other
rvices associated with checking deposits are offered "free," or at least
ow the true cost of producing these services.

(a) How can commercial banks provide these services without charging
for them?

(b) How would the price charged for checking services change if banks
were forced to hold 100 per cent highpowered reserves?

rt IV. (30 minutes)

ritania is a country with a constant population, constant per capita real in-
ne, and a constant real interest rate of δ. On his last visit Professor
rberger estimated the real social cost, C, of obtaining real resources, T,
the government through methods of taxation other than inflation to be

(1) $C = aT + bT^2$ $\qquad$ $a > 0, b > 0$

The demand for real balances is

(2) $\left(\frac{M}{P}\right)^d = \alpha - \beta \Pi$ $\qquad$ $\alpha > 0, \quad \beta > 0$

ere Π is the expected rate of inflation. At a rate of deflation of δ, money-
ders are satiated with real balances.

Calculate the rate of inflation which minimizes the social costs of obtaining
al resources of $\bar{G}$ for the government. (You are expected to obtain an equa-
n for the rate of inflation as function of $\bar{G}$, which you need not solve ex-
citly.)

rt V. (30 minutes)

"It is no accident that Friedman and Meiselman found Keynesian theory to
be a better predictor than the quantity theory only in the 1930's. Keynesian
theory is applicable only in depressions. And since it has shown us how to
avoid depressions, it is no longer of use for the major policy problems."

"If Keynes had known the facts we now know he could not have blamed the
Great Depression on a collapse of the marginal efficiency of capital."

nment on these views.

Part VI. (30 minutes)

"The total deficit run up in the budgets of the Nixon years will amou
to more than $90 billion . . .

(a) " . . . does anyone doubt that the economy would be worse off than
is if the federal government were spending $90 billion less during
the Nixon years? . . .

(b) "If President Nixon had been producing balanced budgets all this
time it's likely he now would have a much higher unemployment rat
than the current 6.1 per cent to be defending before the electorate.
(Wall Street Journal, January 25, 1972)

Give the formal theoretical analysis underlying statements (a) and (b).
Are they equivalent statements? What empirical assumptions, if any, are
required to make them valid implications of that theoretical analysis?

Can you construct an argument that would justify a "doubt" about propo
sition (a)? Do not discuss issue of efficiency of government spending. Lim
your answer to effects on real income, as measured; unemployment; and
prices.

Part VII. (30 minutes)

In connection with Secretary of the Treasury Shultz's proposal at the recent
IMF meeting that standards for international monetary agreements be expressed in terms of an allowable reserve band for each country rather than
exchange rate band, one observer said, "Rigidly fixed exchange rates imply
floating reserves; rigidly fixed reserves imply floating exchange rates.
Mr. Shultz's proposal is therefore a step toward floating rates. "

Explain and evaluate this statement.

Money and Banking
Preliminary Examination
Spring, 1971

ructions: Write your code number at the top left-hand corner of each
, and number the pages at the top right-hand corner. Write the name
e examination at the top of each page. Write only on one side of the
. Write in black ink.)

0 minutes). Indicate whether each of the following statements is true,
lse, or uncertain and provide a brief explanation.

If all major currencies float to their equilibrium dollar values, then
e again fixed in terms of the dollar, the U.S. can expect to stop running
balance of payment deficit.

Inflationary taxes cannot be imposed by the U.S. on foreigners if they
ld their dollar reserves in the form of Treasury Bills.

If the exchange values of all goods and services were known by all
tential traders, and if everyone was willing to accept in exchange any
od or service at its exchange value, would there be any purpose in having
monetary good?

If the dollar appreciated by 10 per cent relative to all other currencies,
e world real money supply would be increased.

Since the West German Central Bank holds virtually no domestic govern-
nt securities, an independent monetary policy is impossible.

If the Regulation Q ceiling on time deposit rates is 6 per cent, a
billion increase in high-powered money will raise M_1 (currency and
mand deposits) by more when the Treasury bill rate is 9 percent than
en it is 3 per cent.

A permanent increase in the rate of monetary expansion will reduce the
al interest rate in the long-run if consumption is a function of wealth.

The standard income-expending model implies that an increase in govern-
nt expenditures financed by borrowing from the public will always

have a larger effect on income than an equal increase in government expenditures financed by increased taxes.

9. If the average and the variance of measured family incomes in two countries are the same at some point in time, and if country A has a much wider variance of family consumption exenditures than country B, then we may conclude that permanent income is less equally distributed in country A than in country B.

10. "But the daily revaluations of the Stock Exchange, though they are primarily made to facilitate transfers of old investments between one individual and another, inevitably exert a decisive influence on the rate of current investment." By this statement in the General Theory, Keynes meant that the marginal efficiency of capital schedule was unstable.

II. (30 minutes) A major strike occurs. The monetary authorities do not permit the strike to affect the time-path of the quantity of money.

(1) On a straightforward income-expenditure analysis, the associated decline in autonomous expenditures would be expected to make national income lower than it otherwise would have been both during and for some period after the strike.

(2) On a straightforward quantity theory analysis, no change in income would be expected either at the time of the strike or thereafter.

Reconcile (1) and (2) on a theoretical level.

III. (30 minutes). Consider the following alternatives.

(1) A federal Reserve open market purchase sufficient to produce as its final effect a $10 billion increase in the quantity of money.

(2) A reduction in bank reserve requirements sufficient to produce as its final effect a $10 billion increase in the quantity of money.

(3) The declaration and distribution of a veteran's bonus amounting to $10 billion financed by printing money, accompanied by a rise in reserve requirements sufficient to prevent any secondary expansion by banks, so that the quantity of money increases by $10 billion.

(4) Same as (3) but the bonus is financed by borrowing from the public with no change in the quantity of money.

Analyze the differential effects on nominal income to be expected from these four measures.

V. (30 minutes) You are operating the Federal Reserve Desk in New York under instructions to produce a 5 per cent per year increase in M_1 on as steady a month-to month basis as possible. What information would you require and how would you use it?

. (40 minutes) Two views have recently been expressed on the roles of monetary and fiscal policy.

(a)"A policy mix consisting of a less rapid expansion of the supply of money combined with a cut in tax rate could produce the same growth in nominal income as the present policy along with a lower rate of inflation."

(b)"It is time to remember that monetary policy should look abroad more and that fiscal policy should concentrate mainly on the home front." (Henry Wallich, Newsweek, May 17,1971).

1. Explain the logical analysis underlying these statements

2. If (a) is rejected, whether on theoretical or empirical grounds, must (b) also be rejected? And conversely?

. (40 minutes) Suppose that a fully competitive banking system were established in the U.S. by releasing commercial banks and other financial intermediaries from all government regulations on maximum allowable deposit rates and minimum reserve requirements and by freeing entry into banking. Explain and analyze the major differences between the hypothetical and present U.S. system as regards:

(a) The theory of the supply of money

(b) The ability of the monetary authorities to control nominal income.

(c) The validity of the proposition that "the monetary system passively supplies the money required by the real sector."

(d) The effect on economic welfare of an increase in the expected rate of inflation.

(30 minutes) It is January 1977, employment is "full," prices are stable, and the Federal budget is balanced. Suddenly the President announces that, after watching an appearance by Professor Milton Friedman on "Meet the Press," he has decided to recommend cutting Federal expenditures by half and tax revenues by an equal amount, and that he has the assurance of the Federal Reserve that they will keep the amount of money fixed.

Assume(unrealistically) that the President's recommendation passes
Congress by acclamation. Using the simplest income-expenditure model
adequate to the purpose:

(a) State the necessary and sufficient conditions for the President's action
to cause a drop in national income.

(b) On the assumption that there is an initial drop in national income,
state the values of the parameters in your model which would imply
a permanent increase in unemployment.

MONEY AND BANKING

Preliminary Examination for the Ph.D. and A.M. Degrees

Summer, 1970

(80 minutes) Indicate true, false, or uncertain and provide a brief explanation.

The full-equilibrium quantities and relative prices of goods and services in a multi-country world under a fixed-exchange-rate (gold standard) system are fundamentally independent of the parities which may be set between individual currencies and gold.

Tax stimuli (such as the investment tax credit) to business investment in plant and equipment can divert investment from other activities to the designated cases, but cannot by themselves increase the total volume of investment.

In a static model with markets for commodities, money, and labor, an increase in the saving/income ratio will reduce the interest rate and increase real balances.

In a monetary system with only a few banks, adjustment to an equilibrium reserve position is much quicker than in a system with many banks.

The current excess of long-term interest rates over short-term rates indicates an excess supply of long-term bonds and an excess demand for short-term bonds.

The assertion that "high interest rates indicate that money has been easy" implies that investment is a positive function of the interest rate.

When the market interest rate is above the regulation Q ceiling on time deposit rates, an increase in that ceiling raises the money multiplier (defined as demand deposits plus currency divided by high-powered money).

8. A government wishing to maximize the budget deficit which can be financed by monetary expansion will always create a positive rate of inflation.

9. In an anticipated inflation as compared to a situation of no inflation, the profitability of petroleum refineries would increase relative to that of supermarkets.

10. Federal Reserve Authorities are correct when they defend increases in the supply of money as an appropriate response to an increase in demand for business loans.

II. Essay questions

1. (35 min) A flow of U.S. bank deposits into Eurodollars:

   a. causes an increase in the U.S. balance of payments deficit.

   b. prevents the Federal Reserve from controlling the U.S. money supply.

   c. prevents European central banks from controlling the money supply of their own nations.

   d. is a necessary and sufficient condition for the existence of a "dollar standard" of international exchange.

   e. gives the Federal Reserve effective control of the world money supply.

Which, if any, of these statements are true? Analyze each, taking care to define terms carefully.

2. (25 min) Assume excess reserves of member banks are increased by billion dollars (a) by the Federal Reserve System acquiring 1_b of financial assets previously held by member banks, or (b) by a reduction in the required reserve ratio for demand deposits sufficient to release 1_b from required reserves. How would you expect the effects of these two policies to differ?

3. (25 min) "The usual assumption [about the demand for real balances] that the substitutability between real balances and capital is perfect, when the opportunity cost of holding real balances is zero. At that point, the marginal utility of real balances has been driven down to zero. On the

margin, they have the same attributes or characteristics and hence are the same good as far as the household is concerned."

Hence, asserts this writer, as the opportunity cost approaches zero, the percentage change in the quantity of money held per unit change in opportunity costs approaches infinity. Put differently, if opportunity cost is plotted on the vertical axis and the quantity of real balances demanded on the horizontal axis, the demand curve will become asymptotic to the horizontal axis as the opportunity cost approaches zero.

    a. What is the opportunity cost of real balances?

    b. Is the above analysis correct? Justify your answer.

4. (25 min) Derive, on the basis of the demand function for real cash balances, a relationship explaining the rate of change of the price level as a function of the relevant variables. Indicate how you would adapt this relationship to take into account the phenomenon of lagged response. What are the fundamental characteristics of the pattern of lagged response of the rate of change of prices to the rate of change of money supply? Explain in detail the theory underlying each of these characteristics.

5. (25 min) The quantity of money in the U.S. has grown at an annual rate of something like 4 per cent a year from December, 1969 to June, 1970--a decidedly higher rate than in the six months from June, 1969 to December, 1969. A number of commentators, however, have argued (a) that this is a highly misleading figure and does not involve an expansionary monetary policy. Prices have risen at the rate of 6 per cent a year since December, 1969, so, they say, the real money supply has been declining, demonstrating that monetary policy is highly deflationary, (b) that in order to reduce the rate of unemployment, they claim, there must be an increase in the real and not merely the dollar money supply.

Comment on each of the above assertions, making explicit your definition of an "expansionary monetary policy" and your interpretation of that relationship between the rate of unemployment on the one hand and the real and nominal money supplies on the other.

6. (25 min) A government in a hypothetical stationary economy has been maintaining a balanced budget and the quantity of money, consisting wholly of government fiat money, has been constant. The government increases expenditures by $X a year, and does not change tax revenues.

Using the IS-LM apparatus, trace the initial and ultimate effects of this new policy, for whatever alternative assumptions about resource utilization and price behavior you regard as pertinent, under the following conditions:

    a.   The government deficit is financed by printing additional money.

    b.   The deficit is financed by sales of interest-bearing bonds to the public.

In each case, make clear how the public is induced to hold the increased supply of money or bonds.

MONEY AND BANKING

Preliminary Examination for th Ph.D. and A, M. Degrees

Autumn, 1969

WRITE THE FOLLOWING INFORMATION ON YOUR EXAMINATION PAPER:

    Your code number and NOT your name
    Name of examination
    Date of examination.

Results of the examination will be sent to you by letter.

The time of the examination is 4 hours. The time allocation suggested
in the left margin corresponds to the grading weights.

I. Indicate whether the following statements are True, False or Uncertain
   and why. Your grade depends mainly on the explanation.

in.) a. Under the new system of reserve requirements adopted by the Federal
         Reserve in September 1968, the Federal Funds market is unnecessary,
         since the deposits subject to reserve requirements and bank vault
         cash are both calculated for the period two weeks in advance of the
         reserve settlement date.

in.) b. When banks purchase stationery or supplies by writing checks on
         themselves, they raise purchasing power in the community and cannot
         be restrained from doing so by Federal Reserve control.

in.) c. An increase in high-powered money will be "neutral" in an economy
         where government deficits have always(since the beginning of time
         until the present) been financed by the issuance in equal proportions
         of high-powered money and long-term bonds.

in.) d. A"humped" term structure of interest rates with short and long rates
         lower than intermediate term rates reflects relatively high anticipated
         rate of inflation in the intermediate run and relatively low anticipated rate of inflation in the short run and in the long run,

in.) e. The 1961-62 U.S. experiment in debt management called "Operation
         Twist" would have been predicted in advance to be a success by proponents
         of the "expectations" hypothesis of the term structure of interest rates.

-175-

(20 min.) II. Some journalists say "The sole source of Eurodollar deposits is U.S. balance of payments deficits." Do you agree? If not, explain other ways in which Eurodollar deposits can be created possibly using T account to clarify your answer.

(20 min.) III. Has the relation of money to income in the U.S. in the last few decades been more stable if time deposits are included in the definition of money than if only currency and demand deposits are included ? What is your explanation for the facts which you cite?

(30 min.) IV. (a) It has been pointed out that there are welfare costs connected with effects on the holding of demand deposits due to (1) failure to pay interest on required reserves and (2) prohibition of interest on demand deposits, the effects being those of a tax on demand deposits. Under the assumptions that there is no actual or expected inflation and the banks do not circumvent the prohibition of interest by changing services to depositors or charging lower interest rates to depositors who are borrowers, show how to estimate the magnitude of welfare costs due to the tax on money. How are the welfare costs affected by an anticipated inflation? Use numerical estimates or guesstimates to arrive at a dollar magnitude for the welfare costs, for the last twelve months in the United States.

(b) Discuss why the magnitude of welfare costs was different ten years ago. About how much different was it?

(c) Now assume that banks respond to the prohibition of interest by changing services to depositors and charging lower interest rates to depositors who are borrowers, and assume further that there is no limitations on entry into banking. Discuss how the answer to (a) is affected.

(30 min.) V. Throughout the history of debates on money, including those leading up to establishment of the Federal Reserve system, the idea of need for an "elastic money supply" recurs. Relate this idea to the real bills doctrine and to seasonality. Analyze the idea more fully using what you consider to be adequate concepts from monetary theory, bringing out what is right if anything and what is wrong if anything with the idea.

(30 min.) VI. (a) Using a simple neoclassical growth model, illustrate the effect on the equilibrium growth rate of income of a change in the ratio of saving to income.

(b) What behavior of the ratio of saving to income is suggested by microeconomic theory based on the relative prices of consumption goods in the present and in the future?

(c) Suppose it were true (as Kuznets in fact has found for the U.S. since 1890) that the ratio of saving to income remains constant in the long run. Does this fact conflict with your answer to (b)? If so how would you reconcile the two?

(in.)   VII.   The following budget constraint for the government sector has been suggested in the literature.

$$G = T + \Delta D + \Delta B$$

where

G = government expenditures
T = tax receipts
ΔD = change in government interest bearing debt to the public
ΔB = change in the monetary base

(a)   If the government transfers deposits from commercial banks to the central bank, how will this transaction be reflected in the above equations?

(b)   Do you think this is a correct statement of the government's budget constraint? If yes, how do you explain your answer to (a)? If not can you suggest a correct specification?

(in.)   VIII.   In a well-known recent article an equation similar to the following was estimated by ordinary least squares:

(1) $$\Delta Y_t = w\Delta B_t + u \Delta (T - G)_t$$

where:

Y = nominal GNP
B = the monetary base, defined as member-bank deposits at the Federal Reserve plus currency.
T - G = the government surplus
w and u = the fitted coefficients
t = time period (quarters)

Since the fitted w coefficient was significantly positive and the u coefficient was insignificantly different from zero, the article claimed that fiscal policy has no effect on national income. As a corollary, an implication is that the quantity theory is more valid as a theory of income determination than the Keynesian theory.

(a)   Write down a simple Keynesian structural model assuming the economy stays at less than full employment with prices unchanging. Assume that investment, government spending, taxes and monetary base are all exogenous (but not necessarily constant).

(b)   Point out differences between your reduced-form equation in (a) and equation (1). Under what circumstances would these differences change the results of the regression experiments?

(c)   Can you think of reasons to believe that, given the institutional arrangements prevailing in the U. S. between 1953 and 1968, ΔB_t might have been an endogenous variable during this period?

(d)   Re-do part (a) assuming the economy is at full employment with prices endogenous.

Preliminary Examination for the Ph.D. and the A.M. Degree
Spring Quarter, 1968

WRITE THE FOLLOWING INFORMATION ON YOUR EXAMINATION PAPER:

Your code number and NOT your name
Name of examination
Date of examination

Results of the examination will be sent to you by letter.

Answer all questions. Time: 4 hours

1. (a) Write down a set of equations for a standard Keynesian model
containing markets for goods, money, and labor. For
simplicity, assume that there is no government sector.

(b) Explain in detail the equations for the labor market and how
they fit in with the other equations under (1) rigid wages,
(2) flexible wages.

(c) In price theory, the demand for labor is regarded as derived
from the demand for goods, or, alternatively, the demand for
goods as an indirect demand for labor (and other factors of
production).

Is this true of your model? That is, does a shift in the investment function or in the consumption function, implying an
increased demand for goods, affect the demand function for
labor? If not, how can such a shift affect employment?
Consider both the rigid and flexible wage case.

The usual analysis assumes a single homogeneous good. Can
you suggest how the analysis might be affected by introducing
more than one good?

2. (a) Explain why a change in the public's holdings of outside money
with no initial change in any other asset <u>must</u> influence the
demand for (or supply of) some commodity besides money
itself (e.g., investment goods, consumption goods, government bonds, corporate stock, labor, etc.), Explain, in other

words, why a model of an economic system would be theoretically inconsistent if the public's holdings of outside money
did not influence any of those demands (or supplies).

(b) Why was the preceding stated in terms of outside money? How,
if at all, would your analysis be altered if the word "inside"
were substituted for the word "outside".

3.   The Federal Reserve Board has just raised the legal limit on
the interest rate that member banks may pay on large time
certificates of deposit (a form of time deposit) from 5 1/2 to
6 per cent. Assume that the underlying forces in the credit
markets make banks want to raise the interest rates they pay
now that they are permitted to do so. In what ways do you
expect this change to influence the economy? Will it
influence only the quantity of time deposits in banks, or might
it influence real factors, such as the quantity of investment
in certain sectors and the quantity of total employment?
Might it influence the structure of interest rates? Why do you
suppose the Federal Reserve made this change?

4.   Suppose a government is committed to a policy of maintaining
a given real deficit financed through the creation of high-
powered money. How would you predict the rate of inflation
resulting from this policy?

State explicitly the assumptions about the institutional arrangements in the creation of money underlying your answer.

Suppose the central bank were to pay interest on commercial
bank reserves. How, if at all, would that alter your answer?

5.   "Much of the dispute in Britain in the early nineteenth century
between the currency and banking schools was about the
proper definition of money." Discuss.

6.   Eurodollars are demand deposits in foreign banks which are
denominated in dollars (the foreign bank promises to pay the
depositer in U.S. dollars), and their use has expanded rapidly
in recent years. Not only do individuals hold deposits in
foreign banks denominated in dollars, but also these foreign
banks are making dollar loans. Comment on this recent development of the Eurodollar market. In what ways is it likely
to influence the U.S. balance of payments both immediately
and in the long run? Should the U.S. encourage this development?

MONEY AND BANKING

Preliminary Examination for the Ph.D. and the A.M. Degree

Winter Quarter, 1969

WRITE THE FOLLOWING INFORMATION ON YOUR EXAMINATION PAPER:

Your code number and NOT your name
Name of examination
Date of examination

Results of the examination will be sent to you by letter.

Answer all questions.   Time: 4 hours

I.   The Federal Reserve has recently altered the method of
     calculating required and actual reserves. Required reserves
     are now calculated on the basis of average deposits two weeks
     earlier. Actual reserves equal average cash in vault two
     weeks earlier plus deposits at Federal Reserve Banks the
     current week. (There are a few other minor technical details
     that can be neglected.)

     Under this new system, the adjustment mechanism of the banking
     system is in principle dynamically unstable (explosive) for
     any one week by itself.

         (a) Explain why the system is dynamically unstable.
         (b) What factors render the system stable in practice?

         How does the new system affect:

         (c) The Federal Reserve's ability to control the money sup
         (d) The significance of excess reserves, free reserves,
             and borrowings?

II. "Central bankers were highly receptive to the Keynesian analys
     of monetary policy because it fitted in with their own precon-
     ceptions, which were based on the real-bills doctrine." Expla
     why you agree or disagree, in the process summarizing the
     history of the real-bills doctrine.

III. A major relationship in most income-determination models is
     the negative interest elasticity of investment. But during th
     post war period in the U.S., falling interest rates have been
     accompanied by declining rates of investment in plant and
     equipment and a rising volume of residential construction.

         (a) Does that suggest that residential construction is mor
             interest-elastic than investment in plant and equipmen

         (b) How far, if at all, has the observed pattern been rela
             to central bank policy and the structure of financial
             intermediaries?

-180-

IV.   (a) Construct a model for the analysis of economic policy
in a closed economy, with an exogenous money supply, an
income-elastic tax system, flexible prices, and saving a
constant fraction of income.
           (b) For a unique equilibrium, which variables do you regard
as determined by this model, and which outside the model?
           (c) Distinguish between monetary policy and fiscal policy
in terms of your model.
           (d) Can monetary policy be used to maintain stable prices?
Can fiscal policy? Indicate the conditions in the model
necessary for only one or the other to be effective.

V.   Consider the problem of explaining the response in a
stationary economy to a change that leads to increased unemployment of resources, such as an unanticipated fall in the
demand for goods and services. Suppose that any increases in
unemployment are temporary, with dynamic properties of the
system such that there will be a return to an "equilibrium" or
"natural" rate of unemployment if no further unanticipated
shocks occur.

           (a) Explain what the "natural rate of unemployment" means.
           (b) Assume that the quantity of money is constant.
Sketch out an explanation of the time path of output, employment of labor, price of goods, price of labor, and interest
rate.
           (c) Indicate what each of the following concepts means
and how, if at all, each is relevant in explaining the
adjustments: search unemployment, labor as a quasi-fixed
factor of production, Phillips curve, expectations.

VI.   The loss in real value of money during inflation has been
likened to a tax. Assume that inflation is fully anticipated.
How much is the tax, who bears it, and who receives the proceeds:

           (a) If there are 100 percent reserves and the central bank
pays no interest on reserves, with commercial banks otherwise
unregulated?
           (b) Same as (a) except there is fractional reserve banking?
           (c) If there is fractional reserve banking and the central
bank pays no interest on reserves, with commercial banks
forbidden to pay a nominal rate of interest on deposits higher
than would be paid in the absence of inflation?
           (d) Same as (c) except banks are also forbidden to charge
nominal interest rates on loans higher than would prevail in
the absence of inflation?
           (e) If there is fractional reserve banking, no interest
rate regulation on commercial banks, and the central bank pays
interest on reserves totaling to the interest payments earned
on its assets?

VII. Assume that the U.S. stops pegging the price of gold and of
other currencies, and in reaction to this measure, the European
common market countries form a currency block linked internally
by fixed exchange rates and permit the exchange rates of the
common market currencies to float relative to the dollar.
Assume that all other currencies float relative to the dollar.

Compare monetary adjustment <u>within</u> the two currency areas
(i.e. adjustment of the fifty states of the U.S. as compared
to adjustment of the six countries of the common market).

MONEY AND BANKING

Preliminary Examination for the Ph. D. and A. M. Degrees

Summer, 1967

WRITE THE FOLLOWING INFORMATION ON YOUR EXAMINATION PAPER

        Your code number and NOT your name
        Name of examination
        Date of examination

Results of the examination will be sent to you by letter.

1. a) "The fallacy in the quantity theory of money is that it allows for the circulation of money but not the circulation of goods. A correct theory would have a velocity of circulation of goods to parallel the velocity of circulation of money." Discuss

   b) According to one writer, one of the "fundamental laws of economics" is that "the inflation rate is approximately equal to the interest rate when averaged over several decades." (Andre Gleyzal, "Theory of Money in a Free Economic System." Discuss (and do not dismiss out of hand).

2. a) What is the "Phillips Curve"?

   b) Give the theoretical analysis on which it rests. Do you regard it as valid? If so, defend it; if not, why not?

   c) What is its relation to the notion of a "trade-off" between unemployment and inflation?

   d) What is your understanding of the present state of the empirical evidence on the Phillips curve?

3. a) Expand the standard analysis of the IS-LM (or EE-LL) curves to include foreign trade and the balance of payments when all economies are operating with fixed exchange rates under a pure gold standard.

   b) Would this analysis be any different under

     i) fixed exchange rates with national currency standards?

     ii) floating exchange rates?

     Why, or why not?

ANSWER ALL QUESTIONS - ALL QUESTIONS HAVE EQUAL WEIGHT

4. a) A once and for all change in the money supply is expected to affect only the price level and not any real economic magnitudes. Yet some economic theorists who accept the neutrality of money in this sense argue that a sudden decrease (say) in the money supply will cause unemployment. How do you reconcile these two positions?

   b) Assume that a country is operating on a classical gold standard. It has a central bank but the bank does not engage in open market operations. It confines its policy to setting an interest rate (discount rate) at which it lends freely. Let important gold discoveries be made in that country such that, at the prevailing price of gold, the rate of gold production increases. Does the neutrality of money still hold true in the long run? Will the increased rate of gold production affect only the price level and not the level of real income in the given country?

5. Most empirical studies of the demand for money that use time series data take the real stock of money as the dependent variable and take measures of real income or wealth and of the interest rate as explanatory variables. However, most monetary theorists treat the nominal stock of money as exogenous. This appears inconsistent with the empirical work. Can you describe a sensible economic model to defend the choice made by the empirical investigators? Assume it is your purpose to predict the increase in the demand for real money balances resulting from an increase in real income. For simplicity, assume that current real measured income is the relevant income variable. Do not discuss the econometric theory of identification, etc. Focus your attention on the economic hypotheses in terms of the price level, the nominal money stock, interest rates, and nominal income. Would it be better to treat real money balances as an explanatory instead of as a dependent variable in estimating the demand for money?

3

6. Comment on the following proposition:

In the portfolios of banks, private loans and government bonds
are alternatives. The smaller the quantity of loans that banks
make (i.e., the tighter the supply of bank credit), the greater
must be the quantity of government bonds the banks are holding
in their portfolios. But the total supply of government bonds
is fixed, and so this implies that the tighter is bank credit, the
smaller the supply of government bonds available to the non-bank
public to hold in their portfolios. But the smaller the quantity
of government bonds available to the non-bank public, the greater
the quantity of other assets they will hold. In other words, the
tighter is bank credit, the greater the supply of private credit
from non-bank holders of wealth, and the portfolio behavior of
banks is largely irrelevant in determining the total supply of
private credit.

MONEY AND BANKING

Preliminary Examination for the Ph.D. and A.M. Degrees

Summer 1966

WRITE THE FOLLOWING INFORMATION ON YOUR EXAMINATION PAPER:

    Your code number and NOT your name
    Name of Examination
    Date of examination

Results of the examination will be sent to you by letter.

Time: 4 hours.

I. Answer the following questions True, False, or Uncertain and
    briefly explain your answer. (Allow 1 hour)

    1. A bank's assets and liabilities are both in nominal terms.
       Hence its earnings are not affected by changes in the price
       level.

    2. An increase in savings accompanied by an increase in the ra
       of price decline is compatible with uninterrupted full empl

    3. A fall in domestic wage rates tends to raise employment in
       export goods industries relative to domestic goods industri

    4. In an economy without outside money the price level is
       indeterminate.

    5. If the demand for real cash balance depends on permanent re
       income then a monetary policy that makes changes in the sto
       of money depend on changes in the level of measured real in
       can produce periodic unemployment.

    6. In an economy in which bond yields exceed stock yields (ear
       divided by stock prices) the quantity of money must be incr

    7. The opportunity cost of holding money is the nominal intere
       rate.

    8. Consider an economy containing homogeneous goods, bonds and
       money: a mathematical model of this economy need not conta
       a demand function for goods.

    9. In an economy containing only inside money, the Pigou effec
       could not exist in the aggregate but could only operate thr
       distribution effects.

    10. In a country whose residents have become accustomed to rapi
        inflation, a decrease in the rate of growth of the money su
        is likely to induce an increase in the real demand for mone

-186-

11. Some money-fixed assets (such as savings deposits and Treasury bills) are riskless as alternatives to cash and, in addition, have a positive rate of return. Therefore, short-term transactions needs are the only grounds for holding money, and Keynes was wrong in arguing that there are strong precautionary and speculative motives in the demand for money.

12. Long-term government bonds generally have a higher rate of return than Treasury bills and are equally free of default risk. Therefore, rational individuals would usually hold bonds in preference to bills.

II. Each of the following questions has equal weight.

1. "Intermediaries . . . collect a portion of current voluntary saving and serve the function of making these funds available for the financing of current expenditures - i.e., they help to channel saving into investment in a broad sense. . . . Commercial banks, on the other hand, are distinctly not intermediaries. That is, the decision to save a portion of current income and to hold the savings in the form of a demand deposit does not make any more funds available to the capital market than would have been available had the decision been made to spend instead . . . "

   a) Explain the meaning of this statement that commercial banks are not intermediaries.

   b) Evaluate it critically.

   (From W.L. Smith, "Financial Intermediaries and Monetary Controls," QJE. Nov. '59)

2. The "Gibson Paradox" arises from the empirical observation that concurrent, secular movements in the price level and in long-term interest rates appear to be in the same direction. Why is this empirical phenomenon called a paradox?

3. "It is distinctly more natural that the immediate cause of a downturn should be real than that it should be monetary. For the actual process of real expansion is very favorable to the expansion of credit. Profits are good and risks appear to be low; even though there is some strain on the ultimate money supply, the opportunities for the development of money substitutes are vast, and the strain is therefore not very likely to be effective so long as the boom continues. It is not very easy to see why a monetary reaction should suddenly appear out of the blue at the top of the boom." Hicks, Trade Cycle, p. 159.

a) What do you think Hicks means by real and monetary factors in the trade cycle. State your analysis in the IS - LM framework.

b) What are some empirical implications of Hicks' reaso? Are these confirmed by U.S. experience?

c) Can you give reasons for the appearance of a "moneta? reaction" at the "top of the boom"?

4. Discussing Japanese developments in the 1870's and 1880's G.C. Allen wrote, "Competition with French and Italian si was assisted . . . also by the depreciation of silver whi conferred a bounty on Japanese exports to gold standard countries." (A Short Economic History of Japan, rev. ed.

Analyze the validity of this assertion in terms of the monetary theory of a country on a commodity standard. Fo purposes of this analysis assume that (a) Japan had no tariffs or other impediments to foreign trade, (b) Japan a silver standard, (c) domestic Japanese prices were fair flexible. (These assumptions in fact correspond very clo to the actual situation.)

5. With reference to the current situation, an economic anal writes, "So long as capacity was not fully utilized, risi demand was reflected in rising output and prices remained But now that excess capacity is negligible, further incre in demand will spill over mostly into prices. That is wh inflation has become so much greater a threat."

From 1933 to 1937, the rate of utilization of capacity wa far lower than at any time from 1961 to 1966, yet wholesa prices rose 50% from 1933 to 1937, more than doubling for products, and rising over 39% for other commodities.

How do you explain the contradiction between these facts the hypothesis implicit in the quotation?

6. a. What is the balanced budget theorem?

b. Use the quantity theory framework (MV = Py) to demons? it, paying special attention to the assumptions requi? for its validity.

c. What additional factors enter on a more sophisticated

MONEY AND BANKING

Preliminary Examination for the Ph.D. and A.M. Degrees

Winter, 1967

WRITE THE FOLLOWING INFORMATION ON YOUR EXAMINATION PAPER

Your code number and NOT your name
Name of examination
Date of examination

Results of the examination will be sent to you by letter.

PART I. True or False: Defend your answer. <u>Two hours</u> (8 minutes each).

- The growth of financial intermediaries which has increased the supply of money substitutes has made control of the money supply a less effective policy instrument to affect employment and the price level.

- Rising prices accompanied by increasing unemployment are inconsistent in the Keynesian system.

- The desired real stock of money is greater when real wages are rising and the price level is constant than when real wages are rising and nominal wages are constant.

- An increase in inventories accompanied by a decrease in the demand for the stock of money implies an increase in the excess supply of bonds.

- An excess demand for money implies an equal excess supply of bonds.

- The desired and actual stock of money must be equal because there must always be equilibrium in the money market.

- If the Treasury permitted a free market in gold to operate in New York, the dollar price of goods imported from abroad into the United States would rise if foreign countries kept the price of gold in terms of their own currencies constant.

The absence of the interest rate as an argument in the demand for money means that the real sector of an economy can be analyzed independently of the monetary sector.

The invention of a money substitute, such as credit cards, implies a decrease in real income because it reduces the equilibrium stock of real money balances.

10. In an economy with no "outside money" there is no Pigou effect.

11. According to the Baumol-Tobin theory of the transactions demand for money, a 10 percent increase of the interest rate accompanied by a 10 percent increase in expenditures would leave the demand for real balances unchanged.

12. An acceleration of the rate of monetary expansion from 5 percent to 10 percent when the growth of output remains at 5 percent, would result in a lower rate of interest.

13. Proposals to allow interest to be paid on demand deposits and on member bank deposits at the Federal Reserve would create an inefficient use of money, if adopted, because the stock of money held, when demand deposits pay a zero interest rate, is optimal.

14. Under a system of fixed exchange rates the supply of money has to be endogenous to the international system in the long run, but under a system of flexible exchange rates, there is scope for an independent national monetary policy.

15. An economy experiencing a balance of payments surplus and inflationary pressure in a fixed exchange system should increase taxes to relieve the balance of payments and raise interest rates to prevent "inflation".

PART II. One Hour

In 1966 the Federal Reserve sharply reduced the rate at which the money supply was expanding at a time when the economy was booming and prices were rising; this occurred at a time when the government spending was rising sharply ahead of tax receipts.

(1) Analyze, on the basis of theoretical model, the likely effects of such a change in policy on:

    (a) the level and structure of interest rates
    (b) the level of employment
    (c) income velocity
    (d) savings and investment
    (e) free reserves

(2) Is there any important difference between the answers you would give to (1) based on a difference between short-run and long-run considerations?

(3) In what sense if any could ti be argued that monetary policy was neutral in the context of the "tight money" squeeze?

(4) What considerations would you regard as important in attempting to determine whether money is "tight" or "easy"?

(5) What balance of payments effects of the tight money policy would you predict?

PART III. One-Half Hour Each

1. Contrast the difference between the effects of a 10 per cent increase in the quantity of money effected through:

    (a) an open market operation, and

    (b) a reduction in legal reserve requirements.

2. Consider a simple model of long-run growth in which the equilibrium growth rate is given exogenously by the (positive) rate of growth in the labor force. For simplicity, assume there is no technical change. There are only two different types of assets that individuals may hold in their portfolios: capital goods and "money" issued by the government and paying no interest. Long-run equilibrium has the properties that the capital-labor ratio remains fixed, the ratio of money to capital goods in portfolios remains fixed, and labor and capital are fully employed. Government spending on goods and services is a fixed fraction of total output. Assume, furthermore, that the government runs whatever deficit (financed by new money) is required to keep the price level constant in equilibrium, and that individuals always want to hold both money and capital in their portfolios.

    (a) Is a long-run equilibrium with a constant price level possible in this non-inflationary economy without the government running a deficit? How is the size of the deficit related to the growth rate?

    (b) Does the fact that individuals want to hold some money in their portfolios tend to increase or decrease equilibrium capital intensity, compared to what it would be if individuals did not hold any money? Why?

    (c) Would an increase in the deficit (causing inflation) increase or decrease equilibrium capital intensity?

Price Theory
The Theory of Income, Employment
and the Price Level

Alternative B of the A.M. Degree

WINTER, 1981

WRITE THE FOLLOWING INFORMATION ON YOUR EXAMINATION PAPER:

Your Code Number, but NOT your name.
Name of Examination.
Date of Examination.

Results of the examination will be sent to you by letter.

TIME: 3 Hours.

ANSWER ALL QUESTIONS.
WRITE ALL ANSWERS IN BLACK INK - ONE SIDE OF EACH PAGE ONLY.

Note: This examination is in two parts. Write your answers in separate parts.

Count the number of pages used, write the number and circle it on the first
page of your answer sheets.

PART A. Price Theory (90 minutes)

I. (5 minutes each). Answer TRUE, FALSE, or UNCERTAIN and EXPLAIN.

1. Robbery is simply a transfer of wealth from one individual to another
    so that from the point of view of one who is interested only in maximizi
    the total wealth of society, there is nothing wrong with it.

2. A firm uses two inputs, x and y in equal amounts. The price of x is
    less than that of y. Therefore, if a law is passed requiring that the
    firm use 1.1 units of x for every unit of y, then marginal cost and
    the price of output will fall.

3. If the owner of firms are discriminatory in the sense that at a given
    price they would prefer to hire a man than an equally productive woman,
    then their demand curve for female labor could slope up.

4. An increase in the price of an inferior factor will reduce the price of
    output in a competitive industry.

5. An increase in the value of land should not be counted in calculating
    national product.

II. 10-minute questions.

1. Suppose that a particular item can be purchased for a price of A and
can be expected to last for N years. An identical item can be rented
on a yearly basis at a price such that the present value of N years'
rent is B. For what sorts of items would you expect a large difference
between A and B? List at least two attributes which an item could
have which might contribute to causing a large difference, and justify
your answer.

2. Nolan Ryan, a famous baseball player, was under a five year contract
to play baseball for the California team of the American League. Upon
expiration of the contract, Ryan became a "free agent", able to sell
his services to whomever he chose. For a considerable increase in
salary ($1 million per year) he signed a contract to play for the Houston
team. If Ryan is most valuable to Houston, why was he not originally
playing for them? Should it matter whether the California Team has
the right to sell his contract or whether Ryan has the right? Does
the fact that Ryan changed teams when he was given the rights to sell
his contract contradict Coase's proposition?

3. Suppose that consumers demand only two goods, X and Y, and that all
consumers have positive demand for both of these goods. Some suppliers
provide X and some provide Y, but no supplier provides both. All markets
are perfectly competitive, and prices are set so as to clear both markets.

Now a law is passed (and perfectly enforced) which requires any consumer
purchasing both X and Y to pay the same price for each of them. How is
that price determined?

III. 15-minute question.

It has been argued that houses in California appreciate in value more rapidly
than do houses in Illinois in order to compensate their owners for the risk
of destruction by earthquake.

Assume a constant rate of interest, assume that the event or non-event of
a California earthquake is determined identically and independently each year,
assume that the rental rates for the two houses are identical in any given
year (say a_k in year k) and assume that all of this is perfectly forseen at any time

a) If a is a constant function of k, explain why you would <u>not</u> expect
the California house to appreciate more rapidly than the Illionis house.

b) In the situation described in (a), are California home-owners compensated
for risk? If so, how? If not, why not?

c) Suppose that $\frac{a_{k+1}}{a_k}$ decreases with increasing k. Show that even with

all individuals risk-neutral, the California house will appreciate
relative to the Illinois house. (If you find this too difficult or
time-consuming, please go directly to part (d)).

d) Would risk-aversion _exaggerate_ or _mitigate_ the effects in (c)?

e) How much truth is there in the original argument?

IV. 20-minute question.

Mr. A and Mr. B have identical endowments of goods x and y, say 50 units of each. Their preferences are somewhat unusual:

$$U^A(x, y) = x + .8y$$

$$U^B(x, y) = x + .5y$$

1) What is unusual about these preferences?

2) In an Edgeworth Box, identify

   (i)   The original endowment
   (ii) The contract curve
   (iii) The region of mutual advantage
   (iv) The competitive equilibrium

3) In part (iv), what precisely do you mean by an equilibrium? Is your equilibrium unique? What is the competitive price ratio?

COMPREHENSIVE EXAMINATION

Winter, 1981

Part B: Income, Employment & the Price Level (90 minutes).

Answer all questions. The point total is the same as the number of
minutes available. Be sure to leave enough time for the higher value
questions at the end.

I. 5-minute questions.

1. (True, False or Uncertain): Rational expectations models are inconsistent
   with serial correlation in the unemployment rate.

2. How will the effects of a constant money growth rule differ from the
   effects of a money growth problem which is erratic, but which is announced
   well in advance?

3. (True, False or Uncertain): If the budget deficit is eliminated, then
   the inflation rate will go to zero .

4. "All I know is that if I buy a car from the Japanese, I've got the car
   and the Japanese have the money. But if I buy a car from an American,
   I've got the car and an American has the money?" Comment.

5. Are the existence of temporary layoffs inconsistent with a market
   clearing economy?

6. Compare the inflationary effects of the following two actions:

   1) Printing 10 billion dollar bills, and giving them randomly to the
      citizens of the U.S. and

   2) carrying out open market operations in which the government buys $10
      billion worth. of government bonds.

I. 20-minute questions.

1. The following regression equation has been estimated using 1954-77
   U.S. data:

   $\Delta \ln W = -1.88 + 7.44 \left(\frac{1}{u} \right) + .79 \, \Delta \ln W_{-1} + .21 \Delta \ln W_{-2}.$

   where $\Delta \ln W$ is the rate of wage inflation, and u is a measure of the
   unemployment rate.

   How can this result be explained?

2. Consider a closed economy that has for some time been in full-e[m]
   equilibrium with a stable price level and zero real growth. Im[p]
   upon that economy a disturbance in the form of an instantaneous
   increase in the quantity of money.

   a) Indicate the likely shapes of and interrelationships among,
      time paths of money, the price level, and real cash balance[s]
      response to this disturbance.

   b) Do the same for the case where the disturbance is a shift t[o]
      steady 20% per annum rate of increase in the quantity of mo[ney]

3. a) Explain how you could construct a consolidated balance sheet
      the entire monetary/banking system of a country.

   b) How do the various definitions of money (currency, high-powe[r]
      money, M_1, M_2) appear, or fail to appear, on this balance sh[eet]

   c) What, if any, is the relationship between M_2 on the one hand
      international reserves plus domestic credit on the other?

Price Theory
The Theory of Income, Employment
and the Price Level

Alternative B of the A.M. Degree

SUMMER, 1980

WRITE THE FOLLOWING INFORMATION ON YOUR EXAMINATION PAPER:

Your Code Number, but NOT your name
Name of Examination
Date of Examination

Results of the examination will be sent to you by letter.

TIME: 3 hours. ANSWER ALL QUESTIONS.

NOTE: This examination is in two parts. Write your answers in separate parts.

WRITE ALL ANSWERS IN BLACK INK - ON ONE SIDE OF EACH PAGE ONLY!

Count the number of pages used, write the number and circle it on the first page of your answer sheets.

PART A. Price Theory (90 minutes)

I. (5 minutes each). Answer TRUE, FALSE or UNCERTAIN and briefly explain. Your grade depends on your explanation.

1. If a per-unit tax is placed on the output of a competitive industry, price will rise by the amount of the tax.

2. If the production function is $y = f(a,b)$, then the demand for 'a' is more elastic than the value marginal product schedule of 'a' if $f_{ab} > 0$ but is less elastic if $f_{ab} < 0$.

3. In consumption theory, the income and substitution effects may be of opposite signs, but in production theory, the substitution and scale effects of an input price change always have the same sign. There can, therefore, be no Giffen factors.

4. A price cieling which is expected to last forever and which is below the equilibrium price is placed on the sale of an exhaustible resource (e. If owners of stocks of this resource maximize their wealth, quantity in the current priod will fall.

5. If a tax is placed on the utilization of an inferior factor by a monop the price of output will fall.

6. A risk averse individual will buy unfair insurance.

7. In a neighborhood of minimum long run average cost, the short-run marg cost curve is steeper than long run marginal cost. Thus, short-run ma cost is below long run marginal cost for reductions in output, so thes reductions are cheaper in the short-run than in the long run.

8. If all goods are gross substitutes, then all uncompensated own price elasticities are negative and greater than unity in absolute value.

PART II. Longer Questions.

1. (15 minutes). Different locales offer different amounts of "amenitie public goods which are consumable only by residents of an area. In wh ways will observable economic variables such as wages, prices, and lar values be affected by the presence of such amenities in a competitive equilibrium?

2. (10 minutes). Suppose that a cieling price is imposed on the sale of domestically produced crude oil. Analyze the effects on:

   (a) the price of gasoline to domestic consumers.
   (b) the price of gasoline to foreign (e.g. European) consumers.
   (c) the world price of crude oil.
   (d) the revenues of OPEC members, and their total barrels produced.
   (e) the profits of domestic refiners.
   (f) the degree of vertical integration in the domestic petroleum indu

3. (10 minutes). Consider a program in which workers are paid an amount if their earnings are less than 1/2; an amount 1/2 if earnings are be 1/2 and G, and nothing if their earning exceed G.

   (a) For a particular wage rate, graph the budget constraint in commod leisure space
   (b) Graph a labor supply function for a representative worker in this

4. (15 minutes). Mr. A. and Mr. B. have the following endowments of x and y

$$E_A = (X_A, \ 0)$$
$$E_B = (0, \ Y_B)$$

Their utility functions are $U^A(x, y)$ and $U^B(x, y)$ with the usual properties. They trade competively.

(a) In an Edgeworth-Bowley Box, illustrate the competitive equilibrium.
(b) Now suppose that before trade occurs, Mr. A.'s endowment of x is increased to $X_A + \Delta X_A$; and consider the following potential outcomes of the new equilibrium as compared to the one you illustrated above.

    (i)   Both A and B are better off.
    (ii)   A is better off, B is no worse off.
    (iii)   B is better off, A is no worse off.
    (iv)   A may be worse off, B is no worse off.

Which, if any of these conclusions is the right one?

MONEY

Exam Questions - M.A. Comprehensive

PART B: Income, Employment & the Price Level. (90 Minutes)

> Answer all questions. The point total is the same as the number of minutes available. Be sure to leave enough time for the higher value questions at the end.

I. <u>True-False-Uncertain.</u> Explain your answer. (5 points each)

1. In a rational expectations model, the real effects of an unanticipated shock cannot persist for more than a single period.

2. Housing construction helps to dampen business cycles.

3. According to the permanent income hypothesis, unemployment caused by c fluctuations does not affect aggregate consumption.

4. Expected inflation has the same effect on the demand for money as the interest rate.

5. With a constant rate of growth of the money supply, technological chang reduce inflation by making more goods and services available to consume

6. Credit cards are inflationary.

7. The recent decline in short-term interest rates indicates a decline in anticipated rate of inflation.

8. National income is inaccurately measured in the national accounts becau of double counting: primary products like cotton are counted once when are sold to clothing manufacturers and again when the clothing is sold public.

9. Changes in OPEC's price of oil do not affect American inflation.

10. Since we owe it to ourselves, the national debt represents no burden for the taxes required to pay interest on it.

11. Unexpected inflation increases business taxes, but expected inflation d not.

II. (10 Points) What is the relation between the quantity of high-powered mone the money supply? How is the relationship affected by a change in the rate inflation?

III. (15 points) Is a tax cut inflationary? Give a Keynesian and a monetarist answer, and bring out the reasons for the difference.

IV. (10 points) What, if any, is the relation between the exchange rate and the real terms of trade in producing goods and services? Do changes in the value of the dollar reflect only changes in the expected rate of inflation in the United States relative to that in other countries?

COMPREHENSIVE EXAMINATION

Price Theory
The Theory of Income, Employment
and the Price Level

Alternative B of the A.M. Degree

Winter, 1980

WRITE THE FOLLOWING INFORMATION ON YOUR EXAMINATION PAPER

Your code number, but NOT your name
Name of Examination
Date of Examination

Results of the examination will be sent to you by letter.

TIME: 3 hours. ANSWER ALL QUESTIONS.

NOTE: This examination is in two parts. Write your answers in
separate parts.

WRITE ALL ANSWERS IN BLACK INK.

Count the number of pages used, write the number and circle it on
the first page of your answer sheets.

Part A. Price Theory (1-1/2 hours)

I. [5 minutes] True or False:

It is meaningless to ask A.C. Frankfurter if he really wants to ship
jobs.

2. [5 minutes] True or False:

Supply slopes up because demand slopes down.

3. [5 minutes]True or False:

The Federal Communications Commission must regulate broadcasting to
prevent the inevitable externalities of one frequency interfering
with another.

4. [5 minutes] True or False:

Gold is a good investment nowadays because it has risen so much in
value recently.

5. [10 minutes]

Several years ago, the government of California restricted the
ability of braceros (seasonal farm workers from Mexico) to enter
the state during harvest time. Defending this policy subsequently,
the Governor pointed out that the value of that year's crop was
higher than previously. Thus, he reasoned, the policy could only
have been beneficial from a social point of view. COMMENT

6. [15 minutes]

According to a well-known consumer advocate, surveys indicate that grocery shoppers tend to use a large portion of the capacity of their grocery carts. According to this same advocate, this is because of the shame people feel if they arrive at the check-out counter with their basket only partially filled. Grocery stores have taken advantage of this social pressure by <u>recently</u> increasing the depth of their carts so they will sell more goods. Construct an alternative theory of grocery cart depth. Is your theory consistent with the recent deepening of carts? How might you test your theory?

7. [15 minutes]

Consider the following average rises of wheat prices month-to-month in England in the 13th and 14th centuries:

Price Rise from the Month Named to the Next Month

September	+7.5%
October	3.8
November	6.4
December	6.3
January	1.9
February	3.7
March	3.6
April	1.2
May	1.5
June	4.2
July	1.5

Average +3.8% per month

Theoretically speaking, what is the full cost of storing a bushel of grain for consumption in the next month. Empirically speaking, in these data what is the cost? What would you expect the August-September figure (not shown) to be, drawing on your knowledge that early September was the wheat harvest?

What would the spring figures look like if farmers got knowledge of their future crop in che spring?

8. [5 minutes] True or False:

The number of firms in an industry has little or nothing to do with the closeness or price to marginal cost.

9. [10 minutes] True or False:

The ratio of the price of (mother) cows to (baby) calves is related to the going interest rate.

Comprehensive Exam
Price Theory

10. [15 minutes] Q

Banks have recently begun to allocate customers to tellers th
the use of feeder lines: All customers stand in one line and
the person at the head of the line proceeds to the first avai
teller. Why do customers prefer this system to one where eac
teller has a line and customers allocate themselves? Why do
and airlines adopt the system but grocery stores do not?
Why does the system break down if it is not compulsory?

Winter, 1980

Money

Exam Questions - M.A. Comprehensive

Part_B. MONEY SECTION: 90 Minutes (Monetary Theory)

Answer all questions.

1. [5 minutes]

    If individuals have perfect foresight, then changes in the
    inflation do not affect any real variables.

2. [5 minutes] True or False:

    Inflation stimulates economic growth by reducing the share of
    their savings which individuals allocate to the accumulation of
    real cash balances.

3. [5 minutes]

    In a closed economy a decrease in the real interst rate will
    lead to a decrease in both private saving and government saving.

4. [5 minutes]

    "An increase in the interest rate on Treasury bills will attract
    foreign capital into the country and tend to appreciate the
    currency." Explain when you would agree and when you would
    disagree with this statement.

5. [5 minutes] True or False:

    The fact that there is serial corelation in the unemployment
    rate is strong evidence against the view that "only unantici-
    pated money matters."

6. [10 minutes]

    Domestic government bonds are not considered to be net wealth
    by domestic residents, since they discount the implied tax
    liability. However, this is not the case for foreign holders
    of domestic government bonds. Hence, a once-and-for-all gift
    of bonds by each government to the other country's residents
    increases world wealth and consequently aggregate demand.

7. [10 minutes]

    The facts that the yield curve (yield on bonds vs maturity)
    is downward sloping and the rate of inflation is about equal
    to the short term interst rate indicates that investors do not
    anticipate the current rate of inflation to be permanently
    maintained.

8. [20 minutes]

    Suppose that in a closed economy, the central bank wants to stabilize income. It is chosing between a policy of pegging the interest rate and pegging the money supply. Using an IS-LM framework

    a) which policy should be followed if the major shocks to the economy are shocks to the money demand function?

    b) which policy should be followed if the major shocks to the economy are shock to the investment schedule?

    c) which policy should be followed if autonomous increases in money demand are associated with autonomous increases in investment demand (and autonomous decreases in money demand are associated with autonomous decreases in the investment schedule)?

9. [10 minutes] True, False, Uncertain: Explain

    The permanent income and life cycle hypotheses of consumption imply that a temporary sales tax on consumption goods will have a smaller contractionary effect than a permanent sales tax of the same magnitude.

10. [5 minutes] True, False, Uncertain: Explain

    The monetary approach to the balance of payments predicts that a rise in the foreign interest rate will necessarily lead to a surplus of the home country's balance of payments.

11. [5 minutes] True, False, Uncertain: Explain

    The existence of long-term labor contracts implies that both anticipated and unanticipated changes in monetary policy have an effect on employment.

12. [5 minutes] True, False, Uncertain: Explain

    "Okun's Law" states that as a fact of nature changes in the unemployment rate will be inversely related to changes in the output growth rate.

COMPREHENSIVE EXAMINATION
Price Theory
The Theory of Income, Employment
and the Price Level

Alternative B of the A. M. Degree

Summer, 1979

WRITE THE FOLLOWING INFORMATION ON YOUR EXAMINATION PAPER

Your code number, but NOT your name
Name of Examination
Date of Examination

Results of the examination will be sent to you by letter.

TIME: 3 hours. ANSWER ALL QUESTIONS.

NOTE: This examination is in two parts. Write your answers in separate parts.

WRITE ALL ANSWERS IN BLACK INK.

Count the number of pages used, write the number and circle it on the
first page of your answer sheets.

Part A. Price Theory (1-1/2 hours)

I. (30 minutes)

You wish to analyze some demand data and need a functional form which will
give a satisfactory approximation to the unknown true form. You are primarily
interested in (own-price) demand curves and Engel curves (quantities vs. income).
You consider initially the utility function $u = \Sigma_i \beta_i \ln x_i$ where the x_i are
commodities. Indicate what general class of demand and Engel curves can arise
from maximization of this utility function subject to a budget constraint
$\Sigma_i p_i x_i = y$ and a normalization $\Sigma_i \beta_i = 1$. How well might these approximate
theoretically plausible demand and Engel curves? Give a graph of an example
for which these are poor approximations. You decide to make the model more
general by adding parameters and come up with

$$u = \Sigma_i \beta_i \ln(x_i - \alpha_i)$$

the Stone-Geary utility function. Again, consider the demand and Engel curves,
using graphs, and discuss their potential as approximations to more complicated
forms. Finally, consider simply taking linear approximations to the demand
functions. Comment wisely on this approach.

II.   (25 minutes)

In the American South before the Civil War there were competitive market
slaves.

   a. How would a planter determine his demand for slaves?
   b. In an empirical study of a slave market, what slave characterist
       would you enter into a hedonic price index (i.e. a regression wit
       slave prices as dependent, and slave characteristics as independe
       variables) for slaves, and what would you expect the signs of the
       estimated coefficients to be? Explain why.
   c. Under what economic conditions would you expect slavery to disapp
       from a society without political intervention?

III. (10 minutes)

If American urban wages are greater than rural wages, would pecuniary co
derations ever lead foreign immigrants to the United States to settle in
rural rather than urban areas?

IV.   (25 minutes)

You are interested in input substitution in a firm producing quantity q
inputs x_1 and x_2. The price of output is p, the input prices are p_1 and
Someone has estimated the following equations

$$\ln x_1 = \alpha_1 \ln x_2 + \alpha_2 \ln q$$
$$\ln x_1 = \beta_1 \ln x_2 + \beta_2 \ln p_1 + \beta_3 \ln p_2 + \beta_4 \ln p$$
$$\ln x_1 = \gamma_1 \ln p_1 + \gamma_2 \ln p_2 + \gamma_3 \ln q$$
$$\ln x_1 = \delta_1 \ln p_1 + \delta_2 \ln p_2 + \delta_3 \ln p$$

Discuss the economic interpretation of these equations and the relations
among them. Pay particular attention to the interpretations of α_1, β_1,
and δ_2 .

Exam Questions – M.A. Comprehensive

(MONEY SECTION: 90 MINUTES)

Answer all Questions.

I. **True – False – Uncertain.** Explain your answer. (5 points each)

1. If the money stock is held constant, the price level will fall at just the right rate to obtain the optimum quantity of money.

2. If the supply of labor is independent of the real wage, then a technological change that raises labor's marginal product at each level of employment will not affect the level of employment, and consequently output and the price level will also be unchanged.

3. The permanent income hypothesis implies that the larger the variance of transitory income, the lower the marginal propensity to consume.

4. If the monetary authority adopts a monetary rule that pegs the interest rate, then there is no determinate price level.

5. The existence of long term wage contracts implies that monetary policy can be effective in influencing the level of employment.

6. The announcement of future Treasury gold sales will depress the current price of gold.

7. An import tax plus an export tax are equivalent to a devaluation provided the proceeds are rebated.

8. Equilibrium theories of the business cycle imply that price forecast errors are serially uncorrelated and hence cannot account for the serial correlation in unemployment rates.

II. (15 points) "Since government bonds are regarded as assets by their holders, an increase in government debt implies an increase in private sector wealth. This increase in wealth will lead to an increase in desired expenditure which, in turn, will drive up output, interest rate and prices. Higher interest rates, however, imply lower investment. Therefore government deficits are expansionary in the short-run but contractionary in the long-run" - Discuss.

III. (10 points) On theoretical grounds, should we expect investment tax credits or personal income tax reductions to provide greater stimulus to aggregate demand per dollar of tax loss to the government?

IV. (20 points) It has been argued that recent oil price rises have had inflationary effects in the United States. It has also been argued that the oil price rises have had adverse balance of payments effects for this country. Yet Germany and Japan which are relatively more oil dependent have had balance of payments surpluses. Present a framework within which you analyze these issues.

COMPREHENSIVE EXAMINATION

Price Theory
The Theory of Income, Employment and
the Price Level

Alternative B of the A.M. Degree

Winter, 1979

WRITE IN BLACK INK

WRITE THE FOLLOWING INFORMATION ON THE FIRST PAGE OF YOUR EXAMINATION PAPER:

> Your code number and not your name
> Name of examination
> Date of examination

Write only on one side of each page

WRITE THE FOLLOWING INFORMATION ON EACH PAGE OF YOUR EXAMINATION PAPER:

> Top left: code number
> Top right: number of page

When you fold your paper at the end of the exam, write your code number on the back, and indicate the total number of pages.

Credit is proportionate to time.

Results of the examination will be sent to you by letter.

Answer all questions.   (PRICE SECTION: 90 MINUTES)

I. (5 points each)
Indicate whether you believe each of the following statements to be TRUE or FALSE. In each case write a few sentences explaining your answer.

1. Because people would not engage in it if they could avoid it, expenditure on health is a bad (not a good), and should not be included in national income.

2. The General Accounting Office concluded that when the Treasury gave approval to a liquor industry proposal to shift to metric sizes for liquor bottles "consumers weren't adequately served," because the shift was accompanied by rises in prices per quart (or litre). What do you conclude?

3. A discriminating monopolist will charge in each market the pric
   that maximizes receipts in that market.

4. A tax of 20 percent on all wages will decrease the supply of la
   by less than a tax of 20 percent on overtime pay alone.

II.a. (12 minutes)
Professor H calculates the welfare loss of monopoly in the American
economy by assuming unit elasticities of demand in the monopolized
industries. Professor S argues that Professor H's calculation is
inconsistent because literal monopolists would not operate at such
a point.

1. Briefly explain Professor S's argument. Professor H replies th
   the "monopolies" in question are not literally single sellers,
   but a few. He points out that the elasticity of a whole indust
   demand is therefore no measure of the firm's elasticity. The b
   havioral economics and the welfare economics are in this case q
   consistent, says Professor H.

2. Explain Professor H's argument.

II.b. (12 minutes)
College professors are inundated with free copies of new texts. Bo
dealers buy up these texts and resell them, when the guilt-ridden
professors will sell. One dealer says that she allays the professo
guilt by arguing that "it's unfair to the students not to sell them
they get a cheaper book when it is resold." But the dealer confess
that she really doesn't believe this argument and would prefer to g
it away at random herself. What would happen? Is there any differ
in result among selling, giving, or keeping?

III. 1. (10 minutes)
Let $c(y, w_1, w_2) = y^\alpha w_1^{\beta_1} w_2^{\beta_2}$ be a cost function for producing
output y when factor 1 receives wage w_1, factor 2 receives w_2.

a. How would you tell if there were constant returns to scale

b. What do we know about the value of $\alpha + \beta_1 + \beta_2$?

c. What do we know about the value of $\alpha + \beta_1$?

d. What do we know about the value of $\beta_1 + \beta_2$?

2. (5 minutes)
Suppose there are constant returns to scale. Calculate the deri
demand for factor 1 holding w_2 fixed when the demand for output
given by Q(p). This derived demand should be a function of w_1 a
w_2 only.

3

3. ((Q minutes)
   Consider the non-U.S. demand for oil, with price elasticity η, and
   the world's supply of oil, with elasticity ε.

   1. What is the price elasticity of supply facing U.S. customers?
      What is it facing the U.S. as a whole?

   2. What happens to the elasticity as the rest of the world's
      elasticity of demand becomes more elastic?

   3. What happens to the elasticity as U.S. demand shrinks towards
      zero?

IV. (15 minutes)
Some people criticize the "meat-axe" approach to cutting the government
budget, i.e., taking a uniform percentage from each government project.
They support a "scalpel" approach, with some luxury programs getting
larger cuts while necessary programs get smaller cuts.

   a. How would a rational government allocate a fixed budget among many
      projects?

   b. If the "meat axe" involved taking $10 from each program, what would
      you think of it?

   c. If it involved taking 1/100 of 1% of each program's budget, what
      would you think?

   d. If it involved taking 30% of each program's budget, what would
      you think?

In short, what do you think about the relative merits of the meat axe
and the scalpel?

V. (6 minutes)
Congestion tolls are not charged on most highways. Many products use
trucks and therefore the price of the product is affected by inefficiency in the market for transportation. TRUE or FALSE: In
calculating the welfare cost from not charging tolls, one must count
not only the deadweight loss that occurs in the market for transport
but also the induced deadweight loss in output market that occurs
because output prices are affected by the distortions in transportation markets.

COMPREHENSIVE EXAMINATION

Winter, 1979

Money

Exam Questions - M.A. Comprehensive

(MONEY SECTION: 90 MINUTES)

Answer all questions.

I. (15 minutes)
Can the central bank peg at a certain rate:

a) the nominal interest rate in the short run?
b) the nominal interest rate in the long run?
c) the real interest rate in the short run?
d) the real interest rate in the long run?

Briefly explain your answers.

II. (10 minutes)
If the probability of bank failures increases, what effects might this have on the money supply? Why?

III. (10 minutes)
How would the equalization of the required reserve rates on demand deposits and time deposits affect the ability of the Federal Reserve System to control:

a) M1?
b) M2?

IV. (10 minutes)
Was it reasonable for the Germans to blame the U.S. for their inflation problems during the fixed exchange rate period of the late 1960's?

V. (15 minutes)
Does stability of the money demand function (in the sense of predictabi[lity]) provide support for the following monetarist propositions:

a) Money is all that matters for the determination of nominal income .
b) In order to minimize fluctuations in output, the Federal Reserve should use a money stock target rather than an interest rate target[.]

VI. (15 minutes)
In an IS-LM, aggregate demand-aggregate supply framework, describe the effects of an increase in government expenditure on real output and the price level in (i) the short run and (ii) the long run when:

a) the demand for money is unaffected by the interest rate and the mon[ey] supply is given.

b) the demand for money is unaffected by the interest rate and the sup[ply] of money is positively related to the interest rate.

VII. (15 minutes)
What explanations can you give for a positive relationship the interest rate and the supply of money?

-214-

COMPREHENSIVE EXAMINATION
Price Theory
The Theory of Income, Employment
and the Price Level

Alternative B of the A.M. Degree

Summer 1978

WRITE IN BLACK INK

WRITE THE FOLLOWING INFORMATION ON THE FIRST PAGE OF YOUR EXAMINATION PAPER:

————————Your code number and not your name
————————Name of examination
————————Date of examination

Write only on one side of each page

WRITE THE FOLLOWING INFORMATION ON EACH FOLLOWING PAGE OF YOUR EXAMINATION PAPER:

————————Top left: code number
————————Top right: number of page

When you fold your paper at the end of the exam, write your code number on the
back, and indicate the total number of pages.

Credit is proportionate to time.

Results of the examination will be sent to you by letter.

Answer all questions

Part A. Price Theory

I. 30 minutes

Tell whether the statement is true, false, or uncertain and briefly explain why.

1. An exogenous increase in the price of output will always cause an increase
   in the derived demand for labor.

2. An individual consumes 5 units of x and 3 units of y in period 0 and 4
   units of x and 4 units of y in period 1. The prices are $P_{x_0} = 10$; $P_{x_1} = 10$;

   $P_{y_0} = 10$; $P_{y_1} = 12$. His behavior is inconsistent.

3. A producer has two plants: one has declining average cost throughout,
   the other has rising average cost throughout. Both plants will never
   be used simultaneously.

4. If technological change occured at the same rate in all industries,
   relative commodity prices would remain constant over time.

I. (continued)

   5. An investment tax credit in 1978 followed by a more lenient tax credit in 1980 will unambiguously reduce investment in 1978 relative to what it would have been in the absence of tax credits.

   6. Despite the fact that a monopolist has control over his prices, he will pass along to consumers a smaller proportion of an excise tax than a competitive firm.

II. 30 minutes.

   Suppose that the economy has only two types of occupations: lawyers and secretaries. Females are unable (either physically or as the result of licensing restrictions) to become lawyers. Males, on the other hand, are free to enter either profession. All males are alike and all females are alike. Assume the output (marriages, divorces, and wills) is sold competitively at price P_Q. Suppose that females are suddenly able to enter the lawyer occupations and perform as effectively as males.

   a). What will happen to the wages of lawyers relative to secretaries if it were the case that before this change some males were secretaries?

   b). Is your answer to (a) altered if you are told that there was a lawyers' union before the change?

   c). Now suppose that all men had chosen to be lawyers before the change. Is it possible that real wages of males and females will rise after the change?

   d). Does your answer to (c) depend upon whether females are substitutes or complements to males in production?

   e). The marginal product of lawyers and secretaries is given as

   $$MP_L = 100 - L$$

   $$MP_S = 5$$

   where L is the number of lawyers, S is the number of secretaries and MP is marginal product. Some males choose to be secretaries. If $P_Q = 5$, what is the competitive wage rate of lawyers? Does it depend upon the number of males in the economy? How many lawyers will there be per firm? Can anything be said about the firm's profits?

III. 30 minutes

Discuss the use of the following quantities for making interpersonal utility comparisons:

a). the marginal utility of income;

b). the income elasticity of the marginal utility of income.

IV. 30 minutes

A consumer in a two period economy enters the first period with m units of the single consumption good and has utility function $U(c_1, c_2) = \log c_1 + \log c_2$.

In the first period he can invest in education e at a unit price (in terms of the consumption good) of p_e; this investment yields $a + b \log e$ units of the consumption good in the second period. Borrowing and lending is possible at a zero interest rate.

a). How much education does the consumer buy?

b). How much of the consumption good does he consume in each period?

c). How do your answers to a) and b) change if the utility function was $U(c_1, c_2) = \log c_1 + 1/2 \log c_2$?

Part B. Income, Employment and the Price Level

I. 30 minutes

Tell whether the statement is true, false or uncertain and briefly explain why.

1. The adaptive-expectations model for the rate of price change is inconsistent with rational formation of expectations.

2. An investment project that costs $100 today and brings a return of $10 a year forever is more desireable than a project which costs $40 today and returns $80 next year and nothing after that.

3. If no component of aggregate demand (e.g., investment in particular) is responsive to interest rates then, if consumers wish to increase the amount they save, they cannot.

4. With fixed wages and prices, the "balanced-budget multiplier" will be above unity only if individuals value government activities at less than their cost.

5. An increase in reserve requirements at commercial banks may be expansionary, since it may reduce the excess demand for high-powered money.

6. If individuals come to expect an acceleration of money supply at some future date, the current price level will rise.

I. (continued)

   7. If the expected real rate of return is constant over time, then an u[ ]
      sloping term structure of interest rates must reflect expectations o[ ]
      rising rate of inflation.

   8. The procyclical pattern of quits supports the non-market clearing
      approach to business cycles.

   9. Increases in GNP represent increases in social welfare.

   10. Technological innovation which introduces credit cards into the econo[ ]
       cause an increase in the money supply producing inflation.

II. 30 minutes

   Consider two countries, A and B, that are identical in terms of size,
   technology, natural resources, etc. Suppose that the two countries adop[ ]
   monetary policies that involve the same mean rate of monetary expansion
   but that the money growth rate is less predictable in country A than in
   country B. (Assume that the world is one of flexible exchange rates.)

   1. What would you predict for the two countries about their relative va[ ]

      a. mean "real income"?

      b. Phillips curve slopes?

      c. dispersion of relative prices?

   2. How would the answers be affected if country A also had a larger (sys[ ]
      countercyclical policy response of money to the lagged value of unemp[ ]

III. 30 minutes

   In the microeconomic competitive equilibrium, a set of prices exists suc[ ]
   that all markets clear -- there is no "macroeconomic problem". The now-
   traditional IS-LM model is designed to consider the macroeconomic proble[ ]
   below full employment income. How do the two models differ in terms of w[ ]
   markets are assumed to clear? State a case for the possible policy usefu[ ]
   of the IS-LM model in a world in which wages adjust to equilibrium slowly[ ]
   "multipliers" exist, and so on. (Hint: social costs are not independent[ ]
   time spent out of equilibrium.)

COMPREHENSIVE EXAMINATION

Price Theory
The Theory of Income, Employment
and the Price Level

Alternative B of the A.M. Degree

Summer 1977

WRITE IN BLACK INK

WRITE THE FOLLOWING INFORMATION ON THE FIRST PAGE OF YOUR EXAMINATION PAPER:

> Your code number (NOT your name)
> Name of examination
> Date of examination

WRITE ONLY ON ONE SIDE OF EACH PAGE

WRITE THE FOLLOWING INFORMATION ON EACH FOLLOWING PAGE OF YOUR EXAM PAPER:

> Top left: code number
> Top right: number of page

When you fold your paper at the end of the exam, write your code number on the back, and indicate total number of pages.

Credit is proportionate to time.

Results of the examination will be sent to you by letter.

Part A. Price Theory (90 minutes)

I. Warmups (5 minutes each, 10 minutes in all)

   1. T or F: The difference in wages between a steam-shovel operator and a (hand) shovel operator can be explained by the theory of marginal productivity

   2. T or F: A tax on the windfall profits of oil companies will have no effect on the industry.

II. Serious Business (7 minutes each, 28 minutes in all)

   3. T or F: If it is literally true that all differences in wages can be explained as returns to differing amounts of human capital or to the disamenities of unpleasant jobs, then no increase in happiness can result from reshuffling the labor force, regardless of how much larger the reshuffling makes the average wage.

   4. Q: "In the professions of law, medicine and the like, it is the reputation of enjoying a large practice which attracts new clients. Thus a successful barrister or physician generally labours more severely as his success increases." (W. S. Jevons, The Theory of Political Economy, c. 1885, 4th ed. [Penguin, 1970, p. 197]). Explain.

-219-

5. **T or F**: If public transport and automobiles are substitutes, then an ex_
   fall in the supply curve of public transport will cause a vicious (or vi_
   circle of continuously declining consumption of both public transport an_
   automobiles.

6. **T or F**: An upper—middle—class mix in Flossmoor's services (schools, par_
   city museums and concerts) will insure that only the upper middle class _
   choose to live in Floesmoor, especially if no one can live in Flossmoor _
   owning property.

III. **More Serious Business** (5 minutes each, 30 minutes in all)

7. **T or F**: The wage that an emigrant from Ireland to America gets in Ameri_
   is likely to be higher than the wage his distant cousins could get in Am_
   if they, too, emigrated to America.

8. **T or F**: A tax on gas—guzzling cars will always reduce national income.

9. **T or F**: Because money is fungible, even if AID demands that the projects
   finances in poor countries earn a social return of 10% a year as a minim_
   it is still true that the social return on the AID money could be much l_
   say 5%.

10. **T or F**: An ability of the landlord to specify the amount of labor to be
    applied to his acre will suffice by itself to make the landlord's income
    under 50% sharecropping identical to that under ordinary renting.

11. **T or F**: Since people are paid their marginal products, shooting them wo_
    have no effect on the rest of society.

12. **T or F**: Since wages in Povertia can only be measured in the principal c_
    the wage statistics are worthless: the sample is too small.

IV. **Final Business** (7 minutes each, 21 minutes in all)

13. **Q**: The elasticity of demand for slaves in Southern cities in the early
    century was fairly high, i.e. 0.9 (there were good substitutes for slav_
    city occupations); the total elasticity of demand for slaves, in city a_
    countryside together, was .08; 96 percent of slaves lived in the countr_
    T or F: Therefore the elasticity of demand for slaves in the countrysi_
    very low, i.e. .05 (there were no good substitutes for slaves in countr_
    occupations).

14. **T or F**: If all goods were perfect (net) complements with each other, t_
    the unweighted sum of all own—price elasticities would be -1.0.

15. **Q**: Crusoe and Friday have differing abilities in producing Housing and
    their only objects of desire. Prove graphically that their consumption
    both goods can always be higher if they specialize than if they insist _
    producing and consuming in isolation from each other.

Money, Income, and Price (90 minutes)

(10 minutes) Define each of the following terms:

1. Real Balance Effect
2. Automatic Stabilizer
3. Neutrality of Money
4. Balanced Budget Multiplier

(40 minutes) True, False or Uncertain. Briefly explain each answer.

1. A change in the government's budget surplus (deficit) necessarily implies that there was a change in fiscal or monetary policy.

2. If unemployment is above the natural rate the rate of inflation must always be falling.

3. Post World War II recessions in the United States have been caused by errors in expectations leading to unanticipated accumulation of inventories. The duration of the recessions has been determined by the length of time necessary to work off these inventories.

4. The findings that housing demand is highly sensitive to interest rates and more sensitive to permant than transitory income imply that housing helps to dampen business cycles.

5. An increase in excise taxes, as on oil, will decrease income tax collections out of any given level of pre-tax income.

6. A tax on oil has pervasive effects raising the costs of producing many commodities and will raise the price level by approximately the ad valorem rate on oil times the weught of oil in GNP.

7. The increasingly widespread use of credit cards and the introduction of electronic funds transfers are factors reducing the demand for hand to hand currency. The reduction in demand for hand to hand currency will free up high powered money and thus have an inflationary effect.

8. The failure to pay interest on hand to hand currency and on demand deposits implies that there is too little money in real terms in the economy.

(15 minutes) Answer as indicated:

1. Consider the following table:

Assets and debts of households, 1969

Income before taxes	% of households	Total Assets	Percent of total assets Monetary	Variable Price	Debts
----- 3,000	17	92	20	80	8
3,000- 5,000	14	119	20	80	15
5,000-10,000	33	350	18	82	23
10,000-15,000	24	420	14	86	29
15,000-25,000	9	359	12	88	21
25,000-50,000	2	177	14	86	18
50,000-------	0.4	105	18	82	10

Would it be appropriate to tax the very rich in order to obtain means to compensate the poor for their losses due to unanticipated inflation?

2. Consider the next table:

<u>Net Debtor or Creditor (or monetary assets) of Major Economic Sectors 19</u>

Households	+ 856	(billions of $)
Unincorporated business	- 115	
Nonfinancial Corporations	- 278	
Financial Corporations	- 130	
Government	- 399	

What is the effect of a 1 percent unanticipated inflation rate on each s
Explain the meaning of the government "gaining" on its outstanding debts

IV. (5 minutes)

An open market purchase by the Federal Reserve involves an exchange in asset
when the private sector gives up a bond and receives a demand deposit in exc
How then can we have any wealth effect of such an operation?

V. (10 minutes)

What are the effects on the time paths of output, general price level, emplo
and interest rates of a once-for-all completely unforeseen increase in the m
supply of 10 percent? Give attention to markets for financial instruments,
and services and labor.

VI. (10 minutes)

Recession and recovery are observed to be world-wide phenomena, with particu
strong correlations between cyclical changes in unemployment in the United S
and Western European countries. What are the major linkages that account fo
correlation? To what extent would the correlation be reduced if every count
completely flexible exchange rates?

Price Theory
The Theory of Income, Employment
and the Price Level

Alternative B of the A.M. Degree

Winter 1977

WRITE IN BLACK INK

WRITE THE FOLLOWING INFORMATION ON THE FIRST PAGE OF YOUR EXAMINATION PAPER:

Your code number and NOT your name
Name of examination
Date of examination

WRITE ONLY ON ONE SIDE OF EACH PAGE

WRITE THE FOLLOWING INFORMATION ON EACH FOLLOWING PAGE OF YOUR EXAM PAPER:

Top left: code number
Top right: number of page

When you fold your paper at the end of the exam, write your code number on the back, and indicate total number of pages.

Credit is proportionate to time.

Results of the examination will be sent to you by letter.

Part A. Price Theory (90 minutes)

I. Three Short Questions (5 minutes each, 15 minutes in all)

1. T or F: The demand curve for food of a man who needs 1 pound of food or more per day to survive is vertical.

2. What is the relation between the law of diminishing returns and diminishing returns to scale?

3. T or F: Free but wretched housing provided by the state can under some circumstances reduce the amount of housing (quality corrected) consumed by the population.

II. Two Longish Questions (10 minutes each, 20 minutes in all)

1. The Hyde Park Co-op invariably has long lines at its checkout counters. Suppose that some of the counters charged 5% more on the grocery bill than the others. Who would use them? Who would benefit from the system?

2. Show that with linear demand curves a monopolist facing two markets in which he can charge different prices will never produce less than he would if he was forced to charge the same price in both.

III. One Long Question (15 minutes)

In addition to a price per drink, bars often impose cover charges (entry fees) or minimum number of drinks. Suppose Jimmy's was the only bar in Hyde Park (but attendance, of course, was not compulsory).

1. In an indifference curve diagram for Jimmy's typical customer between drinks and all other goods locate the bundle that would maximize the net revenue to Jimmy [Hint: Draw the budget line the customer would face if Jimmy (foolishly) sold drinks at what they cost Jimmy; now draw the indifference curve through the customer's pre-drink bundle, i.e. zero drinks and his initial income in all other goods. Now answer the question].

2. Jimmy thinks of imposing a cover charge or, alternatively, a minimum number of drinks. Interpret his thoughts.

3. If the City outlaws these possibilities and requires that Jimmy charge one price for a drink, what does Jimmy do?

IV. More Short Questions (5 minutes each, 25 minutes in all)

1. Draw the indifference curves for Jones, who has priorities in consumpt: i.e. first he buys food; then — when he has enough food — he buys then ... etc., down to electric can-openers and copies of Robert Lekachman's latest work.

2. T or F: Triangles of lost consumers' and producers' surplus underesti: the social loss from price controls, regulation, taxation, and monopol;

3. T or F: Because Brazil produces a third of the world's coffee, the elasticity of demand for coffee is -0.2, and the supply from other countries is virtually fixed, the Brazilian government can make more money by raising the export tax on coffee.

4. T or F: Because medical care is a monopoly society is made worse off by subsidies to medical care.

5. T or F: The Coase Theorem says we live in the best of all possible worlds (from the point of view of efficiency): i.e. that transactions costs are in fact zero.

V. One More Long Question (15 minutes)

Under a federal welfare program a family is given $50 per week when its income is below $15 a week. When its income is greater than $15 the amount over $15 is subtracted from the $50 payment (until, at a pre-gift income of $65, the payment is zero). Show how the program would affect the supply curve of labor.

Part B. Money, Income, and Price (90 minutes)

1. (10 minutes) T or F: If real balances have been going down, the central bank has been decreasing the nominal money stock.

2. (5 minutes) T or F: If consumers were irrational, choosing points on their budget line at random, Walras' law will nonetheless hold.

3. (5 minutes) T or F: The willingness of the Japanese to accumulate American money in exchange for cars and T.V. sets (i.e., to tolerate a surplus in their balance of payments with Americans) is a Good Thing for Americans.

4. (10 minutes) What would be the impact on Gross National Product and the price level if, with fiscal and monetary policy unchanged, the recent cold weather causes severe crop failures? Why?

5. (13 minutes) The usual story of multiple deposit creation indicates that

$$DD = \frac{1}{\delta} H$$

where   DD = demand deposits
    H = monetary base (high-powered money)
    δ = required reserve ratio on demand deposits

If the Federal Reserve dropped its reserve requirements for demand deposits (i.e., δ = 0), would demand deposits expand indefinitely? Explain why or why not.

6. (10 minutes) The standard IS-LM model indicates that an "easy money policy" of rapid money growth leads to lower nominal interest rates, which stimulate the economy; yet we find that countries with the highest rates of money growth tend to have the highest nominal interest rates. How can this apparent contradiction be explained?

7. (15 minutes) Indicate the effect on the money supply of

    a. increased fear of banking failures
    b. legalization of illegal book making (gambling) activities
    c. a rise in the treasury bill rate

8. (12 minutes) The U.S. economy of the late nineteenth century might be characterized as a small open economy with fixed exchange rates, integrated into world capital markets. How might this affect Friedman and Schwartz's argument that changes in the domestic money supply caused U.S. business cycle movements of that period?

9. (10 minutes) Under rational expectations the short run Phillips curve is vertical.

COMPREHENSIVE EXAMINATION

Summer Quarter 1976

Price Theory

The Theory of Income, Employment
and the Price Level

Alternative B of the A. M. Degree

WRITE THE FOLLOWING INFORMATION ON YOUR EXAMINATION PAPER:

Your code number, but NOT your name.
Name of Examination
Date of Examination.
Results of the examination will be sent to you by letter.

Time: 3 hours. Answer all questions.

Note: This examination is in two parts. Write your answers in separate part
Begin Part B of the examination on a new sheet of paper.

WRITE ALL ANSWERS IN BLACK INK

Count the number of pages used, write the number and circle it on the back
of the last page.

A. Price Theory (90 minutes)

1. (5 minutes)
The government supports the price of some agricultural goods by buying
up the surplus at the support price. Putting limits on the amount of
government funds received under these programs by large farmers will
reduce the benefit large farmers get from the price supports. True or
False? Explain.

2. (5 minutes)
Sears, Roebuck should buy its goods, when possible, from its own sub-
sidiary companies rather than from outsiders, because the profits of
its subsidiaries (and therefore of Sears, Roebuck) will increase.
True or False? Explain.

3. (5 minutes)
A shipping company borrows money at 10 percent to invest in a ship and
operates the ship for twenty years. Each year the revenue from operatir
the ship is less than the interest cost on the debt and other costs. The
company was probably acting irrationally when it bought the ship, and
certainly was acting irrationally when it continued to operate it
despite the losses. True, False or Uncertain? Explain.

4. (5 minutes)
   After the South had been defeated in the American Civil War and the slaves had been freed, agricultural output in the South fell by about a third. The supply of labor(formerly slave labor) and of other factors of production except land also fell by about a third. Therefore there was a fall(due perhaps to the abolition of slavery or persistent disorganization occasioned by the war) in the agricultural production function in the South . True, False,or Uncertain? Explain.

5. (5 minutes)
   In Japan, workers cannot be fired once they have been hired. Therefore in Japan a minimum wage law would not cause Unemployment. Ture, False, or Uncertain? Explain.

6. (5 minutes)
   If interest rates generally average 7 percent, tax free municipals give a 3 1/2 percent subsidy to a taxpayer in the 50 percent bracket. True, False, or Uncertain? Explain.

7. (5 minutes)
   Show in an Edgeworth box that a monopolist and his victims would be better off if the victims could bribe the monopolist to charge a competitive price. In view of this, why do you suppose monopolies charging noncompetitive prices persist?

8. (15 minutes)
   1) Slavery was abolished in Brazil in 1888. In the thirty or so years before abolition one could rent a slave for a year in Rio for 330 mil reis. If the rate of return on investments having the same risk was 25 percent and if slaves lived forever(effectively they did: the life expectancy of a 25 year old slave was about 20 years more, and with such high interest rates this is "forever"),what would be the price of slaves?

   2) Slaves "die" when they are freed as far as their owner is concerned. What do you make of the following pattern of slave prices in Rio in the 1880's?

      (prices in mil reis)

      | 1880 | 1233 | 1883 | 589 | 1886 | 543 |
      | 1881 | 1700 | 1884 | 700 | 1887 | 249 |
      | 1882 | 1128 | 1885 | 543 | 1888 | 0 |

9. (20 minutes)
   A furniture manufacturing plant purchases lumber for use in producing standard units of a particular kind of table. A consultant uses monthly data over a ten year period to estimate the following relationship between lumber purchases in board-feet, m_t, and tables produced x_t:

$$\ln(m_t) = \underset{(0.44)}{2.61} + \underset{(.12)}{(.46)} \ln(x_t).$$

The numbers in the parentheses below the coefficients are standard errors. The

R-squared from this regression is .86; the Durbin-Watson statistic is 0.32.

  (i) Is the estimated relationship a satisfactory account of lumber use by the plant? Why or why not?

  (ii) To what extent is this result evidence of increasing returns to scale?

 (iii) Which of the reported numbers would one expect to change if one changed the units in which lumber input is measured?

  (iv) What (if any) other variables should be included in an empirical relationship relating materials purchases and output? Explain.

10. (20 minutes)
A university computation center has purchased a $2,000,000 computer. The terms of sale require that the machine cannot be re-sold, that time cannot be sold to non-campus users, and off-campus time cannot be purchased by campus users. The university is free, however to add additional capacity.

The center is depreciating the machine over five years, at $ 400,000 per year. Operating costs of the center are given by:

$$\$100,000 \ + (\$75) \ H$$

where $H \le 8760$ is hours of use per year.

Campus users purchase time on the computer at a uniform price fixed by the center. The demand for time follows the curve

$$H = 10,400 - (32) \ P$$

where P is the price (dollars) per hour of use. Assume that this demand curve is "correct," in the sense that

$$\frac{10,400 - H}{32}$$

measures the "true" value to the university of an additional hour's use, when usage is at the rate H.

The management of the center observes that at a price of $200 per hour, revenues of the center will just cover costs, defined as operating expenses plus depreciation charges. (Both will equal $800,000.) Accordingly, P is set at $200 per hour.

Comment on this pricing policy, dealing in particular with the following questions:

   (i) Is the computer use at P= $200 efficient? Why not?

(ii) What price will lead to efficient use? Why?

(iii) At the price found in (ii), will the computer center "break even"? What are the implications of this answer for efficiency?

(iv) Was the computer purchase a good investment?

Part B. The Theory of Income, Employment and Price Level (90 minutes)

I.(3 minutes each) True, False or Uncertain. Give a one or two sentence explanation of your answer.

1. An increase in the marginal propensity to consume shifts the LM curve to the right. (T, F or U).

2. An increase of one percent in the expected rate of inflation decreases the demand for money by the same amount as does a one percent increase in the interest rate on assets which are money substitutes. (T,F or U).

3. The crawling peg is the ratchet in the Phillips Curve, when the Phillips Curve is properly specified in real terms. (T, F or U).

4. Cost push inflation is caused when the Fed raises the interest rate above the real rate plus the expected rate of inflation.(T, F or U).

5. The existence of a bequeathment motive for savings hastens the approach of an economy towards the golden age. (T, F or U).

6. If expectations are rational, business cycles will not occur.(T,F or U).

7. The welfare cost of inflationary finance refers to the loss in real value of the government debt as the price level rises.(T,F or U).

8. If consumption is a function only of real wealth in a world with perfect capital markets and perfect foresight, with taxpayers fully aware of the future liabilities imposed by the government debt, a reduction in taxes will not affect consumption.(T,F or U).

9. The statements, that consumption is a function of wealth and that consumption is a function of permanent income, are equivalent. (T,F or U).

10. If the Fed paid a market rate of interest on commercial bank reserves and if commercial banks were allowed to pay a free market rate of interest on deposits, there would be not tax on money. (T,For U).

11. The IS curve becomes perfectly vertical at full employment. (T,F or U).

12. If the economy is at full employment and the government increases expenditures without increasing taxes, inflation must occur. (T,F or U).

II. (8 minutes) Comment on possible effects of inflation on the full employment level of output. What might be their relative strengths? Would it make any difference if inflation is open or supressed? How else can real cash balance affect the "real side" of the economy?

III. (5 minutes) Inflation requires a sustained growth of money supply, but the converse is not true. Why?

IV. (7 minutes). The nominal rate of interest often differs from the real rate of interest. Give reasons why this might be so. What policy would you recommend if the government is interested in lowering the nominal rate of interest? What policy if interested in lowering the real rate of interest ?

V. (8 minutes) Determine the impact on the money supply of a government deficit financed by:

a) Sale of bonds to the public
b) Sale of bonds to the banking system
c) Sale of bonds to the Fed
d) Sale of bonds to foreigners.

VI. (8 minutes) Where a positive externality exists in the employment of labor in a particular import-substituting industry, a tariff on imports can increase welfare, but not by as much as an appropriately-set subsidy to production; and a subsidy to production in turn cannot improve welfare by as much as an appropriately-set subsidy to the use of labor in the affected industry. (True, False or Uncertain? Explain).

VII. (5 minutes) According to Kaynes, Say's Law underlies the whole classical theory, which would collapse without it. Do you think this law is necessary to the classical conclusions?

VIII. (7 minutes) Traditional theory limits itself to the analysis of the effects of monetary and fiscal policy on aggregate demand. Discuss some possible effects of these policies on aggregate supply.

IX. (7 minutes) Unions raise money wages 10 percent in a country where a large fraction of national income is traded internationally. Suppose the country follows a monetary policy which maintains the unemployment level prevailing before the wage increase, and has also a policy of not intervening in foreign exchange markets. Predict the percentage amount by which the following magnitudes will be affected by the money wage increase:

i) the general level of price
ii) the quantity of money
iii) the unemployment rate
iv) the exchange rate.

Price Theory

The Theory of Income,Employment
amd the Price Level

Alternative B of the A.M. Degree

Winter 1976.

WRITE IN BLACK INK

WRITE THE FOLLOWING INFORMATION ON THE FIRST PAGE OF YOUR EXAMINATION PAPER:

>Your code number and NOT your name.
>Name of examination
>Date of examination.

Write only on one side of each page

WRITE THE FOLLOWING INFORMATION ON EACH FOLLOWING PAGE OF YOUR EXAM PAPER:

>Top left: code number
>Top right: number of page

When you fold your paper at the end of the exam, write your code number on
the back, and indicate total number of pages.

You should have ample time to give a careful answer to each question. Where-
ever possible illustrate or verify your answer with either a well-labeled
diagram or appropriate equations.

Results of the examination will be sent to you by letter.

Part A. Price Theory

I. Short questions (10 minutes each)

(i) The Mayor proposes an increase in the fine for illegally parked
(and towed) cars from $20.00 to $30.00. Under the present contract, towing firms get $15.00 per car towed and fined and the
city $5.00. The new arrangement will give the towing firms the
same $15.00 and give the city $15.00. Towing firms, which have
a monopoly for each region of the city, claim that they will lose
money under the new rules. Evaluate their claim.

(ii)Evaluate: For a given consumer all goods cannot be inferior,
superior, luxuries or necessities(the last one implies income
elasticity between 0 and 1).

(iii)Evaluate : " A monopolist producing at constant unit costs will not produce any output if the market demand curve is unitary elastic."

(iv)Product B is produced using product A in fixed proportions. One government sets a price ceiling for A below the present equilibrium price. What will happen to the price of B?

(v)A research and development lab turns out 12 new product ideas per year, about half of which are judged good enought to be produced and marketed. Average " life" of these products is five years. Average net revenue (sales less direct costs) is $80,000 per product per year.

Operating costs of the lab are $1,500,000 per year. The lab has plant and equipment valued at $5,000,000. The lab is one division in a company which has an overall pre-tax of return on capital of 20 percent.

What is the annual economic profit of the lab?

2.(20 minutes)
Two individuals, A and B, live on an island. They want to divide the island in three parts: each one will be given a part of the island to produce food for himself and the third part will be set for a common park. How would they divide the island?

(Formal Hint): Let the total size of the island he equal to 1 unit of land. Assume you can write the indirect utility of A as $U^A(x_A,y)$ where x_A is the amount of land he gets for private use, and y is the amount of parkland. Similarly, let B's utility be given by $U^B(x_B,y)$. Assume both utility functions are concave.

3. (20 minutes)

A competitive industry contains 100 firms. It is initially in equi-librium,with an industry output of 4,000 units per month, and price = $2 per unit. The smallest firm produces 10 units ; the largest, 120.

a. State two models of industry and firm cost functions which are consistent with these facts.

b. Compare the predictions of these two models with regard to firm and industry response to an increase in demand; to the imposition of a lump-sum license for remaining in the industry.

Begin Part B on new Page.

Part B. Theory of Income, Employment and the Price Level

1. (20 Minutes)
   In the following questions, assume that the economies involved are initially at " full employment" (have output near its normal trend line) and that prices initially are stable. Each question postulates a "shock" affecting one or more economies, and then lists some possible short run consequences.

   Answer each part TRUE or FALSE. No explantaion is required, but if you wish to qualify your answer indicate by an asterick and do so below your answers to all the parts of this question.

   A. If the U.S. troops now stationed in Germany are immediately re-turned to the U.S. and discharged:

       (i)   the U.S. inflation rate will fall
      (ii) the German inflation rate will fall.
    (iii) U. S. unemployment will increase.
     (iv) German unemployment will increase.

   B. If U.S.government expenditures increase, taxes remain constant, and the deficit is entirely financed by a bond issue,

       (i)   U.S. inflation will increase.
      (ii) U.S. unemployment will increase
    (iii) U.S. interest rates will decline
     (iv) Japanese inflation will increase.

   C. If the U.S. government expenditures increase, taxes remain constant,and the deficit is financed entirely by an increase in the money supply,

       (i)   U.S. inflation will increase
      (ii) U.S. unemployment will increase
    (iii) U.S. interest rates will decline
     (iv) Japanese inflation will increase.

   D. If the U.S. and Mexico agree to free immigration across national boundaries,

       (i)   U.S. GNP will increase relative to trend
      (ii) U.S. inflation will increase
    (iii) Real wages in the U. S. will increase.
     (iv) Real wages in Mexico will increase.

   E. If the U.S. money supply should contract sharply,

       (i)   U.S. interest rates will decline
      (ii) U.S. inflation will decline
    (iii) U.S. GNP will decline
     (iv) British inflation will decline.

2. (20 minutes)
What do you consider to be the most important effect on the U.S. economy of an increase in the foreign price of oil(the U.S. is a net importer of oil). Explain.

3. (20 minutes)
Reconcile the following statements:

a. An increase in the quantity of money reduces nominal interest rates.

b. An increase in the rate of expansion of the money supply increases nominal interest rates.

4. (30 minutes)
On the following page, you are given time series on GNP per unit of capital, and manhours per unit of capital. You are also given the results of a regression of $\ln(Y_t/K_t)$ on $\ln(L_t/K_t)$ and time.

On the basis of this evidence, plus the general knowledge you have of the U.S. economy (recall that the average share of GNP going to labor was roughly constant at .65), evaluate the following three hypotheses:

(a) The economy is roughly competitive and the "true" aggregate production is the Cobb-Douglas:

$$Y_t = \gamma K_t L_t^{1-\beta} \lambda^t, \quad \lambda > 1, \gamma > 0, \ 0 < \beta < 1;$$

(b) The production function is Cobb-Douglas, but the economy as a whole exploits labor, so that the real wage rate is less than the marginal product of labor;

(c) The production function exhibits "fixed proportions" of labor and capital, or:

$$Y_t \leq \alpha L_t \lambda^t, \quad \lambda > 1, \quad \alpha > 0$$

$$Y_t \leq \beta K_t, \quad \beta > 0,$$

and product and labor markets are roughly compeitive.

Year	Y/K	L/K		Year	Y/K	L/K
1929	.424	.243		1950	.673	.299
1930	.373	.224		51	.680	.300
31	.346	.208		52	.666	.292
32	.302	.190		53	.670	.287
33	.310	.203		54	.637	.269
34	.354	.215		55	.658	.268
35	.402	.237		56	.640	.262
36	.465	.268		57	.623	.251
37	.489	.282		58	.595	.237
38	.459	.262		59	.616	.245
39	.507	.281		1960	.612	.242
1940	.550	.296		61	.604	.234
41	.626	.325		62	.625	.236
42	.681	.352		63	.626	.232
43	.779	.404		64	.636	.230
44	.857	.431		65	.642	.229
45	.861	.419				
46	.765	.373				
47	.703	.347				
48	.685	.331				
49	.636	.299				

Regression results:

$$\ln(Y_t/K_t) = .441 + \underset{(0.025)}{(1.009)} \ln(L_t/K_t) + \underset{(.000+)}{(.016)t}$$

The adjusted R^2 is .9976. The Durbin-Watson Statistic is .6483.
The signs of the residuals are as follows:

Positive(underpredication): 29-31,41-42,45,50-58,64-65

Negative(overprediction) : 32-40,43-44,46-49, 59-63.

Price Theory
The Theory of Income, Employment
and the Price Level
Summer 1975
Alternative B of the A. M. Degree.

WRITE THE FOLLOWING INFORMATION ON YOUR EXAMINATION PAPER:

> Your code number, but NOT your name.
> Name of examination
> Date of examination

Results of the examination will be sent to you by letter.

> TIME: 3 hours. ANSWER ALL QUESTIONS.

Note: This examination is in two parts. Write your answers in separate parts.
Begin Part B of the examination on a new sheet of paper.

WRITE ALL ANSWERS IN BLACK INK

Count the number of pages used, write the number and circle it on the back
of the last page.

A. Price Theory

Credit is in proportion to time. Equalize your marginal point product
on each question.

I. Warm Ups (5 minutes each, 20 minutes in all)

Indicate whether each of the following assertions is True(T), False(F),
or Uncertain(U), and explain briefly why.

1. No private firm undertook to set flying and operate the system of
communication satellites. Therefore this project was socially
undersirable.

2. Henry Smith, by all accounts a dynamic business genius, leaves
General Motors and goes to Ford. Nothing happens to the price of
General Motors stock relative to Ford stock. Apparently Smith is
not as much of a genius as he is supposed to be.

3. Cigarette smugglers and museum thieves in Italy are usually casual
laborers and farm workers when not engaged in crime. One would
expect their hourly wage in these crimes to be equal to their wage
as casual labor and farm workers.

4. An employer will never invest in training a worker if the worker can
move to another employer after being trained.

II. Joe Palooka Revisited (15 minutes)

Joe Palooka has a real property income of $200 per year and faces a market real wage of $2.00 per hour. Joe's health is a bit poor and he must spend 4,056 hours per year (out of a total of 8,736) in sleeping and other personal care time, leaving him 4,680 hours per year to allocate between market work and household consumption(or"leisure") . He chooses to work 1,560 hours per year.

a. For reasons beyond his control, his health improves enough so that he must spend only 3,856 hours per year(200 less than before) in sleeping and personal care time. By how many hours per year(more than 200? less than 200? less than zero?) will his hours of market work increase? Explain.

b. Instead of the improvement in health assumed in (a), his real property income increases by $400. How many hours will Joe now choose to work, if in (a) he would have chosen to work 1,660 hours per year ? Explain.

III. More Short Questions (7 minutes each, 14 minutes in all)

1. The immigration of raw labor(immigrants possess no capital of any kind) raises the total income of the natives.

2. In a last effort to save itself before it went out of business, Life magazine in 1970 reduced its circulation from 8.5 million to 5.5 million copies and raised its subscription price. This behavior contradicts the common assertion that economies of scale are substantial in publishing.

IV. Legal Constraints on Factor Combinations (25 minutes)

Each of the actual and potential firms in a competitive industry has the following production function

$$X = Min(\ell^{\frac{1}{2}}, \ k^2)$$

where x is output, ℓ is labor input, and k is capital input. (Read

Min $(\ell^{\frac{1}{2}}, k^2)$ as "the smaller of $\ell^{\frac{1}{2}}$ and k^2.") This industry is so small a part of the economy that to it the prices of the inputs are given. Let the price of labor services be unity and that for capital services be 2.

a. Draw a diagram showing the shape and position of the isoquants for x=1 and x= 4.

b. Prove that when total factor cost is minimized at the given factor prices, the following propositions hold.

$$x = \ell^{\frac{1}{2}} = k^2$$
$$c = 2x^{\frac{1}{2}} + x^2$$

where c is the total factor cost.

c. Describe the shape of the <u>average</u> cost curve. At what output is average cost a minimum?

d. Part of the industry output is sold to the government, which has the following demand curve

$$X_G = 300 / P_G$$

where X_G is its quantity demanded and P_G the unit price it pays. The rest of the output is sold to non-government buyers who have the following demand curve

$$X_N = 150 / P_N$$

where X_N is quantity and P_N the price.   In the long run equilibrium what are the values of P_N and P_G ? X_N and X_G? The number of firms in the industry?   The total quantity of labor employed in the industry? Of capital?

e. Now assume that a law is passed requiring that in the production of all of the output sold to the government the labor/capital ratio cannot be less than 8.   In the new long run equilibrium what are the values of P_N and P_G? X_N and X_G?   The number of firms in the industry? The total quantity of labor employed in the industry? Of capital?

V. Still More Short Questions(5 minutes each, 15 minutes in all)

1. Population increased by 50% in 16th. century Europe, driving up the price of land-intensive commodities, in particular grain. Grain had a very large share of total consumption. Therefore the population increase contributed to the inflation of the general price level.

2. A landlord in a tight housing market does not raise his rents on his apartments but demands instead that his tenants pay for some of the regular redecoration (painting,etc.) than before the market was tight. He is evidently irrational.

3. A Law setting maximum hours to be worked per week will reduce hours of work per week per employee and raise the wage rate.

4

Part B. The Theory of Income, Employment and the Price Level.

I. (35 minutes) Indicate whether each of the following statements is True(T), False (F), or Uncertain (U), and indicate briefly your reason.

1. An increase in government spending financed by reduced transfers so as to maintain budgetary balance at the new equilibrium level of income will be more expansionary the higher the income tax rate.

2. In the classical quantity theory, the income elasticity of the demand for money is unity unless velocity depends on the rate of interest.

3. The inventory theory of transactions demand for money predicts that the quantity of money demanded will increase less than in proportion to income, and therefore that the rate of inflation will exceed the rate of monetary expansion(ignoring growth of real output).

4. A central bank is a necessary condition for a balance of payments problem.

5. Models of "rational" expectations are impractical since they do not allow for mistakes in predicitions.

6. In a closed economy the steady-state capital-labor ratio is independent of the rate of inflation.

7. When the marginal product of capital is less than the natural rate of growth, it is Pareto optimal(across generations) to decrease current saving.

8. In a closed economy, the money multiplier generally exceeds the reciprocal of the reserve requirement.

9. If one observes that the level of GNP is historically constant while government spending moves cyclically, one may infer that fiscal policy has no effect.

II. Define briefly (5 minutes)

1. Okun's law

2. Walras law

3. Gresham law

III. (15 minutes)

During the German hyper-inflation, when interest rates were high, there were complaints about a "shortage" of money. Interpret.

In your inperpretation explain:

(a) What the term money means in this complaint.

(b) In what sense was there a "shortage" of money? Assume no complaints of "shortage" existed before the inflation.

(c) How the "shortage" was created.

(d) How your answer relates to the view that a stable demand function for money exists.

IV. (10 minutes)

It has been observed that the Phillips curve for England lies below that for the U.S.

(a) Define the Phillips curve.

(b) Present a theoretical justification for the negative slope.

(c) How might one explain the difference between the American and English Phillips curves? (Give at least two explanations.)

V. (10 minutes)

Evaluate the following proposition:

"Under full employment, a reduction in the rate of personal income tax accompanied by a rise in the corporate income tax rate which leaves total tax revenue unchanged will lower the rate of interest."

VI. (15 minutes)

Analyze the effects of the rise in the relative price of oil on consumers' and corporate spending.

COMPREHENSIVE EXAMINATION
Price Theory
The Theory of Income, Employment
and the Price Level

Alternative B of the A.M. Degree

Winter 1975

WRITE IN BLACK INK

WRITE THE FOLLOWING INFORMATION ON THE FIRST PAGE OF YOUR EXAMINATION PAPER:

    ------------Your code number and not your name
    ------------Name of examination
    ------------Date of examination

Write only on one side of each page

WRITE THE FOLLOWING INFORMATION ON EACH FOLLOWING PAGE OF YOUR EXAM PAPER:

    ------------Top left: code number
    ------------Top right: number of page

When you fold your paper at the end of the exam, write your code number on the back, and indicate total number of pages.

Results of the examination will be sent to you by letter.

Part A. Price Theory

I. Short Questions (6 minutes each, 30 minutes in all)

Indicate whether each of the following assertions is True (T), Fales (F), or Uncertain (U), and explain briefly why.

1. Joe Palooka had initially no income except what he earned in the market as a sparring partner for Muhamed Ali at $2.50/hour. The government now offers him $37.50 a week plus half of whatever he can earn in the market. Under this plan he chooses to work 30 hours a week. He would work less in the absence of the government plan.

2. Comment on the following: "A 10% Hicks-neutral technological change in the growing of peanuts results in a 10% rise in the marginal physical products of labor, land, seed, machinery, and so forth, but also results in a 10% decline in the price of peanuts. Therefore the value of the marginal product of the inputs does not change. Therefore such a technological change has no effect on unemployment."

3. The owner of a small firm making pocket calculators finds it pleasing to maximize his output rather than his profits, but doesn't want to

actually lose money. If the demand for pocket calculators declined he might increase his output.

4. If two kinds of money, ordinary money and ration coupons, were required to buy goods, and if the required ratio of ration coupons to money varied from good to good, a rise in the money income of a consumer could raise the amount he consumed of, say, automobiles and a rise in the coupon income of a consumer could lower it.

5. A lump sum tax on firms does not affect marginal costs. Therefore it does not affect allocation.

II. Quotas on Oil (25 minutes; part 3 by itself is 15 minutes)

1. In the dear, dead days of cheap world oil the United States erected an import quota to protect domestic oil fields from (unfair and ruinous) foreign competition. If the quota were effective, and fixed at a certain level, call it M, who would benefit from the quota and by how much would they benefit if the quota were allotted randomly to oil companies?

2. If, as many economists then proposed, the rights to import foreign oil at the low world price, P_f, and sell it at the high domestic price, P_d, were auctioned off by the government to the highest bidder, who would benefit and how much?

3. But suppose that, as was in fact the case, the amount Q_f a single company could purchase of foreign oil at the low foreign price P_f were in some fixed proportion, k, of its production of oil from domestic wells, Q_d. The company drills some in the U.S., buys some abroad, and sells both to American customers at the high domestic price, P_d.

   a. Explain intuitively (and verbally) why under this version of the quota system oil companies would bid down the domestic price of oil (for a given size of the total quota, M) below that which would obtain under (1) or (2).

   b. Write down the equation for total profits on all sales for a single oil company as a function of Q_d (i.e. using $Q_f = k \, Q_f$). Write down the first-order condition for profit maximization with respect to choices of Q_d (use "MC" for the rate of change of costs of domestic wells with respect to Q_d: that is, don't bother with the functional form of the cost function).

   c. Solve the first-order condition for P_d expressed as a function of MC and P_f. Using a straight line through the origin for MC, draw a diagram corresponding to this equation and tell what it says about the intuitive argument in (3.a.) above.

III. More Short Answers (5 minutes each, 35 minutes in all)

1. Effective minimum wages in trucking increase the demand for truck-driving schools, which are good substitutes for on-the-job training.

2. The president of the Chicago Teachers' Union proposes, as a solution to the problem of too few teachers in the Chicago school system, that internships be adopted, whereby beginning teachers would be employed at low wages for two years before graduating to full teacher status. He says that this will be good for the many unemployed teachers in the community. T, F, or U: His plan can also be interpreted as an attempt to blockade entry to teaching in Chicago for the benefit of present Chicago teachers.

3. "Commodities with higher income elasticities have higher price elasticities of demand" (Stigler, Theory of Price, 2nd ed., p. 45).

4. The market for assistant professors in economics is now relatively good (for the professors) and relatively bad for full and associate professors (who cannot be fired). This situation arises from the bad financial state of universities.

5. In the presence of a perfect capital market people would never buy insurance against disaster, because if disaster struck they could borrow all the money they required to recover from it from Household Finance.

6. The rate of change of real wages is equal to the rate of change of output per man.

7. A newly formed monopoly of an exhaustible natural resource (such as oil in the Persian Gulf) would allocate supplies equally to each year over the N years it calculated its reserves would last.

Part B. Income, Employment and the Price Level

I. True-False-Uncertain (5 points each)

Indicate whether each of the following assertions is True (T), False (F), or Uncertain (U), and explain briefly why.

1. Apart from any change in the level of economic activity, replacement of the corporate income tax with a value-added tax of the same yield would lower national income relative to national product in the U.S.

2. Given the rate of monetary expansion, an exogenous increase in the rate of growth of real output will reduce inflationary pressures by making more goods and services available for final consumers.

3. If taxpayers realize the government debt is fully their liability, there will be no Pigou effect.

4. At less than full employment, an increase in the quantity of money causes interest rates to go down, whereas at full employment an increase in the quantity of money causes interest rates to go up.

5. In an open economy with a fixed exchange rate, the nominal monsupply is determined by the monetary authorities.

6. An increase in oil taxes accompanied by income tax reductions
   leaving total government tax collections unaffected is inflati

7. The balanced budget multiplier will differ from zero only when
   consumers are unable to save a portion of the income produced :
   the public sector.

8. An increase in Federal oil taxes will lower income subject to
   and will therefore lower income tax collection thereby partial
   if not wholly offsetting the increased collections from the o:

II. Long Answers

1. (30 minutes) Among President Ford's proposals for dealing wit
   current recession, is the recommendation for a $16 billion per
   income tax rebate to be paid in 1975:

   a) Drawing on macroeconomic concepts, make three estimates (h:
      low, and medium) of the effect of adopting this recommenda
      on real GNP in 1975. Assume the recession continues so th
      any effect of the tax cut on aggregate demand raises real
      with no effect on prices. Assume further that monetary po
      is perfectly accomodating in the sense that the demand for
      resulting from the tax cut will be met with money supply i
      without any effect on interest rates.

      Explain the reasons for the differences between your high,
      and medium estimates.

   b) Same as a) except assume monetary policy does not accomoda
      all, i.e., the Fed has a fixed money supply growth target
      it adheres to regardless of the tax rebate.

   c) How are the answers to a) and b) affected if by the time t
      is response to the tax cut the economy has recovered so th
      effect of an increase in aggregate demand is to raise pric
      no effect on real output?

2. (20 minutes)

   Define each of the following terms:

   Phillips Curve
   Natural rate of Interest
   Hoarding
   Pigou Effect
   Real Bills Doctrine
   Walras law

COMPREHENSIVE EXAMINATION
Price Theory
The Theory of Income, Employment
and the Price Level

Alternative B of the A.M. Degree

Summer 1974

WRITE IN BLACK INK

WRITE THE FOLLOWING INFORMATION ON THE FIRST PAGE OF YOUR EXAMINATION PAPER:

    ————————Your code number and not your name
    ————————Name of examination
    ————————Date of examination

Write only on one side of each page

Write the following information on each following page of your exam paper:

    ————————Top left: code number
    ————————Top right: number of page

When you fold your paper at the end of the exam, write your code number on the back, and indicate total number of pages.

Results of the examination will be sent to you by letter.

———

Part A. Price Theory. Credit is in proportion to the time.

I. Short Questions (4 minutes each, 24 minutes in all)

    Indicate whether each of the following assertions is True (T), False (F), or Uncertain (U), and explain briefly why.

    1. If the division of labor within firms rises with their size, then the division of labor is limited by the extent of the market.

    2. An increase of 10 percent in an economy's endowment of labor and capital per capita will increase real income per capita by 10 percent, but will leave the real prices of labor and capital unchanged.

    3. [continuation of 2] On the other hand, an economy-wide Hicks-neutral technical improvement of 10 percent will increase real income and the real prices of the factors by 10 percent.

4. If leisure is required in fixed proportions to consume commodities, then a tax in kind on all commodities (the revenue from which is thrown away) will increase hours of work.

5. [continuation of 4] If the tax revenue is returned in lump sum payments, then the hours of work will remain the same as before the tax.

6. In response to complaints that large farmers were getting enormous payments from the government under governmental purchases to support the price of cotton, Congress enacted a dollar limit to the amount a single farmer could be paid. There are circumstances under which this limit would have no effect on the revenues of any farmer.

II. George's Pill (12 minutes)

Indicate whether each of the following assertions is True (T), False (F), or Uncertain (U), and briefly explain why.

1. If George invents a pill for his own use that enables him to reduce his nightly sleep by 50 percent, George will work more.

2. If George then distributes the pill to everyone free of charge and if everyone has the same tastes as George, then George will still work more than before the pill, but may work less than before he distributed it.

3. If George is sufficiently different from everyone else, he may be worse off after inventing and distributing the pill than he was initially.

III. Price Ceilings and Taxes (17 minutes)

Assume that a competitive industry in long-run equilibrium faces an elasticity of demand of 1.0, that its elasticity of substitution between labor and capital (the only factors) is 1.0, that the share of labor is .5, that the elasticity of supply of labor to the industry is 4.0, that the elasticity of the supply of capital to the industry is 500, and that the industry is producing 1 percent of national income. In answering the following questions, justify your answers.

1. What is the numerical value of the industry's elasticity of demand for labor?

2. In what direction and by what percent will the employment of labor in the industry and the wage rate received by labor change if:

a. A price ceiling 1.0 percent below the initial price
is imposed on the price of the output of the industry?

b. A wage ceiling   2.0 percent below the initial wage
is imposed on wages in the industry?

c. A 5.0 percent _ad valorem_ tax is imposed on the output of
the industry?

d. A 5.0 percent payroll tax is imposed on the industry?

IV. More Short Questions (7 minutes each, 14 minutes in all)

Indicate whether each of the following assertions is True (T), False (F),
or Uncertain (U), and explain briefly why.

1. Let σ denote the average elasticity of substitution in consumption
between beer and other commodities. Then if real income (money
income divided by the cost-of-living index) is held constant along
the demand curve for beer, the own-price elasticity of this
demand curve is −σ.

2. Assume that the market wage rate for physicians is $20 per hour
and for dentists $15 per hour. If a 20 percent income tax is
imposed, a smaller fraction of all those who would choose to be
either a physician or a dentist will choose to be a physician.

V. John Doe's Work (13 minutes)

John Doe has an annual income of $200 from some land that he owns.
He works in the labor market 1,500 hours per year at $2.00 an hour.

1. Draw a diagram illustrating his choice of hours of work.
Now suppose that a law is passed providing that any person
whose total income is less than $3,200 is eligible to receive
from the government half of the difference between $3,200 and
his income.

2. Draw John Doe's new budget line on the diagram of (1).

3. Will Doe still choose to work 1,500 hours per year? Explain.

4. Is it possible that Doe might now choose not to work at all?
Explain.

VI. Final Short Questions (5 minutes each, 10 minutes in all)

Indicate whether each of the following assertions is True (T), False (F),
or Uncertain (U), and explain briefly why.

1. The proposal to extend the territorial limits of nations (for fishing in particular) 200 miles from their shores has been attacked by the <u>New York Times</u>, among others, as a selfish move that will impoverish a world dependent on fish for protein. There is, however, an economic argument that the extension will increase the supply of fish.

2. After the South had been defeated in the American Civil War, agricultural output in the South fell by about a third. The supply of labor (formerly slave labor) and of other factors except land also fell about a third. Therefore, there was a fall in the agricultural production function in the South.

Part B.   The Theory of Income, Employment and the Price Level

I.   (35 minutes)

Indicate whether the following statements are True (T), False (F),
or Uncertain (U), and briefly explain why.

1.   An expected inflation rate of 4 percent per year reduces the demand
     for deposits by the same amount as reduction in the interest paid on
     deposits from 5 percent to 1 percent.

2.   The optimum quantity of money is achieved when there is no cost of
     holding money.

3.   One hundred percent reserve requirements are untenable because banks
     would be unable to make a profit under this system.

4.   It is inflationary for the government to introduce a regulation per-
     mitting notes to be issued by non-banking institutions which are
     payable on demand at whatever interest rates they choose to pay,
     while maintaining ceilings on interest rates that can be paid by
     banks and savings and loan institutions.

5.   If the demand for money is insensitive to the interest rate, then an
     increase in the stock of money cannot affect the interest rate.

6.   An increase in government spending financed by taxes will have a
     larger effect on GNP the more of a substitute government spending
     is for private consumption.

7.   A tax cut financed by an increase in government debt issue can be
     deflationary if the tax cut motivates an increase in the supplies
     of factor services.

II.   (25 minutes)

Suppose that the government reduces taxes while holding fixed its
demand for commodities. Analyze the immediate and longer run
effects on income, employment, and the price level assuming that:

A.   The deficit is financed by money creation, and

B.   The deficit is financed by the issue of interest-bearing debt.

III.   (15 minutes)

It is often contended that an inflation cannot be stopped without
causing a recession. Which of the following concepts are needed
to analyze this issue: demand for money, supply of money,

III. (15 minutes) cont.

demand for commodities, supply of commodities, demand for labor, suppl
of labor; expectations. Using the concepts chosen, provide an analys?
of why it could be difficult to stop an inflation without a recession.

IV. (15 minutes)

In a two-country world connected by fixed exchange rates with free
trade, one country inflates through exogenous increases in its
domestic money supply. The other country follows a policy of maintaining a stable price level for itself. Discuss what will happen
to prices and output of the two countries and to trade between them.
What events in the inflating country might cause the policy to break
down? What events in the country with the stable price level might
cause the policy to break down?

COMPREHENSIVE EXAMINATION
Price Theory
The Theory of Income, Employment
and the Price Level

Alternative B of the A.M. Degree

Winter 1974

WRITE THE FOLLOWING INFORMATION ON YOUR EXAMINATION PAPER

    Your code number, but NOT your name
    Name of Examination
    Date of Examination

Results of the examination will be sent to you by letter.

    TIME: 3 hours. ANSWER ALL QUESTIONS.

NOTE: This examination is in two parts. **Write your answers in separate parts.**

    WRITE ALL ANSWERS IN BLACK INK.

    Count the number of pages used, write the number and circle it on
    the first page of your answer sheets.

_____

Part A. Relative Price Theory (1+1/2 hours). Credit is in proportion to
        the time allotted.

I. (7 minutes each, 14 minutes in all)

    Indicate whether each of the following assertions is True (T), False,
    (F), or Uncertain (U), and explain briefly why.

    1. The proposal to permit only drivers with license plates ending in
       even digits to buy on even-numbered days of the month and odd on
       odd will have no effect on the length of queues caused by price
       ceilings on gas.

    2. In December, 1973 the automobile industry agreed, in exchange for
       decontrol of its prices, to increase mileage per gallon of gasoline
       for the average American car by 50 percent in 10 years. Without
       a change in the technological possibilities of producing cars (with
       various amounts of mileage on the one hand and of other qualities
       on the other) or without a change in the preferences of buyers, it
       will be unable to fulfill its promise.

5) The choice among occupations is not affected by a proportional income tax.

6) Suppose that in the absence of price controls and rationing the price of gas would be 80¢ a gallon. Suppose further that an effective rationing schema is imposed, with freely transferable ration coupons and that the price of gasoline then is 50¢ per gallon. Therefore the price of a one-gallon coupon will be 30¢.

7) Raising standards for admission to medical school is defended on the grounds that it raises the average quality of doctors. Even if this were true, however, it does not follow that the higher quality is a net gain to society, considering the opportunity cost of the higher quality medical students.

8) A technical change that raises the schedule of the marginal product of labor in a competitive industry will always cause employment of labor in the industry to rise.

II. (14 minutes)

Indicate whether each of the following is True (T), False (F), or Uncertain (U), and explain.

a) The effect of a given percentage increase in the price of a commodity on the real income of a consumer is greater the greater the share of his income he spends on the commodity.

b) The share of his income spent on a commodity will increase as his real income increases if the commodity is a luxury, technically speaking.

c) It follows, therefore, that there is no presumption that an effective price ceiling will redistribute real income towards the poor unless the commodity is a necessity (again, technically speaking).

III. (22 minutes)

Telephone Tariffs

Illinois Bell charges 10¢ for each of the first 40 telephone calls per month from a home telephone and 5-1/4¢ for each additional call. It could be compelled to charge 7¢ for all calls. Use indifference curve diagrams to answer the following questions.

a) Which price system makes a customer better off? Under what conditions, if any, will the customer be indifferent between the two systems?

b) Which system leads the customer to buy the most calls? Be explicit about the various possibilities in your diagrams.

c) If the marginal cost of a call were in fact 5-1/4¢, which system would maximize the profit earned by Illinois Bell from this customer? Again, be explicit about the various possibilities.

IV. (5 minutes each, 40 minutes in all)

1) The welfare cost of an effective price ceiling on gasoline is the same as the welfare cost of an excise tax having the same effect on the output (equal to the consumption) of gasoline.

2) Hours of work per week per employee tend to rise in booms and fall in depressions. This fact contradicts the common assertion that the supply curve of labor to the market is backward-bending.

3) An excise tax on some commodity can never raise its price including the tax by as much as the tax itself.

4) An increase in the price of diesel fuel will tend to lower the employment and wages of truck drivers.

Part B. The Theory of Income, Employment and the Price Level

I.   (40 points)

Indicate whether the following statements are True (T), False (F), or Uncertain (U), and briefly explain why.

1. If a universal credit card system were established, under which all transactions for every person were charged, there would be infinite inflation.

2. The implication of simple Keynesian models that the balanced-budget multiplier is unity results from the assumption that the marginal propensity to spend is greater in the public than in the private sector.

3. If consumption is a function of wealth, the inflationary tax on money will reduce the demand for consumption goods at a given real interest rate.

4. As IS is a function of the real rate of interest and LM is a function of the nominal rate, expectations of inflation are self-fulfilling.

5. If the price level is expected to rise at an exponentially increasing rate, the velocity of money will rise at an exponentially increasing rate also.

6. In the context of a simple neo-Classical growth model without technical change, per capita consumption is maximized by setting the saving rate equal to the real rate of interest.

7. If all bonds, mortgages and loans were of the purchasing power variety (repayment specified in real rather than nominal terms), the price level would be indeterminate.

8. If the government were trying to maximize the revenue from money creation, it would never deflate the economy at a rate greater than the rate of growth of real income times the income elasticity of demand for real cash balances.

II. Discussion Questions:
1. (30 points)

A. In a closed economy with a fiat currency and a banking system, the nominal money supply, M, can be expressed as the product of high-powered money, H, and the money multiplier, the latter depending upon the currency-deposit and reserve-deposit ratios.

5   Theory of Income, Winter 1974

a) What is the effect on the nominal money supply of
    an increase in the currency-deposit ratio? Of the
    reserve-deposit ratio? Explain your answers fully.

b) How does one define "high-powered" money in this
    case?

B. If the same economy is now opened to trade and capital movements with the rest of the world, but maintains her own
currency and banking system, the quantity of M can still be
expressed as the product of H and the multiplier. What are
the determinates of H in this case when:

a) the exchange rate is fixed;

b) the exchange rate is freely determined by market forces.

C. If the same open economy now chooses to use a second country's
currency as unit of account and circulating medium, and
assuming a fixed exchange rate with all other countries,
what changes would you anticipate in

a) the definition of H;

b) the magnitude of the money multiplier;

c) the relevance of the distinction between H and M;

d) the ultimate determinants of M.

2. (20 points)

Suppose that real government expenditures exceed real taxes
(other than tax on money) by a constant percentage of national
income and that the deficit is financed by borrowing from the
central bank so that high-powered money increases by the
amount of the deficit. What is the equilibrium rate of
inflation under alternative assumptions (s) and (b):

a) The demand for goods and services is perfectly
    elastic at a given real interest rate, and the
    demand for money is perfectly inelastic with
    respect to the interest rate.

b) Same assumption as a) about the demand for goods and
    services, but the demand for money is such that
    increasing the rate of interest on alternative assets
    by one percent would reduce the amount of real
    balances held by 2 percent.

c) How does the absolute price level under a) and b) compare?

COMPREHENSIVE EXAMINATION

The Theory of Income, Employment
and the Price Level

Alternative B of the A.M. Degree

Summer; 1973

WRITE THE FOLLOWING INFORMATION ON YOUR EXAMINATION PAPER

      Your code number, but NOT your name
      Name of Examination
      Date of Examination

Results of the examination will be sent to you by letter.

      TIME: 3 hours. ANSWER ALL QUESTIONS.

NOTE: This examination is in two parts. Write your answers in separate parts

      WRITE ALL ANSWERS IN BLACK INK.

      Count the number of pages used, write the number and circle it on
      the first page of your answer sheets.

Instructions:

Please begin answers to Part A on a new sheet of paper.

I.
Economics of Sharecropping
(25 minutes)

There are three tenures under which agricultural land can be worked: landlords hire laborers at a fixed wage to work the land; laborers hire the land at a fixed rent; and sharecropping, in which landlords and laborers, instead of taking a fixed rent or a fixed wage, take a fixed share of the output. It has often been alleged (by Alfred Marshall, for example) that sharecropping leads to inefficiency by comparison with the other two tenures. Consider two identical acres of land, on one of which the landlord hires labor at a fixed wage (determined, we shall assume throughout the problem, elsewhere in the economy) and on the other of which he enters a sharecropping agreement with laborers.

a.) Draw a diagram exhibiting the marginal product of labor on one of the acres, showing the equilibrium amount of labor employed on the acre when the landlord hires labor. Identify the total output, the wage bill, and the implicit rent.

b.) In the traditional analysis sharecropping is supposed to have the same effect as a proportional tax on agricultural output, the idea being that the laborer who enters a sharecropping agreement receives only a fraction (two-thirds for example, if one-third is the share that the land-lord gets under the agreement) of his marginal product. On a diagram similar to the one in part (a.) exhibit the equilibrium under sharecropping. If the analogy with a proportional tax is correct, what happens to the amount of labor employed on the sharecropped acre, the total output of the acre, the wage bill, and the payment to the landlord by comparison with the case in (a.)? Identify the social loss.

c.) In this model, what is being assumed about who chooses how much labor is to be applied to the sharecropped land? If landlords had no control over the amount of labor applied to the land, would a rational landlord ever offer land for sharecropping when they could keep it and hire labor themselves? Suppose you were told that in the American South after the Civil War, in China during the 1930s, in Europe during the nineteenth and twentieth centuries (1) sharecropping existed in the same villages as owner-occupation with hired labor and (2) output per acre was the same on sharecropped as on other acres. What, in sum, would you conclude about the traditional analysis of sharecropping?

II.
(15 minutes)

Suppose an American manufacturer of military tanks has a monopoly in the United States and is initially not permitted to export his product to other countries. Now suppose he is permitted to export it (imports of foreign tanks are still not permitted) and suppose he makes a small portion of the outside world's supply of tanks.

a.) Compare his profits before and after he is permitted to export.

b.) Compare American welfare before and after he is permitted to export.

c.) What is the effect on profits and welfare of a technological change specific to the American manufacturer, both before and after exports are permitted?

III.

(50 minutes)

Indicate whether each of the following statements is true (T), false (F), or uncertain (U) and state your reasoning concisely.

<u>A.</u> If monopolies are costly to maintain, the usual triangular area of social loss is an understatement of the social cost of monopoly.

<u>B.</u> There is a clear-cut economic case for a tax (or a subsidy) whenever an external diseconomy (or economy) creates a divergence between private pecuniary marginal cost as seen by a firm and true social marginal cost.

<u>C.</u> In 1348 (before the "Black Death") the population of England and Wales was 4 million. By 1400 it had fallen to 2 million. Real wages rose about 40%, wages were always about half of national income, England and Wales were agricultural countries, and no new land or capital was employed in agriculture over the half-century. One can conclude

from these facts that technological change was nil in England and Wales and that the fall in population by itself explains the rise in wages. (You may find it helpful to know that the square root of .5 is .71)

D. If redwood lasts forever and if cardboard that looks and acts like redwood lasts for one year, a fall in the interest rate will lower the price of redwood relative to cardboard.

E. "The expansion of the cotton textile industry allowed each firm to spread fixed costs over a larger output and to produce cotton textiles more cheaply."

F. People are granted funds for xeroxing in the Social Science steno pool. Therefore the elasticity of demand for xeroxing in the steno pool is one.

G. If the demand for gasoline is inelastic, an effective price ceiling (maximum) on gasoline will cause consumers of gasoline to spend more in total real outlays for gasoline.

H. If each consumer of bread and butter consumes them in fixed proportions that may vary from one consumer to another, then a rise in the price of bread caused by a shift in the supply curve for bread will surely cause the consumption of both to fall, but bread consumption will fall more (in percent) than butter consumption.

_I._ Savings and loan associations in the U. S. typically offer prospective savers "gifts" in the form of real commodities for opening a savings account or increasing their savings deposits by specified amounts. The explanation for this practice is that by buying these gifts in large quantities, they can offer them to savers at lower "prices" in effect than the savers otherwise would have to pay.

-- ----- ---- --

Part B

I. (30 minutes) Indicate whether the following statements are true (T), false (F) or uncertain (U), and briefly explain why.

1. Monetary policy has less effectiveness the lower is the fraction of their income people choose to hold in the form of money.

2. In order to determine the supply of money, the Federal Reserve needs the authority to fix at least two of the following three variables: high-powered money, reserve requirements, and the rediscount rate.

3. The aggregate amount of the inflationary tax on money is the rate of inflation times the amount of high-powered money.

4. High interest rates may be caused by either a low capital-output ratio or a high rate of inflation, but rapidly rising interest rates are due to changing expectations of inflation.

5. In the short run policymakers can trade off less unemployment for more inflation but in the long run they cannot affect the unemployment rate and gain nothing from inflation.

6. If knowledge is recognized as one of the forms of capital, the golden age result that a steady level of per capita income will be realized no longer holds.

II. Answer the following:

1. (30 minutes) Consider the following economy:

   (1) $\frac{M}{p} = ay - bi$

   (2) $y = \alpha + \beta y - \gamma p + \delta \frac{M}{p}$

   (3) $i = r + \pi^e$

   (4) $y = \bar{y}$

where M/p is real balances, y is real income, i the nominal interest rate, r the real interest rate, π^e the expected rate of inflation, and $\bar{y}$ the full employment level of income, and the other letters are parameters.

   (a) Suppose there is an autonomous increase in the expected rate of inflation. Analyze, graphically or algebraically, the effects on i, r and M/p.

   (b) Suppose there is a one-time increase in M but expectations of inflation are unaffected. What happens to i, r and M/p?

   (c) Suppose the growth rate of nominal balances increases and expectations of inflation respond with a lag to the behavior of the actual rate of inflation. Analyze in as much detail as you can the resulting behavior of P, i and r.

2. (15 minutes) Explain in detail the results of an increase in regulation Q ceilings on time deposit rates. You should discuss the resultant changes in M_1, M_2, other interest rates and real output and prices.

3. (15 minutes) The purpose is to consider proposals to eliminate redistributional effects of inflation.

   (a) Suppose all government debt were henceforth issued in real terms, e.g., government bonds had cost of living escalator clauses so that they were always worth the same real amount regardless of when redeemed. Would this change make monetary policy more effective in stabilizing price level and employment? Would it render fiscal policy more effective in achieving these aims?

(b) Same as (a) except all debt, both public and private, is henceforth issued in real terms.

COMPREHENSIVE EXAMINATION
Price Theory
The Theory of Income, Employment
and the Price Level

Alternative B of the A.M. Degree

Winter, 1973

WRITE THE FOLLOWING INFORMATION ON YOUR EXAMINATION PAPER

Your code number, but NOT your name
Name of Examination
Date of Examination

Results of the examination will be sent to you by letter.

TIME: 3 hours. ANSWER ALL QUESTIONS.

NOTE: This examination is in two parts. Write your answers in separate parts.

WRITE ALL ANSWERS IN BLACK INK.

Count the number of pages used, write the number and circle it on
the first page of your answer sheets.

Part A. Relative Price Theory (1½ hours)

I. (70 minutes)

Indicate whether each of the following statements is true (T),
false (F), or uncertain (U) and state concisely the reasoning for
each of your responses.

1. The smaller the share of a factor of production in total factor
   cost, the lower is the own-price elasticity of demand for the
   factor.

2. The marginal productivity of labor is greater, the greater is
   the capital/labor ratio. Therefore, steel workers in Chicago
   who work with much capital per worker will have higher wages
   than workers in Chicago who work with little capital per worker.

3. If the price elasticity of demand for coal is 2.0 and the price
   elasticity of demand for all fossil fuels (coal, oil, natural gas)
   is 1.0, then the price elasticity of demand for non-coal fossil
   fuels (oil, natural gas) must be less than unity.

4. If the share of cigars in consumers' budgets is very small, the
   area under the ordinary (money-income constant) demand curve
   for cigars between two levels of consumption is an approximately
   unambiguous measure of consumer surplus.

5. An ad valorem (proportional) tax on the rent of agricultural
    land will not affect the amount of land in use.

6. Taxes on commodities will leave a competitive economy on its
    production-possibility curve.

7. Taxes on the factors of production used to produce the commodities,
    however, will push a competitive economy off its production-
    possibility curve.

8a. The equilibrium output in a competitive industry is not changed
    if an ad valorem tax on the output of the industry is replaced
    by a specific tax (in which the tax is a fixed amount per unit
    of output) that yields the same tax revenue.

8b. The same is true if the industry is a monopoly.

9. If in the economy as a whole the share of labor in the national
    income is 0.8, a 10 percent increase in the capital/labor ratio
    will cause real wages to rise by 2 percent.

10. In equilibrium the market wage of a married woman must be equal
    to her household or shadow wage. An increase in her husband's
    wage will increase the demand for her time in household activities
    and thus cause both her shadow wage and her market wage to
    increase.

II. (10 minutes)   of land
     In 1891, David A. Wells, remarking on the recent decline in the value/
     over large areas of the earth's surface, gave the following case in
     point: "Formerly Paris obtained its fruits and vegetable supply
     entirely from lands in its own neighborhood . . . but now the rail-
     ways bring the same commodities from very distant places for the
     same or a less price, and the value of land in the neighborhood of
     Paris has actually declined."

     Assume that the cost of producing vegetables and fruits can be
     neglected, but the cost of transporting them cannot. Show the
     demand and supply curves for fruits and vegetables at Paris before
     reduction in transport costs. Identify the land rent to which
     Wells refers and the total rent to all lands producing fruits and
     vegetables. Show how the reduction in transport costs alters the
     rent. Under what conditions will the total rent to all lands
     increase?

III.   (10 minutes)

In 1706, 1707, and 1708 Robinson Crusoe's daily schedule of his
sixteen waking hours and his daily output of his two sources of
pleasure were:

	1706	1707	1708
Coconuts, Hours per day devoted to collecting:	4 hours	14 hours	8 hours
Output of coconuts per day	5 coco.	14 coco.	16 coco.
Grass shirts, Hours per day weaving:	12 hours	2 hours	8 hours
Output of grass shirts per day	15 shirts	4 shirts	10 shirts

True, False or Uncertain:

(a)   Between 1706 and 1707 Crusoe's tastes definitely changed.

(b)   Between 1707 and 1708 Crusoe's technology definitely
        changed.

PART B. The Theory of Income, Employment and the Price Level

in.) I. Indicate whether each of the following statements is true (T),
false (F), or uncertain (U), and explain briefly why.

1. The current attempt of the Federal Reserve to hold down
interest rates will reduce inflationary pressures in 1973, since
interest expense is part of business cost, and any increase in the
interest rate is passed on in the form of higher prices.

2. The inflation tax is different in kind from an income tax,
since an individual can avoid it simply by reducing his holdings
of real money balances to zero.

3. An increase in the interest rate ceiling on time deposits, with
no change in the interest rate ceiling on savings and loan deposits,
is deflationary.

4. Accelerated depreciation on apartment houses, which reduces the
effective corporation income tax, shifts investment from other
sectors to apartment houses but does not raise aggregate investment.

5. A positively sloped yield curve indicates the existence of a
liquidity premium on short-term bonds.

6. "Funding" the U. S. public debt (i.e. lengthening its average
maturity), is deflationary but as an offset tends to reduce the
U. S. balance of payments deficit.

7. Foreign-exchange speculation which reduces the number of yen
which can be purchased with a dollar, simultaneously redistributes
income from American to Japanese consumers, and from Japanese to
American exporters.

8. Because uncertainty increases the precautionary motive for holding
money, the demand for money is greater under erratic inflation than
under expected steady state inflation.

9. After a disturbance which increases unemployment, the return to
the natural rate of unemployment is faster the more specific human
capital there is in the labor force.

10. Under a strict life cycle theory where there is no bequeathment,
permanent consumption equals permanent income.

in.) II. Answer the following:

1. It has been argued that the prohibition against paying interest
on demand deposits should be abolished. Why? According to the
usual argument, what determines the optimal level of interest to
be paid on demand deposits? Show graphically the gains in going
from a prohibition of interest to the optimum level of interest.

2. What determines the optimum level of interest to be paid
currency? Assume the optimum level of interest on currency is
greater than zero. Then, if interest were paid on demand dep
but not on currency, would non-optimality be introduced into t
choice between demand deposits and currency? Contrast the ga
in abolishing the prohibition of interest of demand deposits
and without simultaneously abolishing the prohibition of inte
on currency.

(25 min.) III. Consider an economy in which banks hold reserves in the form
high-powered money with a reserve requirement (r) set by the
bank; no interest is paid on high-powered money; any differenc
between bank revenue and expenses accrues to owners of common
in banks; the government issues interest-bearing bonds which a
by the Central bank, commercial banks, and the public.

(a) What part of the bank-created money in this economy is pa
the net wealth of the private sector on the following conditic

(i) $r > 0$ and the interest paid on demand deposits is
$(i_D = 0)$.

(ii) $r > 0$ and $i_D > 0$.

(iii) $r = 0$ and $i_D = 0$.

(iv) The banking system is perfectly competitive.

(b) Under what conditions, if any, are the interest-bearing
government bonds held by the public part of the net wealth of
private sector.

(c) Explain the difference, if any, between cases (a)(iv) and

COMPREHENSIVE EXAMINATION
Price Theory
The Theory of Income, Employment
and the Price Level

Alternative B of the A.M. Degree

Summer, 1972

WRITE THE FOLLOWING INFORMATION ON YOUR EXAMINATION PAPER

Your code number, but NOT your name
Name of Examination
Date of Examination

Results of the examination will be sent to you by letter.

TIME: 3 hours. ANSWER ALL QUESTIONS.

NOTE: This examination is in two parts. <u>Write your answers in separate parts.</u>

WRITE ALL ANSWERS IN BLACK INK.

Count the number of pages used, write the number and circle it on the
first page of your answer sheets.

Part A. Relative Price Theory (1-1/2 hours)

. (45 minutes) Indicate in the space provided whether each of the following
statements is true (T), false (F), or uncertain (U) and state your reasoning
concisely.

1. (6 minutes) When labor leaves a country, the share of that country's
national income earned by the remaining labor rises because the
capital/labor ratio rises.

2. (8 min.) The imposition of an effective minimum on wages of labor
employed in a particular industry in the long run will cause industry
employment of labor and industry output to rise and industry employment
of capital to fall, if the industry is monopsonized.

3. (6 min.) A technological improvement in agriculture will cause both
agricultural output and output in other sectors of the economy to
increase.

4. (8 min.) If the elasticity of demand for labor in agriculture is 0.5 and if the demand for labor in agriculture does not depend upon the supply conditions for other agricultural inputs, the elasticity of demand for agricultural output is also 0.5.

5. (8 min.) The mining of coal is more difficult, the deeper is the mine and the thinner is the seam of coal. Therefore, there is reason to expect that at any given time and locality, deep mines will tend to have thick seams and shallow mines thin seams.

6. (4 min.) If the elasticity of demand for a commodity is 2.0 at every price of the commodity, then a 100 percent increase in the price of the commodity will cause the quantity demanded of the commodity to fall by 200 percent.

7. (5 min.) If the elasticity of demand for meat is unity, then an effective ceiling on the price of meat will have no effect on the aggregate expenditures of consumers on meat.

II. (10 min.) Railways and long-haul trucking are substitutes in demand for transportation while short-haul trucking is complementary to both.

   a. Suppose that there is a technological improvement in long-haul trucking. What effects will this have on the prices and quantities of each of the three types of transportation services?

   b. Suppose that the demand for short-haul trucking increases for reasons external to the long-haul trucking and railway industries. What effects will this have on the prices and quantities of each of the three types of transportation services? Explain your answers.

III. (15 min.) Suppose that the government of a country were to adopt the following policy of subsidizing the housing of its population:

Every household is given the option of living in <u>rent-free</u> housing (of given amount and quality) provided by the government rather than in whatever housing (provided by the private housing market) the household otherwise would choose.

Are there any circumstances under which the government policy in the long run will reduce the quantity of housing services consumed by the population of the country? Explain carefully.

IV. (20 min.) Slaves in ancient Rome were used interchangeably with free labor in most occupations.

1. Assume that the supply of slaves is inelastic. Describe the determination of equilibrium in the market for slaves.

2. Now assume that slaves are permitted to buy their freedom and can accumulate the money to do so. Describe the total demand curve for slaves and the equilibrium in the market. Under what circumstances would slavery disappear entirely? Explain.

Part B. The Theory of Income, Employment and the Price Level

I. Indicate whether each of the following statements is true (T), false (F), or uncertain (U), and explain briefly why. (35 minutes)

   1. The issuance of Kennedy fifty-cent pieces and Eisenhower silver dollars having souvenir value is deflationary.

   2. A government deficit resulting in a 10 percent increase in the quantity of money would reduce the value of the dollar by 10 percent if there were freely fluctuating exchange rates.

   3. An increase in the demand for money will increase the natural rate of interest.

   4. With perfect certainty and no inflation, the investment demand function can be written

   $$I = (bc/i)^{1/a} N - K$$

   if the aggregate production function is of linear homogeneous Cobb-Douglas form (where I is real investment, i is rate of interest, a is share of capital, b is share of labor, N is amount of labor, and K is amount of capital at beginning of period).

   5. A return to full employment is assured if, in response to unemployment, wages fall faster than expected prices.

   6. Fluctuations in long term interest rates would have a smaller amplitude and would lag those in short term rates if people's expectations about interest rates are fully realized.

   7. An expansion of the money supply accomplished by a bombardment of dollar bills from a heliocopter is identical in principle to one accomplished by a Central Bank purchase of gold previously hoarded in the form of tooth fillings by domestic residents.

II. Answer the following. (25 minutes)

   1. "It is universally assumed that (ruling out a liquidity trap) an increase in the money supply (M) increases nominal income (Y). Yet this conclusion ignores the government budget constraint, which states that government expenditures (G) including interest payments on debt (iB) must be financed by one of three methods: tax revenue (T), sale of bonds (ΔB), or printing of money (ΔM):

$$G + iB = T + \Delta M + \Delta B.$$

Assume that all tax revenue is generated by a proportional income tax ($T = tY$), government expenditure $\bar{G}$ is fixed, and the budget is initially balanced ($\bar{G} + iB_o = tY_o$), and a condition of long-run equilibrium is that $\Delta M = \Delta B = 0$. Therefore a one-time expansion of money ΔM, followed by $\Delta M = 0$ subsequently, cannot permanently raise nominal income. The initial increase in nominal income ΔY raises tax revenue by $t\Delta Y$, which causes a government surplus and retirement of bonds. Since equilibrium requires a balanced budget nominal income continues to drop until the government surplus is eliminated. This requires nominal income to fall below the initial level Y_o since bonds outstanding (B), and hence the interest portion of government spending (iB),has fallen and hence tax revenues must be lower than initially. "

This argument appears to contradict the ordinary quantity theory result that an increase in M raises Y and claims that Y falls instead. Do you regard the quantity theory as overthrown or can you find a flaw in the above reasoning?

Carry out your analysis in two sections:

i. Assume that the price level is fixed.

ii. Assume that the price level is flexible.

2. (30 minutes)

   (a) Define each of the following:

      i.   traditional Keynesian marginal propensity to consume
      ii.   marginal propensity to consume out of transitory income
      iii. marginal propensity to consume out of permanent income
      iv.   Pigou effect
      v.   effect on consumption of inflationary tax on money.

   (b) Suppose the true relationship governing behavior is that real consumption is a linear function of expected real wealth, $C = a + bW$, and that expected real wealth is the discounted sum of expected future income, i.e.,

$$W = \Sigma Y_t / (1 + i)^t$$

where t is summed over all future time periods to infinity. Note, from the well-known formula for an infinite series, that if income is expected to be the same in all future time periods, the expression for expected real wealth becomes $W = \bar{Y} / i$ where $\bar{Y}$ is the uniform expected future income.

-273-

Suppose that income is in fact expected to be the same
in all future time periods, and that this uniform level of
income rises in the current period by one unit. That is,
income rises by one unit and is expected to stay at this
higher level in all future periods.

Using the symbol b and any other symbols needed, indicate
what will happen to the time stream of consumption.

Using the symbol b and any other symbols needed, indicate
the magnitude of the five responses in (a) for an income
change of this type. Each of the five responses is a ratio
of a change in consumption to a change in an income of
wealth concept. Therefore, you need to divide change in
consumption by change in income or wealth concept considered in each response. For the fifth response, assume
that the change in income is due to a reduction in the rate of
inflation reducing the tax on money.

(c) Now suppose that real income rises by one unit for the current
period, after which time it is expected to fall back to its
original level and remain at the original level for all future
periods.

Indicate what will happen to the time stream of consumption.

Indicate the magnitude of the five responses in (a) for this type
of change. For the fifth response, assume the income change
is due to a one period change in the inflationary tax on money.
(If you have difficulty calculating the third response, discuss
the nature of the difficulty instead of attempting to carry out
a calculation.)

(d) In contrast to (b) and (c), what is a more usual type of assumption
about changes in income in the literature on consumption? Still
assuming that real consumption is a linear function of real
wealth, discuss the differences among the five responses under
the more usual type of assumption.

COMPREHENSIVE EXAMINATION
Price Theory
The Theory of Income, Employment
and the Price Level

Alternative B of the A. M. Degree

Winter, 1972

WRITE THE FOLLOWING INFORMATION ON YOUR EXAMINATION PAPER:

Your code number, but NOT your name
Name of Examination
Date of Examination

Results of the examination will be sent to you by letter.

TIME: 3 hours. ANSWER ALL QUESTIONS.

NOTE: This examination is in two parts. Write your answers in separate
parts.

WRITE ALL ANSWERS IN BLACK INK

Count the number of pages used, write the number and circle it on
the first page of your answer sheets.

Part A. Relative Price Theory (1-1/2 hours)

I.   (10 minutes)

This question is worth 10 points out of 90. Show how a rational man
would allocate his time between this question and the rest of the
examination. You may find it helpful to describe the utility function
to be maximized and the constraint under which the rational man
operates.

II.   (60 minutes; a little over 5 minutes each, on average)

Indicate whether each of the following statements is true (T), false (F), or Uncertain (U), and explain briefly why.

a. _____ If consumers can buy books only from retailers, not from wholesalers, they pay two profit margins and therefore pay a higher price.

b. _____ A cartel that wishes to maximize the income of its member firms should distribute output among them so as to equalize their average variable costs.

c. _____ When marginal cost is constant, average cost is also constant, and is equal to average cost.

d. _____ Jones consumes only Cigars and Whiskey. His income elasticity of demand for Whiskey is 2.5 and he spends half of his income on Cigars. Therefore, Cigars are an inferior commodity for him.

e. _____ One would expect the elasticity of demand for transportation (by airplane, say) to be greater for college students than for business executives.

f. _____ There is a presumption on economic grounds that there is under-investment in the acquisition of additions to the world's stock of useful knowledge.

g. _____ One would expect the elasticity of the supply of exports of wine from France to be higher than the elasticity of supply of French wine in total.

h. _____ The whiskey industry, which is competitive, is to be taxed. A tax expressed as a fixed dollar amount per gallon will have the same effect on output as a tax expressed as a fixed percentage of the price of a gallon if the two tax rates are set to yield the same revenue to the government.

i. _____ If an economy with an unchanging technology produces output with labor and land, land being fixed and earning 1/3 of output, then a 12 percent rise in the labor force will reduce output per laborer by 4 percent.

III.   (10 minutes)

Consider a firm that is a monopolist and has constant average costs
of production. The elasticity of demand for the firm's product is 2.
Suppose the monopolist experiences factor-neutral technological
progress that enables it to produce 5 percent more output for the
same inputs. Now, true (T), false (F), or uncertain (U).

a. _____ The price in the market will fall 5 percent.

b. _____ Output will increase 10 percent.

c. _____ All inputs employed will increase 5 percent.

d. _____ The firm's profits will increase by 5 percent.

IV.   (10 minutes)

True (T), false (F), or uncertain (U), as usual.

a. _____ Supply and demand analysis applies to conditions in a
market of monopoly and monopsony as much as to
conditions of perfect competition.

b. _____ The value that a wife places on an hour of her time,
whether in market or non-market activities, is greater,
the greater is her husband's income.

Part B.   The Theory of Income, Employment and the Price Level
(1-1/2 hours. Answer all questions)

I.   (35 minutes) Indicate whether each of the following statements is
true, (T), false (F), or uncertain (U), and briefly explain why.

1. _____ Assuming that money is the only asset in the
economy, it follows from Walras' Law that an
excess demand for money implies an equal excess
supply of goods.

2. _____ Permitting banks to pay interest on demand deposits
would tend to increase market interest rates because
of the increase in the cost of the banking business,
but would tend to lower them because of the increased
demand for demand deposits and hence the supply of
credit.

3. _____ An increase in the deficit of the postal system will
result in a rise of national income relative to
national product.

4. _____ If the demand for real cash balances depends upon
the nominal (expected) rate of interest but expenditure
depends upon the real rate of interest, then expectations
of increased inflation will tend to be self-fulfilling.

5. _____ An increase in the quantity of money induced by an
open market purchase of government bonds is not
itself expansionary as the Central Bank merely bids
up the prices of the bonds until the public willingly
exchanges them for money.

6. _____ In a country where the public sector produces only
consumption goods, the balanced-budget multiplier
would be zero.

II.   (20 minutes) Define each of the following terms:

> Built-in stabilizers
> Full employment surplus
> High-powered money
> The term structure of interest rates
> Government saving
> The savings gap

III.   (20 minutes)

Derive the relationship between the quantity of high-powered money and the money supply. Within the framework of that relationship, indicate the effects on the money supply of the following:

   a.   The rate of inflation rises permanently from zero to 10 percent per annum.

   b.   The government suddenly eliminates minimum legal reserve requirements.

   c.   The government permits deposits held by one bank in another bank to be used to meet the legal minimum reserve requirement.

IV.   (15 minutes)

What do you think would happen to the volume of transactions effected by currency relative to those effected by demand deposits if all restrictions on the payment of interest on demand deposits were lifted? Explain your answer carefully.

COMPREHENSIVE EXAMINATION
Price Theory
The Theory of Income, Employment
and the Price Level

Alternative B of the A.M. Degree
Winter, 1971

WRITE THE FOLLOWING INFORMATION ON YOUR EXAMINATION PAPER:

Your code number, but NOT your name
Name of Examination
Date of Examination

Results of the examination will be sent to you by letter.

TIME: 3 hours. ANSWER ALL QUESTIONS.

NOTE: This examination is in two parts. Write your answers in separate p

WRITE ALL ANSWERS IN BLACK INK

Count the number of pages used, write the number and circle it on
first page of your answer sheets.

Part A   Relative Price Theory (1 1/2 hours)

SHORT QUESTIONS (5 minutes each, 55 minutes in total)

Indicate whether each of the following statements is true (T), false (F),
or uncertain (U), and explain briefly why.

_____ 1. The marginal physical product of each input for a competitive
firm in equilibrium is declining.

_____ 2. If today or at any time in the next ten years (1971 to 1981)
you can make an investment of $1000 that will yield a return
of $2,718 ten years from now (in 1981, that is), then you wi
make the investment today rather than later.

_____ 3. A price maximum imposed on a monopolist and effectively enfor
causes the price charged by the monopolist to fall by 10 per
but has no effect on his output. Therefore the elasticity o
demand for the monopolist's output is 10.

_____ 4. In competitive equilibrium the share of materials in the tota
cost of a product is equal to the elasticity of output of the
product with respect to inputs of materials.

-280-

5. The working members of a newly formed union will always make enough from acting as monopolists to be able, if they wish, to fully compensate those thrown out of work by the union, given that the supply of labor is perfectly elastic.

6. Mr. O'Malley consumes only two goods, Cigars and Telephone Calls. His income elasticity of demand for Cigars is 2.5 and he spends half his income on Cigars. Therefore a Telephone Call is an inferior good to him.

7. Discriminatory pricing of Housing, with two prices permitted, will always increase national income in terms of Housing and All Other Goods over that attainable with one-price monopoly.

8. If the elasticity of demand for automobiles and the elasticity of substitution between labor and all other factors in the automobile industry are both unity, then the elasticity of demand for labor on the part of the automobile industry is also unity.

9. The following two market observations for a community consuming only guns and butter violate the assumption of rational behavior of individuals:

	Price of Guns	Number of Guns	Price of Butter	Pounds of Butter
a)	$10	5	$10	1
b)	5	2	15	3

10. If the two commodities, Brandy and Cigars, are consumed by everyone in a single fixed ratio, say 1 Cigar for every 2 glasses of Brandy, no more tax revenue can be collected by taxing both commodities than by taxing only one of the two.

11. A 100 per cent increase in the price of a commodity for which marginal revenue is zero at every quantity demanded will cause the quantity demanded to decrease by 50 per cent.

Part B. Longer Questions

1. Property Taxes (15 minutes)

The City of Chicago proposes to raise property taxes by 30 per cent. Renter groups are alarmed by this development, for they agree with the landlords that this higher cost will be reflected in an approximately 30 per cent increase in rents. Analyse their economics, for both the long and short run, answering along the way who will pay what when.

2. The Slave Trade (20 minutes)

The attempt by the British after 1807 to stop the slave
trade from Africa to the New World has been viewed by historians
as perhaps noble but certainly futile. The main instrument
of this policy, the capture of slave ships by the British
navy, succeeded in recovering only 160,000 slaves out of a
total of 1,900,000 imported into the Americas from 1811 to
1870. Is this small number of slaves recovered really evidence
for the futility of the British policy? How would you go
about estimating the true effect of the policy on the number
of slaves imported? What sorts of data would you need to
make the estimate? Consider in your answer both cost changes
and the uses to which slaves were put (growing sugar, primarily).

Part B.   The Theory of Income, Employment and the Price Level

I.   (20 minutes--<u>5 minutes each</u>)

Indicate whether the following statements are true (T) false (F), or uncertain (U), and briefly explain your answer.

    a.   Recent reductions in the short term interest rate reflect a drop in the anticipated rate of inflation.

    b.   Over the past year the money stock has risen at an annual rate of about 5 per cent. In the long-run, if real output grows at an average rate of 3 per cent, inflation will fall to 2 per cent per year if the 5 per cent annual growth in money is continued.

    c.   Under the procedures of the U.S. National Income Accounts, returns to real money balances held by firms do get counted in national income, whereas returns to real money balances held by consumers do not get counted in national income.

    d.   Assuming no offsetting open-market operations by the Federal Reserve, an airline strike would increase the supply of money.

II.   (70 minutes)

1.   "The significant character of money is that ownership of it by an individual automatically increases or decreases as a result of any difference between his payments and receipts, <u>without altering its aggregate quantity</u> or having an effect on the market for loans."

        This definition of money has been offered to justify the identification of money with currency plus demand deposits. Explain the definition and criticize it.

2.   Consider a <u>temporary</u> increase in government expenditures financed by borrowing from the public, followed by a return in these expenditures to their former level. State as carefully as you can the conditions under which, as a result of this <u>temporary</u> event:

    a.   There is a <u>permanent</u> increase in nominal income.

b. There is a _permanent_ decrease in nominal income.

c. There is no _permanent_ change in nominal income.

3. Explain and criticize the following statement:

> Rapid growth in the money supply does not increase expenditures in periods like late 1970 when the demand for loans is falling, since under these circumstances banks issue liquid demand deposits to the public in exchange for equally liquid short-term U.S. government securities, and the public's behavior is unchanged.

4. Which of the following events would increase demand deposits and why?

    a. an increase in the Federal Funds rate

    b. an increase in the interest rate actually paid on time deposits

    c. an increase in the Federal Reserve System discount rate

    d. a desire by consumers to reduce the fraction of deposits held in the form of currency

    e. the shift of $1.00 from a time deposit in a U.S. bank to a deposit in a savings and loan institution.

5. Derive the balanced budget government multiplier in a simple Keynesian model and explain the conditions necessary for this multiplier to be equal to 1.0. Show the effect, if any, on this multiplier if consumers treat government expenditures as if they were perfect substitutes for private consumption expenditures.

COMPREHENSIVE EXAMINATION

Price Theory
The Theory of Income, Employment
and the Price Level

Alternative B of the A. M. Degree
Summer, 1970

WRITE THE FOLLOWING INFORMATION ON YOUR EXAMINATION PAPER:

Your code number, but NOT your name
Name of Examination
Date of Examination

Results of the examination will be sent to you by letter.

TIME: 3 hours. ANSWER ALL QUESTIONS.

NOTE: This examination is in two parts. Write your answers to the separate
parts in separate blue books.

Part A.   Relative Price Theory (1 1/2 hours). Answer all questions.

I. (About 40 minutes)

Indicate whether each of the following statements is true (T), false (F), or
uncertain (U), and explain briefly why.

_____ a. For each 1 per cent increase in the real income of consumers the
fraction of their income spent on theater tickets rises by 0.5 per
cent. The income elasticity of demand for theater tickets therefore
is 1.5.

_____ b. If the elasticity of demand for the output of a monopolist is 3.0 at
the equilibrium output, the price charged by the monopolist will
exceed his marginal cost at the equilibrium output by 50 per cent.

_____ c. If the elasticity of demand for the output of a competitive industry
is 2.0 and labor costs comprise half of total costs, the elasticity
of demand for labor by the industry must be at least 1.0.

____ d. If all of the firms in a competitive industry produce under condit of constant returns to scale, the industry's supply curve is infin elastic.

____ e. An increase in the price of a factor of production will increase th marginal cost of the product.

____ f. Because it can buy directly from the manufacturers, eliminating n iddleman's profits, Polk Brothers, a large discount store, can sell air conditioners cheaper than a small store in Hyde Park.

____ g. Time is money, it is said. Therefore, it is equally efficient fro the social point of view to use time (waiting lines at stores, congestion at airports, traffic jams on the road) to allocate som commodity as it is to use money.

____ h. If the elasticity of demand for coffee is 2.0, the elasticity of den for Brazilian coffee, assuming that Brazil produces about one-th of the world's crop, must be over 6.0.

II. (20 minutes)

Jones' income consists of his earnings from labor market employment plus welfare payments to him for which he is eligible. He is eligible for welfar payments if his annual earnings E are less than a specified minimum amou M where M, of course, is a positive amount. The annual amount P of welf payments to him is

$$P = \lambda (M - E), \text{ if } M > E$$

$$P = 0, \text{ if } M \leq E$$

where $0 \leq \lambda < 1$. In the absence of the welfare payments scheme he would E^* annually by working h^* hours per year.

   a. On an "income vs. leisure" diagram show Jones' budget rest when $\lambda = 0$ and alternatively when $\lambda = 1/2$.

   b. Assume that $\lambda > 0$ and that Jones chooses not to be eligible for welfare payments. What then is the sign of $E^* - M$? Of $E - M$? If M were larger would he still choose not to be eligible? If λ were larger? Explain your answers.

c. Assume that $\lambda > 0$ and that Jones chooses to be eligible for welfare payments. What then is the sign of $E^* - M$? Of $h^* - h$ where $\underline{h}$ is his annual hours of work when he receives welfare payments? What will happen to $\underline{h}$ as $\underline{M}$ increases? As $\underline{\lambda}$ increases? Explain your answers.

d. Is this welfare scheme a "guaranteed minimum annual income" scheme? If so, what is the guaranteed minimum annual income? Is the scheme a "negative income tax" scheme? If so, what is the negative income tax rate? The marginal tax rate on Jones' earnings? Explain your answers.

III. (30 minutes) Explain your answers.

All the land of a typical European village ten centuries ago was divided into two large fields. Each year wheat was grown in one field and the other was left uncultivated (to restore its fertility). The next year the roles of the two were reversed. No one was permitted to deviate from this pattern, but aside from that each man cultivated his own land in his own time as he saw fit and owned its crop. There were definite technical advantages to holding your land in one plot, fenced off from other men's plots. Despite this advantage:

1. Men usually held half their land in one of the large fields and half in the other. The traditional explanation for this peculiar scattering of ownership is as follows: if a man held all his land in one field, he would go hungry when the turn came for that field to lie uncultivated; therefore, he made sure that he had land in both fields. If there was a market for wheat in the village, what is wrong with this argument? Given that a man's labor-time was limited, what alternative explanation is there? Given the market in wheat, if there is also a market in labor, what is wrong with the alternative argument? What does the continued existence of this peculiarity of the system suggest about the costliness of transactions in wheat or labor?

2. Within each of the two fields a man would hold his land in many small, unfenced, scattered plots. Historians have argued that this scattering arose and persisted in order to give each man a fair share of the good and bad land in the field. In view of the large inequalities that existed in the villages between rich and poor landowners, what is peculiar about this explanation? Supposing that the village _was_ concerned with equality and distributed land in scattered plots to achieve it, how would

the situation change if there was free trade in land (recall that there were technical advantages to a consolidated plot)? Is the desire for equality, then, an adequate explanation of the persistence of scattered plots? Does there appear to actually have been free trade in land?

3. The landowners of the village were permitted to graze their cattle on the cultivated fields after the harvest was in, the number of cattle permitted being in proportion to each man's holding of land in the field. Historians have argued that this common right was the chief support of the system: if one man wanted to remove his land from the common grazing (to use it better as he saw fit by fencing it, he would not be able to get the agreement of the other villagers, because they would lose grazing land. Given the description of the grazing right, would the others really object? Does it appear that rights to grazing were exchangeable?

In view of your previous answers, would it surprise you that the system broke down most rapidly in the vicinity of large cities and in regions with simple laws of land ownership?

Part B. The Theory of Income, Employment, and the Price Level (1-1/2 hours).

I. (40 minutes) Indicate whether the follwoing statements are true (T), false (F), or uncertain (U). In each case, give a brief explanation of your answer. Your grade depends heavily on the explanations.

1. An increase in government expenditures, financed by borrowing, will not increase nominal income, since the bond purchasers must cut back their expenditures to obtain funds to buy the bonds.

2. The central bank can only vary the nominal quantity of money; it cannot affect the real supply of money.

3. If the reserve requirement on demand deposits were raised to 100 percent, a shift of one dollar of Treasury deposits from its tax and loan accounts to its account at the Federal Reserve would raise high powered money by one dollar.

4. The demand for money is different from that for any other commodity because its price is fixed.

5. In a simple neoclassical growth model with no technical change, per capita consumption is maximized when the real rate of interest equals the saving rate.

6. The money multiplier (demand deposits plus currency divided by high-powered money) will increase if an open market sale is carried out when the market interest rate is above the regulation Q ceiling.

7. Saving always equals investment, except in those cases where mistaken sales expectations cause involuntary inventory accumulation or deaccumulation.

8. If wages and prices are flexible but the demand for commodities is not a function of real wealth, the economy will always return to full employment after a decline in government spending.

II. (50 minutes) Answer each of the following questions.

1. a) Special conditions are required for the Keynesian government spending multiplier to be equal to the inverse of the marginal propensity to save. What are these conditions and what evidence determines the degree to which these conditions are met?

   b) What is the government spending multiplier in a quantity theory model? In such a model, what other important aggregate variables besides nominal income would be affected by an increase in government spending?

2.   "Given the existence of bonds and time deposits which bear interest one can hardly rationalize the demand for money on grounds of risk aversion. The same argument rules out the speculative motive. Therefore only by the transactions motive can we rationalize the demand for money. However in this case the demand for money will not be interest elastic."

Discuss each sentence of this quotation from a famous economist, specifying reasons for your agreement or disagreement.

COMPREHENSIVE EXAMINATION

Price Theory
The Theory of Income, Employment
and the Price Level

Alternative B of the A. M. Degree
Summer, 1969

WRITE THE FOLLOWING INFORMATION ON YOUR EXAMINATION PAPER:

Your code number, but NOT your name
Name of Examination
Date of Examination

Results of the examination will be sent to you by letter.

TIME: 3 hours. ANSWER ALL QUESTIONS

NOTE: This examination is in two parts. Write your answers to the separate
parts in separate blue books.

Part A. Relative Price Theory (1 1/2 hours). Answer all questions.

1. (About 35 minutes)

Indicate whether each of the following statements is true (T), false (F), or
uncertain (U) and explain briefly why.

____ a. If the ratio of capital input to labor input is higher in the chemical
industry than in the steel industry, the wages of labor in chemicals
will be higher than in steel.

____ b. A given output of wheat will be produced at least cost if the output
is divided among farms in such a way that the marginal cost of
wheat is exactly the same for each farm.

____ c. In 1959 Smith spent $5,000 and in 1969 he spent $7,000. Smith's
tastes did not change. The goods he bought in 1959 would have
cost him $7,000 in the prices of 1969. Therefore, Smith was
better off in 1969 than in 1959.

2

d. The ratio of wages in occupation A to wages in B is 2. After the imposition of a payroll tax of 10 per cent on both occupations, the ratio will be higher.

f. Cigarettes and whiskey are always consumed in the ratio of one carton of cigarettes to one bottle of whiskey. The market price of cigarettes is $2 per carton, of whiskey $3 per bottle. A tax of $1 per carton cigarettes will yield the same total tax revenue as a tax of $1.50 per bottle of whiskey.

II. (About 30 minutes). Two parts.

Indicate whether each of the following statements is true (T), false (F), or uncertain (U) and explain briefly why.

1. Mr. Smith consumes only two commodities, Applies and Cigars. The rates of consumption of the commodities are denoted by A and C, their prices by P_A and P_C, and his money income by M. His demand function for Apples is

$$A = \frac{M}{4 P_A}.$$

Therefore,

a. The elasticity of substitution between Apples and Cigars in his utility function is unity.

b. Cigars are an inferior commodity to him.

c. If the price of Cigars increases by 100 per cent, C will decrease by 50 per cent.

2. A law that fixes rents for renter-occupied housing below the level that would otherwise prevail will in the long run:

a. Increase the fraction of the total stock of housing that is owner-occupied.

b. Increase the fraction of the renter-occupied portion of the stock in which the renters own the furniture.

c. Increase the fraction of young married couples who live with relatives.

III. (About 25 minutes). <u>Explain</u> your answers.

Great Britain has a free health service, the only charges being for false teeth and spectacles. The government spends about $4 billion a year on this service.

1. Making the usual assumptions, use a supply and demand diagram to define what is meant by "efficiency" in the provision of health services. What are the "usual assumptions" about the interpretation of the supply and demand curves that are necessary to use the diagram to make valid comparisons with inefficient situations?

2. Suppose that the government distributed a certain quantity of health service coupons to the poor and permitted rich and poor to buy and sell these coupons. Assume that health service is provided only in exchange for coupons. Describe the equilibrium. How would the equilibrium change, wealth effects and transaction costs aside, if the government distributed the coupons equally to the rich and poor? Illustrate the loss from the inefficiency of the coupon system. Is it ever efficient?

3. Suppose the government did not issue coupons, but simply provided the health service consumers wanted. Describe the equilibrium. Illustrate the loss from inefficiency and compare it with the coupon system. If consumers felt they needed a certain quantity of health service, neither more nor less, what is the loss from inefficiency?

Part B. Theory of Income, Employment and Price Level (1 1/2 hours).
Answer <u>all</u> questions.

1. (25 minutes, 5 minutes for each question).
Answer true, false, or uncertain, and give a very brief reason for
your answer.

   a) It is impossible for all people taken together to avoid paying an inflationary tax.

   b) Increasing the money stock at 4% per annum would have eliminated
   the great Depression.

   c) If a commercial bank is in equilibrium and then loses a dollar of demand deposits, it must sell between five and fifteen dollars worth of
   earning assets to reach a new equilibrium.

   d) The concept of national income in the national accounts is faulty
   because of double counting, since primary products like steel are
   counted once when they are sold to automobile makers and again when
   the automobiles are sold to the public.

   e) A long holiday weekend will expand the supply of money if no offsetting
   action is taken by the Federal Reserve.

2. (25 minutes, 5 minutes for each question).

   If the following events occur will the nominal money stock (currency
   plus demand deposits plus time deposits) increase, decrease, remain
   constant? Explain your answer briefly using "T" accounts.

   a) The public increases its currency holdings relative to its demand
   deposit holdings.

   b) The Treasury shifts deposits from its accounts in commercial banks
   to its accounts in Federal Reserve banks.

   c) The Treasury sells securities to Federal Reserve Banks.

   d) The U.S. experiences a gold inflow.

   e) The U.S. experiences a gold outflow, and the Federal Reserve System
   purchases securities equal to the amount of this gold outflow.

3. (10 minutes, short essay)
   The introduction of credit cards will raise market interest rates.
   Discuss.

4. (30 minutes, essay)
   "Increases in government expenditures financed by borrowing can have
   no effect on income."

   a) In a Keynesian framework, using IS-LM curves, explain under what
      conditions this statement is true.
                         within the Keynesian framework
   b) The statement is false under at least two conditions. Explain care-
      fully.

   c) Using a quantity theory of money framework, under what conditions
      will the statement be true and under what conditions false?

Price Theory
The Theory of Income, Employment
and the Price Level

Alternative B of the A. M. Degree
Summer, 1968

WRITE THE FOLLOWING INFORMATION ON YOUR EXAMINATION
PAPER:

    Your code number, but NOT your name
    Name of Examination
    Date of Examination

Results of the examination will be sent to you by letter.

    TIME: 3 hours. ANSWER ALL QUESTIONS

NOTE: This examination is in two parts. Write your answers to the
    separate parts in separate blue books.

PART I: Price Theory

A. (50 minutes) Indicate whether each statement is true (T),
   false (F), or uncertain (U), and state concisely the reason
   for each answer.

   1. Goods X and Y are either substitutes, complements, or
      independent if an increase in the amount of X either re-
      duces, raises, or leaves unchanged the margin.l utility
      of Y.

   2. A competitive firm with a constant returns to scale pro-
      duction function will have infinitely elastic factor demand
      curves when they are derived holding constant the supply
      price of other factors and the price of output.

   3. Suppose there are two occupations in the community, A
      and B, and that wages in each change by the same pro-
      portion. The relative amounts of labor supplied to A
      and B would be unchanged.

   4. A labor-saving technological change in a competitive
      industry will lead to a reduction in the employment of
      labor services per unit of time.

   5. The elasticity of demand for labor in the automobile
      industry will be greater, the larger is the wage bill
      as a percent of total cost of that industry.

   6. A competitive industry can have a backward bending
      supply curve if there are external technical disecono-
      mies to each firm in the industry.

   7. Congress considers two ways of taxing a competitive
      industry's output:
      a) An ad valorem tax of s% on producers price
      b) A specific tax of $t per unit of output such that at
         the original pre-tax output both taxes would yield
         the same revenue
      The specific tax will result in a smaller reduction in
      output than the ad valorem tax.

8. Suppose the increase in prices from period A to period B is measured by a Laspeyres price index. The change in the price index is then used to estimate the change in money income required to maintain the consumer on the same indifference level. Such an index would over-estimate this required rise in money income.

9. If a competitive industry is producing subject to a Cobb-Douglas production function, a trade union cannot increase total labor income by setting a different wage rate.

10. Since all firms in a competitive industry have equal marginal costs at the equilibrium output, it is meaningless to speak of more or less efficient firms.

B. (25 minutes) Indicate how you would measure the welfare costs of the following possible policies. Assume in each case that the rest of the economy is in competitive equilibrium, and free of any distortions. Indicate in each case how the welfare cost depends on the supply and demand e;asticities in the industry in question.

1. A subsidy on the production of bread.

2. A quota limiting production of oil to a level below the free market equilibrium level.

3. A price ceiling, below the free-market equilibrium price of meat.

4. A price ceiling on the product of a monopolist, below the the price which would maximize his profits and above the minimum average cost.

C. (15 minutes) Suppose a proportional tax is placed on earnings, and leisure is a superior good. Indicate in each case the effects on average hours worked in the market when the proceeds of the tax are used in the following ways:

1. To give a proportionate subsidy to the sale of all goods and services.

2. To pay for the construction of useless goods (e.g., digging holes in the ground).

3. To give relief to the poor.

PART II: The Theory of Income, Employment, and the Price Level
(1 hour and 30 minutes) Answer all questions.

A.   (50 minutes) Indicate whether the following statements are true,
false, or uncertain, and briefly explain your answer.

1. In a model with downwardly rigid money wages it is possible
to have underemployment equilibrium even though the demand
for money is interest inelastic.

2. If people decide to switch from savings and loan deposits to
bonds, the drain on member bank reserves is greater than if
they decide to switch from time deposits to bonds.

3. As an accounting convention, the value of government expenditure on goods and services is used as a measure of the value
of final output.   This convention has theoretical difficulties
because part of government output represents intermediate
goods and services.

4. The growing use of credit cards can be expected to increase
the velocity of circulation of money.

5. The internal rate of return on an investment project is defined
as that rate of interest which makes the present value of the
project zero.   It follows that in comparing alternative investments, the project with the higher internal rate of return is
also the one with the higher present value.

6. An increase in the quantity of money can shift the aggregate
demand function, but it cannot increase employment if both the
supply of and the demand for labor are functions of the real
wage.

7. While a tax on foreign travel may help the U.S. balance of
payment, it is likely to cause inflation in the country.

8. In a non-barter economy with stable prices, the interest
rate cannot be negative.

9. The instability of the growth equilibrium in Harrod-Domar
models can be attributed to the particular assumption made
about the production function.

10. The transactions demand for money is independent of the interest rate.

B. (40 minutes) Essay questions.

1. The Phillips curve literature investigates an alleged permanent trade-off between the rate of inflation and the rate of unemployment.

   a) State as precisely as you can the original Phillips hypothesis.
   b) Sketch a theoretical argument to rationalize the relationship.
   c) Sketch an argument for why we should not expect a permanent trade-off between inflation and the rate of unemployment.

2. Consider a stationary economy that is at full employment. Assume that the demand for money is completely interest inelastic.

   a) What is the effect of a 10 percent increase in the quantity of money on the price level and on interest rates?
   b) What is the effect of a 10 percent upward shift in the consumption function on the price level, on interest rates, and on the composition of output?
   c) How are the answers to parts a) and b) affected if the demand for money is not completely inelastic?

(In answering the above questions indicate whether the variables in question are increases, or decreased and indicate the magnitude of the change where possible. Also indicate the forces that operate to produce a new equilibrium, but do not try to explain the dynamics of the adjustment process.)

Price Theory
The Theory of Income, Employment
and the Price Level

Alternative B of the A.M. Degree
Winter, 1968

WRITE THE FOLLOWING INFORMATION ON YOUR EXAMINATION PAPER:

    Your   your name
    Name   n
    Date examination

Results of the examination will be sent to you by letter.

    TIME. 3 hours

NOTE: This examination is in two Parts. <u>Write your answers to the separate
    parts in separate blue books.</u>

PART A. Price Theory (3 1/2 hours)

I. (50 minutes) For <u>eight</u> of the following ten statements, indicate whether
    statement is true (T), false (F), or uncertain (U) and state concisely th
    reasons for each answer. (No extra credit will be given for answering me
    than eight.)

    1. The stability conditions require that the marginal utility of at leas
       one d be declining.

    2. A secular improvement in the productivity of working time would induc
       persons to work fewer hours.

    3. Over time in the U. S. income per capita has risen but the number of
       children per household has fallen. This means that children are an
       inferior good.

    4. An individual with increasing marginal utility of income throughout
       all ranges of income will never take out unfair insurance.

    5. Product A is one of the major inputs used in the production of produc
       B. Price control is imposed on A but not on B, at a level below the
       equilibrium price of A. This will produce a fall in the price of B.

    6. If two firms are identical except that the marginal physical product
       of labor schedule of the first firm is more sharply downward sloping,
       the marginal cost curve of the first firm will have a greater upward
       slope than does the marginal cost curve of the second firm.

7. An unemployment compensation law (in which all unemployed are eligible for benefits) would reduce the wage rate in seasonal industries relative to that in nonseasonal industries.

8. In a cartel which tries to maximize the income of its members, output should be distributed among different members (firms) so as to equalize the average variable cost of the different firms.

9. Neutral technological change will produce a secular decline in relative wage differentials between skilled and unskilled workers, after all labor supply adjustments have occurred.

10. Assume penalties were initially imposed on users and suppliers of marijuana. Legalizing the use and sale of marijuana will reduce total expenditures on this commodity if its demand elasticity is less than one.

II. (20 minutes) Consider a situation in which there are two goods: x and all others. The income elasticity of demand for x is 1, and the own-price elasticity of demand for x is $-\frac{1}{2}$. One-fourth of income is spent on x. In answering the following, use the budget constraint condition implying that changes must obey the relation that total spending adds up to income:

   (a) What is the income elasticity of demand for all other goods?
   (b) What is the elasticity of demand for all other goods with respect to a change in the price of x?
   (c) What is the elasticity of demand for x with respect to a change in the price of all other goods?
   (d) What is the own-price elasticity of demand for all other goods?

III. (20 minutes) Suppose there is a permanent increase from zero in the number of accidents to employees in a given industry. Further, assume that workers and employers know the probabilities and costs of accidents, all persons maximize expected income, no safety devices are available to reduce accident and all factor supply curves to the industry are perfectly elastic. Assume also that wages in alternative employments are unaffected and workers are perfectly mobile. Distinguish the effects on resource allocation and the distribution of income (between workers and employers, and accident victims and nonvictims) for the following three alternative liability rules.

   (1) Firms are always liable for accidents to employees and by law must compensate employees for all work accidents.

   (2) Firms are never liable (i.e., workers are liable) and hence by law need not compensate employees for any work accidents.

   (3) Firms and workers share accident losses by a fixed legal formula; e.g., firms pay 70 percent and workers 30 percent of all losses.

PART B. Aggregative Economics (1 1/2 hours)

I. (20 minutes) Give definitions of a few words each for __five__ of the foll
six items:

   (a) High-powered money
   (b) Net national product
   (c) Gold sterilization
   (d) Credit rationing
   (e) Balance of payments surplus
   (f) Distributed lag

II. (50 minutes) For __seven__ of the following ten statements, indicate wheth
you believe the statements to be True, False or Uncertain. In each cas
give a brief explanation of your answer. Your grade depends heavily on
the explanations. (No extra credit will be given for answering more th
seven.)

   1. A higher dollar price of gold need not mean a change in exchange ra

   2. An investment project that costs $100 today and brings a return of
       a year forever is more desirable than a project which costs $40 tod
       and returns $80 next year and nothing after that.

   3. Changes in interest rates can influence investment spending only af
       a long lag (if at all) because (a) interest rate changes influence
       the capital intensity of production and (b) producers are slow to c
       their capital intensity.

   4. In the long run, a change in the level of interest rates has a grea
       proportional effect on the demand for investment goods than on the
       demand for real balances.

   5. If labor unions force an increase in the nominal wage rate when the
       is unemployment, this will raise the total income of individuals an
       stimulate consumption, thereby reducing unemployment.

   6. If savings does not depend on the interest rate, and if prices are
       rigid downward, a decrease in the level of aggregate consumption sp
       will be associated with a decrease in the interest rate.

   7. To the extent that inventory demand consists of replacement demand,
       value of the multiplier is reduced.

   8. The wealth effect of a change in the rate of interest will be great
       the greater is the quantity of interest-bearing government debt hel
       the public.

9. Walras' Law implies that it does not matter whether one uses the bond market or the money market to study the dynamic adjustment behavior of the interest rate.

10. An increase in the rate of growth of the money supply may raise the nominal rate of interest.

II. (20 minutes)

(a) Suppose the Fed increases the required reserve ratio on demand deposits. Discuss the factors influencing whether this raises or lowers the total real income of banks from their loan and securities portfolio. Distinguish between immediate effects and effects after real income and interest rates have adjusted to the change. (Assume no change in price level in this question.)

(b) The following equations form part of a simple economic model that can be solved to show the way in which aggregate income, the interest rate, the money supply, and the level of bank portfolio earnings depend on the required reserve ratio. Assume prices are fixed.

1. How are equations (1) and (2) derived? What assumptions are implicit in them?

2. What additional equation or equations are required to complete the model?

3. Solve the model for the expression that shows how bank portfolio earnings change when the required reserve ratio changes.

4. Explain the meaning of your result. Does it support your answer in part (a)?

Variables

E = total bank portfolio earnings
H = high-powered money
M = money supply
Y = aggregate real income
r = interest rate
k = required reserve ratio

Model

(1) $M = \frac{H}{k}$

(2) $E = r(1 - k)M$

(3) $M^* = gY^a r^b$ (money demand)

(4) $C^* + I^* = hY^d r^e$ (consumption and investment demand)

Price Theory
The Theory of Income, Employment, and the
Price Level

Alternative B of the A. M. Degree
Summer 1967

WRITE THE FOLLOWING INFORMATION ON YOUR EXAMINATION PAPER:

Your code number, but NOT your name
Name of Examination
Date of examination

Results of the examination will be sent to you by letter.

TIME: 3 hours.

NOTE: This examination is in two Parts. Write your answers to the separate
parts in separate blue books.

Part I. Relative Price Theory (1 1/2 hours)

Time for Part I: 1 hour and 30 minutes. Answer all questions.

I. (Approximately 60 minutes). Indicate in the space provided whether
each of the following statements is true, false, or uncertain and
explain your answers concisely.

a. In year 1 your income is $2,000; in year 2 your income is $4,000.
The "market basket" of goods that you bought in year 1 for $2,000
would cost you $4,000 at the prices prevailing in year 2. Your
welfare (utility) therefore must be greater in year 2 than in year 1.

b. A country will never at the same time export a commodity that it
also imports.

c. Assume that the elasticity of demand for meat (taken numerically)
is unity. The government institutes a program of non-price
rationing of meat that reduces the consumption of meat by 5 per
cent. Therefore, the price of meat received by sellers is caused
to increase by 5 per cent and the total receipts of the sellers is
unchanged.

d. If a union succeeds in raising wages in an industry, it will cause
the ratio of labor cost to total cost also to rise.

_____ e. If a one per cent increase in the real income of consumers causes them to increase the fraction of their income that they spend on automobiles by one per cent, then the income elasticity of demand for automobiles is 2.0.

_____ f. If the elasticity of demand for the output of a monopolist is 2.0, then a law fixing the price charged by the monopolist could not cause the price to fall by more than 50% without causing the monopolist to reduce his output.

_____ g. In a competitive industry the derived demand curve for the factor A is identical to the value of the marginal prduct curve of A.

_____ h. If a competitive firm maximizes not income but its sales subject to the constraint that it does not make any losses, then a reduction in the demand for its product might not lead it to reduce output.

_____ i. The supply curve of persons to any occupation is independent of a proportional income tax.

_____ j. A monopolist who practices perfect price discrimination has no effect on income distribution but worsens resource allocation.

_____ k. A given output of wheat will be produced at least cost if the output is divided among wheat producers in such a way that average variable cost is the same for each producer.

_____ ℓ. Simultaneous increases in the prices of first-class surface mail from 5 to 6 cents and air-mail from 8 to 9 cents would not alter the proportions in which persons use both types of mail.

2. (Approximately 30 minutes)

Crusoe, Viernes, and Sabado are three men who comprise a closed economy. They produce and consume only fish and berries. Their maximum outputs per month if they devote their entire capacities to producing fish are

Crusoe	100
Viernes	150
Sabado	300

They may, of course, devote all or part of their efforts to producing berries, sacrificing fish output as they increase berry output. For each reduction in his fish output of 1 fish per month, Crusoe can produce 1 quart of berries per month. The corresponding figures for the other men are:

Viernes 1.5 quarts of berries per fish
Sabado 2.0 quarts of berries per fish

a. In column 2 of the table below show the maximum berry output of the economy for each specified fish output:

1 Fish output per month	2 Berry output per month
0 fish	quarts
100 fish	quarts
101 fish	quarts
250 fish	quarts
251 fish	quarts
550 fish	quarts

b. The three men have the same tastes. Furthermore, for each the income elasticity of demand for fish is unity and each would consume berries and fish in the ratio of 3.5 quarts of berries to 1 fish if the price of fish were 1.5 quarts of berries per fish. Assume free exchange among them. Find the fish and berry output and consumption of each man. Explain your answer. In your answer show that both Sabado and Crusoe gain by trading.

Price Theory
The Theory of Income, Employment, and the
Price Level

Alternative B of the A.M. Degree
Winter 1967

WRITE THE FOLLOWING INFORMATION ON YOUR EXAMINATION PAPER:

> Your code number, but NOT your name
> Name of Examination
> Date of examination

Results of the examination will be sent to you by letter.

> TIME: 3 hours.

NOTE: This examination is in two Parts. <u>Write your answers to the separate parts in separate blue books</u>.

PART A. Price Theory (1 1/2 hours)

I. (60 minutes) Indicate in the space provided whether each of the following statements is true (T), false (F), or uncertain (U) and state concisely the reasons for each answer.

_____ a. An industry is in long run equilibrium with an output of 1 million units per year, a price (including tax) of $11 per unit, and an excise tax of $1 per unit; the output of the industry and the price (including tax) would not be changed if this tax were repealed and replaced by a tax amounting to 10% of the value of output before tax.

_____ b. It is observed that an individual spends 10% of his real income on commodity X when his real income is $5,000 per year and 15% of his income on the same commodity when his real income is $10,000 per year. Therefore, for this individual the income elasticity of demand for the commodity is 2 and for him all other commodities taken together are inferior.

_____ c. The elasticity of demand for labor by an industry will be greater, the more elastic is the demand for the output of the industry, the more elastic is the supply to the industry of cooperating factors, and the higher is the ratio in the industry of labor cost to total cost.

_____ d. If a firm requires all of its employees to buy their groceries at a store owned by the company, one can be sure that the employer is a monopsonist in buying labor services.

_____ e. Wage rates will tend to be highest in industries in which the capital/labor ratio is highest.

_____ f. The government imposes a maximum on the price of a commodity produced in a particular industry. As a consequence the total receipts of the industry decline. Therefore, one can safely assume that the industry is competitive and that the elasticity of demand for the output of the industry is less than unity.

_____ g. Assume a competitive firm uses two factors, L and C. A reduction in the price of L will lead to an increase in the employment of both L and C.

_____ h. There is no incentive to monopolize a competitive industry when the industry is operating along the elastic portion of its demand curve.

_____ i. Over time in the U. S. the output of the service industries increased at about the same rate as that of goods. Since the price of services increased at least as rapidly as that of goods, the income elasticity of demand for services must be greater than for goods.

_____ j. Labor saving technological change in the computer industry has led to an increase in the employment of labor in this industry. This is inconsistent with economic theory.

_____ k. Long run marginal cost may equal but may never be above short run marginal cost.

II. (10 minutes) Evaluate this statement: "The long run equilibrium position of the competitive industry is where each firm operates at the minimum point on its average cost curve and, therefore, earns zero expected profits." Consider two cases: (a) all firms are identical with respect to the minimum price at which they will enter the industry and (b) firms differ with respect to the minimum price.

III. (20 minutes) Consider two occupations: A requires a college degree and B, only a high school diploma. A person will be indifferent between the two occupations if the present value of the absolute earnings differentials between A and B after the investment period equals the full costs of a college education.

    (a) If government subsidies pay the costs of tuition and books, would the absolute earning differential between A and B fall to zero?

    (b) Would a proportional tax on earnings affect the supply of persons entering A and B?

(c) In what way would a progressive tax on earnings differ from a proportional tax as to effect on persons entering A and B?

(d) Would you expect more able persons to enter A? Why?

PART B. The Theory of Income, Employment, and the Price Level (1 1/2 hours)

I. (20 minutes) Give definitions of a few words each for <u>four</u> of the following five items:

(a) balanced budget multiplier
(b) accelerator
(c) warranted rate of growth
(d) operation twist
(e) Accord

II. (50 minutes) For <u>seven</u> of the following ten statements, indicate whether you believe the statements to be true (T), false (F), or uncertain (U). In each case, give a brief explanation of your answer. Your grade depends heavily on the explanations.

_____ 1. The only ways the amount of high-powered money can change are through open market operations or rediscounting.

_____ 2. The ratio of a change in high powered money to a change in the money supply is equal to the ratio of commercial bank reserves to their deposit liabilities.

_____ 3. In a model in which the demand for money does not depend on interest rates, the monetary authorities would not be able to manipulate interest rates in the short run.

_____ 4. The genuine opportunity cost of holding money is the difference between the nominal rate of interest and the real rate of interest.

_____ 5. For given levels of interest rates and nominal income, the demand for money tends to be higher when the money supply is falling than when it is rising.

_____ 6. A country which attempts to correct a chronic balance of payments deficit through devaluation will have a greater fall in internal prices than if it adheres to a strict gold standard making money supply changes proportional to gold flow.

_____ 7. We expect an increase in interest rates to be associated with a decline in investment spending.

_____ 8. A shift of the investment function will lead to a change in the distribution of total product between consumption and investment.

4

_____ 9. Even if money wages are prevented from declining below a certain
        minimum level, an economy will tend to return to full employment
        after a decline in the money supply if prices are perfectly flexible.

_____ 10. In the 1958 recession in the U. S., total employment declined while
        real wages remained roughly constant. Textbook theory says that
        the aggregate quantity of labor demanded is the quantity that brings
        the marginal product of labor down to the prevailing real wage, and
        therefore, it must be true that a shift in the labor productivity
        schedule caused the decline in employment.

III. (20 minutes) Suppose, due to a disturbance such as a war, there is an
     autonomous increase in government spending of $15 billion per year.
     Further, suppose policies are considered to try to just offset any effects
     of the increased spending on employment or the general level of prices.
     Two alternatives are considered: (a) tax increase, which in view of
     independent central bank policies does not affect the money supply; or
     (b) rely entirely on actions of the central bank, with no tax increase
     or other fiscal efforts to reduce aggregate demand. Using numerical
     parameter values you believe to be reasonable, estimate the amount of
     increase in taxes that would be needed under alternative (a). Estimate
     for (b) the needed change in the money supply from what it would other-
     wise have been. Estimate the change in level of interest rates expected
     under policy (a); under policy (b).

THE UNIVERSITY OF MICHIGAN
Department of Economics

Preliminary Examination
Monetary Theory and Stabilization Policy   May 7, 1981

Answer all questions.

1. Contrast the effects on investment, productivity, and saving of

    a) the liberalization of depreciation allowed for tax purposes
    b) the liberalization of investment tax-credits
    c) cuts in the basic rate of the corporate-profit tax
    d) cuts in high-bracket personal-tax rates
    e) cuts in capital-gains taxation

2. Federal Reserve policy has evolved rapidly in recent years. Describe
    major recent policy changes and indicate and evaluate the major events,
    developments, and ideas that have contributed to them. In discussing
    these changes, be sure to distinguish among ultimate goals, intermediate
    targets, and operating targets for monetary policy.

3. Standard IS-LM theory provides a vehicle for the derivation of various
    static expenditure, tax-transfer, and financial multipliers. Recently
    there has developed a good deal of interest in the role of the government
    budget constraint in this analysis. Through what variables or channels
    is the budget constraint interrelated with the rest of the model? How
    does the inclusion of this constraint affect the multiplier derivations
    and policy debates based on this model?

4. Outline the development and current status of the theory of inflation,
    and of the trade-off between inflation and unemployment. (Be sure to
    consider the roles of expectations and forecasts.)

The student must answer all questions.

I

Evaluate the requirement or encouragement of indexation as a policy response to inflation.

II

The possible "crowding out" of income increases as a consequence of policy shifts has received an increasing amount of attention in the literature. Recently the possibility of "crowding in" has also been noted. Describe at least three types of crowding out (in) consequent on expansionary policy impulses. In what respects do monetary policy and fiscal policy differ as regards these effects, and in what respects do they parallel each other? How do these concepts relate to other topics such as the term structure of interest rates and the monetarist-Keynesian dispute?

III

Models of the demand for money usually assume a zero nominal rate of return on money holdings. Describe the implications for the economic system of allowing a market-determined nonzero yield on money.

IV

(a) Define forecast, multiplier, and instrument uncertainty. What is the implication of each for the use of discretionary policy versus rules?

(b) What are the implications of "inside" versus "outside" lags for the choice between monetary policy and fiscal policy?

(c) What are the implications for this choice of the size of prospective gap between actual and target values of target variables?

The student must answer all questions.

I

Discuss the likely effectiveness versus the probable costs of various forms and techniques of "incomes policy" used or proposed to deal with inflation.

II

Recently the Federal Reserve System appears to have changed its policy targets as between interest rates and monetary aggregates. Describe these changes and discuss the theoretical and practical considerations faced by the central bank in choosing between these targets.

III

The rational expectations theory generally rejects the notion of forming expectations by exclusive reference to the past history of the variable in question. Yet economists have made wide use of such an expectations-formulation procedure; e.g., in studying the expectations theory of the term structure of interest rates.

To what extent—that is, in what particular set of circumstances, application, or run—can this widely-used approach to quantifying expectations be said to be consistent with rational expectations? Discuss as generally as you can.

IV

What is the theoretical argument for the view that our present "pay-as-you-go" social security system reduces private saving? Assuming this result to be correct, how might it be altered if e.g. private mechanisms for the intergenerational transfer of wealth are assumed to be available?

Money & Stabilization
Preliminary Examination

September 11, 1979

Answer all four questions

1. It has become popular in some circles to claim that rational expectations on the part of the public will prevent the government from conducting a successful stabilization policy. What is meant by "rational expectations"? What are the key arguments of the proponents of this view? What kinds of evidence could shed light on this question?

2. Keynesians have tended to focus on M1, while Monetarists (especially Friedman) have emphasized M2. Recent innovations in financial markets have tended to blur the distinctions between these concepts. Describe these developments, and discuss their implications for the conduct of monetary policy.

3. Describe and criticize the various measures of "fiscal impact" (e.g. full-employment surplus, etc.).

4. "Bills Only" was the name applied to the Fed's practice, during the fifties, of conducting open market operations only in very short term securities. In 1960 the Fed changed its behavior and began to conduct some operations in longer securities. Using theory as a guide, what effects might you find from that change in behavior?

THE UNIVERSITY OF MICHIGAN
Department of Economics

Preliminary Examination
Monetary Theory and Stabilization Policy   May 7, 1979

ANSWER ALL QUESTIONS

1. Write an essay on the <u>concept</u> of "stabilization policy", presenting--without
    detailed assessment--some of the basic presumptions that must underlie the
    advocacy of its use by governments.

2. Provide a theoretical and empirical critique of two theories of inflation.
    Indicate what each theory implies for government policies to prevent inflation.

3. Comment on this "headline" taken from the <u>Wall Street Journal</u>: "Money Supply
    Fell in March 1 Week, Easing Pressure for Rise in Interest Rates".

4. For a number of years, economists, from A. W. Phillips to R. S. Holbrook,
    have analyzed problems related to the development of an optimal feedback
    mechanism from the current economic situation to economic policy. Describe
    the major problems identified by these analyses, and evaluate the present
    state of such proposals.

-317-

THE UNIVERSITY OF MICHIGAN
Department of Economics

Preliminary Examination
Monetary Theory and Stabilization Policy

May 12, 1978

Answer all questions.

1. Define the term "crowding out." Describe and analyze critically three
   distinct ways in which crowding out might occur.

2. Banks may soon be permitted to pay interest on demand deposits. Analyze
   the effect of this change on the Fed's ability to conduct monetary policy

3. Write an essay identifying and discussing the central issues which divide
   monetarists and neo-Keynesians. Distinguish these core issues from the
   false or trivial issues which have also been raised.

Preliminary Examination
Monetary Theory and Stabilization Policy   September 15, 1978

The student must answer all questions.

I

Write an essay on the current execution of monetary policy by the Federal Reserve
System, explaining (a) its current conception of the role and goals of its policy (b)
how it currently operates to further these goals, and its rationale for operating in this
way rather than another; (c) the major criticisms currently made of these goals and or
operating methods by economists, and (d) your own evaluation of recent Fed performance.

II

The following statements on U. S. anti-inflation policy have appeared recently in
the Wall Street Journal:

(1) "Money growth has a direct and immediate effect on inflation. Its effects
on production and unemployment are far more complicated and problematical,
but monetary theory has always held that money growth stimulates production,
and therefore reduces unemployment, to the extent that it causes unanticipated
inflation." (WSJ, May 5, 1977.)

(2) "The rate of inflation will not come down so long as pressures of demand
pushing on supplies are strong enough so that higher prices and higher wages
have no adverse effect on sales volume and employment. Indeed, holding
prices and wages below these market-clearing levels by some sort of brute
force or ad hoc process would produce the queue line economy.

"The rate of inflation will embark on a downward trend when the result of
posting inflationary price increases or extracting excessive wage increases
is a painful loss of sales and employment." (Paul McCracken in WSJ, August 1
1978.) [By "some sort of brute force or ad hoc process," McCracken apparently
means both the "jawboning" of wages and prices and any form of "tax-based
incomes policy" (TIP).]

Compare and contrast the theories of inflation implied in these quotes with that
implied in jawboning or TIP.

III

Standard IS-LM theory predicts that an increase in government spending financed by
issuing bonds will affect income positively, but that the effect will be smaller than
if the same spending change were financed by an increase in the money stock. Monetarists
claim that the effect on income in the bond-financed case is approximately zero. On
the other hand, some economists (e.g., Blinder and Solow) hold that the bond-financed
expenditure multiplier on income is _larger_ than the money-financed one.

Discuss the sources of the differences in these views on fiscal policy efficacy.

IV

What are the chief points of view with respect to the determinants of changes in
the term structure of interest rates, and what is the supporting evidence?

THE UNIVERSITY OF MICHIGAN
Department of Economics

Preliminary Examination
Monetary Theory and Stabilization Policy   September 16, 19?

The student must answer all of the following questions.

I

Under current procedures, the Federal Reserve System's Board of Goverr
announces each quarter a set of "target ranges" for the growth rates of M1,
and M3 over the coming four quarters. At each monthly meeting, the Board a
defines "tolerance ranges," covering the current and coming month, for the
rates of M1, M2, and the federal funds rate; these presumably are thought b
Fed to be consistent with the longer-run aggregate target ranges. If the s
run targets for M1, M2, and the federal funds rate are inconsistent with ea
other, as sometimes happens, the trading desk usually holds the funds rate
'ts range rather than the aggregates.

Write an essay on the virtues and defects of this system of long- and
       rt-run targeting.

II

There has recently been a growing emphasis, in analyses of macroeconom
policy, on the relationship among flows and stocks, and on so-called "budge
constraints." Discuss these issues and their relationship to the effective
of fiscal and monetary policy.

III

Does an increase in the rate of monetary expansion raise or lower inte
ates? Discuss various views on this question. Can these views be reconci

IV

Write an essay on the topic of automatic stabilizers, and include a
discussion of those stabilizers subject to "formula flexibility."

THE UNIVERSITY OF MICHIGAN
Department of Economics

Preliminary Examination
Money and Stabilization

May 13, 1977

Answer 4 of the following 5 questions.

1. The "crowding out" hypothesis has been receiving increasing attention from economists, policymakers, and the press during the last few years. Discuss the meaning(s) of the term "crowding out" and the consequences of "crowding out" for stabilization policy as analyzed within the IS-LM framework. Why has the subject received so much attention recently?

2. Explain the tabulation of the sources and uses of member bank reserves, indicating what the individual sources and uses are and how the tabulation is derived. How could this tabulation be altered to convert it into one which gives the factors affecting M1 or M2?

3. A former Chairperson of the Council of Economic Advisors recently maintained: "The surest way of keeping interest rates at tolerably low levels is to expand the money supply by about two percentage points more than its current rate of expansion." At approximately the same time another distinguished economist wrote: "How can we lower the interest rate? That's really very simple. For each percentage point decrease in the rate of growth of the money supply the interest rate will decline by one percentage point." Are these two statements consistent? If so, explain. If not, what test would you propose to see which is the more correct?

4. Write a critical essay on the various measures of the impact of the government budget on the economy which have been proposed.

5. Discuss the problem of policy choice in the presence of uncertainty. Your discussion should include, but not be limited to, the following topics: What are the sources of uncertainty that might be present? How (if at all) can they be dealt with? What effect does the presence of uncertainty have on optimal policy?

THE UNIVERSITY OF MICHIGAN
Department of Economics

Preliminary Exam
Money and Stabilization

September 20, 1976

The student must answer all questions.

I

Since the beginning of the current recovery in April 1975, real output
has grown at about a 7 percent annual rate, prices at a 6 percent rate, and
the money stock at about 4.5 percent. Interest rates have remained at the
same level as they were at the upswing's beginning.

If you were in charge of monetary policy, how would you interpret these
developments and how would they influence your approach to the planning and
evaluation of current policy?

II

Discuss the theory of portfolio choice under uncertainty. Under what
circumstances will this theory provide a suitable rationale for the holding
of money balances? If those circumstances are not realized, what phenomena
does this theory explain?

III

In the context of a static equilibrium analytic framework, is the rate
of interest determined by "real" or "monetary" factors? Discuss thoroughly.

IV

Write an essay on the development and current status of the theory of
inflation in a closed modern industrial economy. What are the implications
of this theory for stabilization policy under a regime of adaptive expectations?
Under rational expectations?

THE UNIVERSITY OF MICHIGAN
Department of Economics

MONETARY THEORY AND STABILIZATION POLICY

Preliminary Examination

May, 1975

The student must answer all of the following questions.

I

Write an essay on the demand for liquid assets, focusing on
(a) the modern transactions theory of the demand for money and (b) the
theory of portfolio choice under uncertainty. Discuss the implications of
(a) and (b) for the appropriate rate of monetary expansion in an environment like the present that involves substantial uncertainty (perhaps
temporary) and a large anticipated government deficit.

II

Recently a good deal of attention has been paid to the so-called
"government budget constraint." Discuss the nature of this relationship
and the role it plays in macroeconomic analysis. How is this concept
related to the Keynesian-Monetarist controversy?

III

Discuss some of the key problems associated with the choice of
macroeconomic policy in the presence of uncertainty. Give a critical
evaluation of a few of the techniques that have been suggested for dealing
with these problems.

Department of Economics

Preliminary Examination

MONETARY THEORY AND ECONOMIC STABILIZATION

May 31, 1974

Answer all three questions.

I

It has been said that the crucial point at issue between the Monetarists and the Keynesians is not whether money matters, but whether government spending matters. Do you agree or disagree? Describe the key issues in the controversy as you see them, cite the major evidence available on them, and state and defend your own conclusions.

II

Static macroanalysis suggests that, assuming the parameter values are known with reasonable certainty, output and other goals can be attained by once-for-all changes in the stabilization instruments; furthermore, the choice among instruments depends only on the configuration of ultimate goals. In the real world, however, policy makers operate under uncertainty with respect to the structure, and are concerned with the shorter-run dynamic consequences of their decisions as well as the comparative static results.

Write an essay on the ways in which dynamic considerations and the presence of uncertainty affect the selection of appropriate stabilization policies.

III

It is widely believed that, at least in the shorter run, a reduction in the unemployment rate can be obtained at the cost of an increase in the rate of inflation (although some economists feel that there is no long-run tradeoff available). Discuss the analytical structure on which these conclusions rest, making explicit the underlying behavioral relationships and giving attention to the serious omissions in as well as the positive features of that theory. Is the analysis consistent with recent events (e.g., an increase in the unemployment rate without a change in the inflation rate, or contemporaneous increases in both the unemployment rate and the rate of inflation)? What policies would you recommend to deal with our current problem of rapid inflation and declining real output, and why?

PART I: ANSWER THE FOLLOWING QUESTION.

Explain how an open market purchase by the Federal Reserve may set in motion a sequence of wealth and portfolio effects which may ultimately lead to an expansion of output and employment. To what extent and at what points would Keynesians and Monetarists be likely to disagree concerning the process you have described?

PART II: ANSWER **THREE** OF THE FOLLOWING FOUR QUESTIONS.

1. Discuss the issues underlying the current argument concerning "rules **vs.** discretion" in monetary policy. Describe the type of empirical research you believe would help resolve the questions raised by the argument.

2. One of the goals of the Federal Government is to bring about a large increase in the rate of housing construction in the next few years. This is reflected, for example, in the Housing and Urban Development Act which set a target of 26 million houses for the ensuing decade-- a marked contrast to the average level of housing starts of 1.4 million per year over the last five years. What problems do you see in providing financing for such a large increase in housing construction? Indicate the kinds of policy actions and/or financial reforms that might need to be undertaken by the Federal Government to solve these problems.

3. Chairman Arthur Burns of the Federal Reserve Board indicated last week that he favored "a serious reexamination" of the use of interest rate ceilings as an instrument of monetary policy. Describe carefully how the rate ceilings operate to restrict and to allocate credit in periods of tight money, indicate the types of adjustments and financial innovation banks have been induced to adopt as a result of the ceilings, and give the arguments pro and con for use of the ceilings as a monetary policy instrument. In the course of your answer, present and defend your own view on this issue.

4. Explain and evaluate various arguments that have been developed in connection with the discussion of "targets and indicators" for monetary policy.

Answer **all four** questions.

I

"Most students of monetary policy seem to be agreed that the authorities must employ some intermediate monetary target (or targets) if they are to carry out an effective discretionary monetary policy. However, there is a good deal of controversy about the choice of an optimal intermediate target." Discuss this statement, being sure to indicate some of the chief targets that have been advocated and to explain the theoretical and strategic arguments that have been advanced by advocates of the various approaches. What further research would you suggest which could cast light on this problem?

II

At various times since the early sixties two short-term instruments, CD's and commercial paper, have experienced extraordinary rates of growth (both positive and negative). Discuss the nature of these instruments, the reasons for their fluctuations, and their implications for the effectiveness of monetary policy.

III

To the extent that Milton Friedman has discussed the transmission mechanism of monetary policy, his views seem not greatly different from those of economists who might be described as neo-Keynesians (for example, James Tobin). In view of this, how do you account for the fact that there appears to be so substantial a difference between the views of Friedman and those of the neo-Keynesians regarding the relative potency of monetary and fiscal policy?

IV

Evaluate Keynes' contribution to the theory of the demand for money. Contrast and compare his views with those who currently refer to themselves as "neo-Keynesians."

MACROECONOMICS

FIELD EXAM

AUTUMN - 1980

Write the following information on the first page of your exam paper:
- Name of examination
- Date of examination
- Your code number and NOT your name.

- Answer all questions in both Parts I and II
- Time: 4 hours

Part I   4 points each   Total: 40 points

Indicate whether each of the following statements is true, false or uncertain and explain why. Your score depends entirely upon your explanation.

1. If the Fed permitted interest rates to fluctuate freely in response to supply and demand conditions on the money market, this would reduce fluctuations in the U. S. dollar price of foreign currencies.

2. A return to the gold standard would stabilize prices.

3. Unanticipated shocks can be successfully neutralized through indexing of all nominal contracts.

4. The Fed could cause interest rates to fall by a sufficiently large reduction in the discount rate.

5. An implication of rational expectations is that official announcements of policy changes are more important than the policies themselves.

6. A central bank which does not allow its intervention in foreign exchange markets to affect the money supply will help to stabilize exchange rates.

7. A tax cut in 1981 would be inflationary.

8. If the rate of unemployment falls we know that more people have jobs.

9. The natural rate hypothesis is the same as the accelerationist hypothesis.

10. A pattern of higher real output during election years would be inconsistent with an equilibrium model of the business cycle.

1. Assume: (a) A sudden doubling of the U. S. population;
               (b) The average skill level of the population is not
                   directly affected by the doubling.
               (c) The initial level of physical capital remains
                   constant. Hold constant the money supply and the
                   nominal stock of government debt.
    Examine the impact on: (a) real wages, (b) employment,
      (c) nominal interest rate, (d) inflation rate and (e) the <u>real</u>
      exchange rate.

    For each variable consider the effect during the first year;
    after 5 years.

2. Suppose you were told that since the mid-1970's, U. S. money demand
    had become "unstable."
               (a) What evidence would you require to support the inference
                   of unstable money demand?
               (b) What possible reasons might be given for such instability?
               (c) Given that the monetary authority cannot remove the
                   source of "instability" how can it minimize the impact
                   on prices of financial assets arising from unstable
                   money demand?

3. The Government of Venezuela has experienced an enormous increase
    in its revenues due to sharp oil price increases which have
    occurred since 1973. The inflation rate in Venezuela has been
    well above the U. S. inflation rate. The exchange rate of its
    currency against the U. S. dollar has remained virtually constant
    since 1973. Explain.

4. Even though money is "neutral," i.e., money does not matter in
    the long run, it is not "superneutral," i.e., its rate of change
    matters.
               (a) Explain why this is so.
               (b) What is the role of superneutrality in the claim that
                   "with rational expectations the monetary authority
                   cannot expect to exploit the Phillips curve even
                   for one period"?
               (c) What is the role non-superneutrality in the Fisher
                   Hypothesis debate?

-328-

ANSWER ALL QUESTIONS IN AT MOST <u>FOUR</u> HOURS

1. (20 points)
Even though money is "neutral," i.e., money does not matter in the long run, it is not "superneutral," i.e., its rate of change matters.

   a. Explain why this is so.
   b. What is the role of this non-superneutrality in the Fisher Hypothesis debate?
   c. What is its role in the Phillips curve debate?

2. (20 points)
During the period from October, 1979 - March, 1980, money growth has slowed in the United States. At the same time, inflation has accelerated, the rate of unemployment has remained steady, interest rates have risen sharply and the dollar has either remained steady or strengthened against most major currencies.

   a. <u>Without</u> resort to arguments about the accuracy of money supply measures, can <u>economic theory</u> account for each of these results? Consider each event singly.
   b. In the light of your answers to part (a), are these events consistent with each other? Explain carefully.

3. (15 points)
The "Lucas supply equation" is now beginning to be evaluated empirically.

   a. Critically analyze information-cost and contractual arguments behind the proposition that monetary "surprises" can have "real" effects on employment or output.
   b. Analyze key problems in designing empirical tests of such supply behavior propositions.
   c. Analyze implications for testing Lucas supply equations which arise if one drops the assumption of auction markets where price adjustments clear the market.

4. (15 points)
The behavioral relations (a) consumption function, (b) investment function, (c) demand for money, (d) supply of money, are all crucial components of the typical modern macroeconomic framework. How can they be derived from theories which rely on the rational behavior of individual agents?

5. (30 points)
Walter Heller, writing in the February 27 Wall Street Journal, stated that "fiscal-monetary policy has to take a bitter toll... a loss of $200 billion of GNP (and three million jobs) to knock one percentage point off the underlying inflation rate. Study after study has confirmed the mountainous costs and mouse-like benefits of sole reliance on monetary-fiscal policy to fight inflation."   (<u>rest of question 5. is on next page</u>)

a. Do you agree with Heller's characterization of the empirical evidence on the response of unemployment and inflation to fiscal-monetary policy variables? (We are not concerned about the exactitude of the $200 billion number).

b. Summarize concisely what you understand to be the implications of the empirical literature bearing on the nature, dynamics and essential magnitudes of these trade-offs. You should make specific reference to particular relevant articles, but of course it is not expected that you recall exact numbers. What we are interested in is how you would characterize the weight of empirical evidence on these issues and how the leterature has dealt with such problems as the role of expectations in measuring the effectiveness and costs of policy actions.

MACROECONOMICS FIELD EXAM

September 28, 1979

INSTRUCTIONS:

1. **Time:** 3½ hours, 9:30 a.m. to 1:00 p.m.

2. **Choice:** **Only** in Section II where you may choose to answer any **one** of the questions.

3. **Weight of Questions:** As indicated on each section.

4. **Write in ink.**

SECTION I. (30 percent)

When inflation becomes "excessive" concern over the conduct of monetary policy focuses upon trying to avoid slowing money growth "too quickly" in a manner that would cause a recession.

a. Based on monetary theory, is this concern justified? Explain why or why not.

b. Is there any body of empirical evidence which can help to indicate whether such concern is justified?

c. What, if any, additional evidence do you believe would be important in assessing validity of concern over effects of sharp changes in money growth?

d. Given the stated objective of the Federal Reserve to lower and stabilize money growth, how do you account for continued high and volatile money growth?

SECTION II. (30 percent) (Choose <u>one</u>)

1. Suppose that the money wage is fixed and that there is abnormally high unemployment. Suppose that the FED sells treasury bills in the open market.

   a. Show <u>precisely</u> how this action will lower both the price level and unemployment.

   b. Show the effects, if any, of this policy on the bill rate, the loan rate, the stock market, and the relative price of machine tools.

   c. How in broad terms would the result be different if instead the required reserve ratio were raised?

2. Recent contributions to macro theory have analyzed the role of expectations in the long and short run.

   a. Show that rapid revision of expectations of inflation could destabilize the system both in the short and long run, being careful to explain what you mean by "destabilize."

   b. Show that this instability could be removed through monetary policy.

   c. Discuss the relationships between employment and (i) expected inflation and (ii) unexpected inflation in the short and long run.

3. Recent contributions to monetary growth theory examined the effects of monetary policy on an economy's real variables.

   a. Explain why an increase in the rate of growth of the money supply will change the economy's capital intensity.

   b. Explain the role of the above result in the debate whether there is or there is not a long-run trade-off between employment and the rate of inflation.

The same contributions increased our understanding of the role of expectations and speeds of adjustment in economic stability.

   c. Show that rapid revision of expectations of inflation could destabilize the system both in the short and the long run.

   d. Show that this instability could be removed by an appropriate monetary policy.

SECTION III.   (40 percent)

You are given the enclosed paper to evaluate concisely in respect macroeconomic content.   You are not asked to evaluate the econometric You   should be careful to comment on

1.   the use of "real" policy instruments

2.   the practical relevance of the policy simulations reported

3.   the probable outcome of attempts to target real GNP by manipulat the real money supply.   What if nominal money were the instrumen

4.   What explanations can you give for the empirical results obtaine

March 31, 1978
Department of Economics
University of Washington

. . . . . a four-hour exam . . o notes or references may be brought
into . . . . . . Choose three of the four parts. Note that there may
be . . . . . . in a part. Read each question carefully before answer-
in . . The . . rts will be weighed equally in grading. All members of the
. . . . . . grade all answers. You will have to be concise and to
. . . . . . rder to finish. Good luck!

PART I. An . . r both questions.

.. Explain why an increase in the rate of growth of the money supply
will change the economy's capital intensity. Does this result have
any effect on the slope of the long run Phillips Curve?

?. What will be the effects, if any, of an open market purchase (by
the Central Bank) of treasury bills on

(a) the rate of return on capital
(b) the loan rate
(c) price level
(d) employment level.

PART II. Answer any two of the three questions.

1. (a) . . . ment of the Fisher Hypothesis has been said also to imply
an absence of the inflation-unemployment trade-off described by
the Phillips Curve. Indicate whether you agree or disagree and
explain why.
(b) If changes in the nominal supply of money cannot affect real
variables, does this mean that the neoclassical dichotemy holds?
Explain your answer carefully.

2.   Policy-makers in the United States have recently announced an
intention to intervene in foreign exchange markets in order to
support the dollar. In addition, Federal Reserve Open Market
Committee directives have been aimed at keeping nominal interest rates from rising above seven percent. Are these policies
consistent? Carefully explain why or why not.

3. Some economists have argued that the only way to reduce unemployment with monetary policy is to mislead the public regarding the
future course of monetary policy.

(a) Explain carefully why this might be necessary.
(b) Would such a policy be viable in the long run? Why or why not?

-2-

PART III. Answer all three questions.

1. Short answer--do all three.

   (a) The higher the rate of inflation, the lower the level of
       unemployment. True or false? Explain.
   (b) The more nearly useless are government expenditures, the
       greater will be their effect on income. True or false? Explain.
   (c) Can the Consumer Price Index rise while the GNP deflator falls?
       Can the GNP deflator rise while the Consumer Price Index falls?
       Explain.

2. During World War II a large fraction of Germany's capital stock
   was destroyed compared to the number of its soldiers who were
   killed. The U.S., however, lost a large number of soldiers relative to the fraction of its capital stock that was destroyed.
   Under the assumptions that the production functions and the steady
   state savings ratios and growth rates of labor are the same in the
   two countries, what can you predict about the growth rate of real
   income in the two countries during the post-war period? Explain.

3. A recent study has compared the performance of two sets of economies. The first set, referred to as Group S, has a history of
   steady growth in the money supply. The second set, referred to
   as Group E, has a history of erratic growth in the money supply.
   This study found the following results:

   (a) In Group E countries, the short run effects of a change in the
       growth rate of the money supply were reflected primarily in
       the growth rate of nominal income and very little in the growth
       rate of the ratio of cash balances to income. In Group S
       countries, the short run effects of a change in the growth
       rate of the money supply showed up primarily in the growth rate
       of the cash balance ratio and very little in the growth rate
       of nominal income.

   (b) Short run changes in the growth rate of nominal income in
       Group E countries were mostly changes in the growth rate of
       prices, while short run changes in the growth rate of nominal
       income in Group S countries were primarily changes in the
       growth rate of real income.

   (c) In steady state equilibrium, real per capita income in Group
       E countries is lower than in Group S countries.

   How do you explain these findings?

PART IV.

Consider an economy in which suppliers are located in scattered competitive markets. Quantity supplied in each market departs from trend depending on the perceived relative price of the output and past departures from trend. Suppliers know only their own output price in the current period, so relative price is perceived in relation to the expected general price level based on information available at the beginning of the period. Also assume that actual prices in individual markets deviate randomly each period around the actual general price level. Suppliers are rational and prices are flexible. Aggregate demand in nominal terms is assumed to shift randomly from period to period.

Discuss briefly:

1. the form of the aggregate supply function
2. determinants of the slope of the aggregate supply function
3. the reduced form relations between (a) output deviations and change in aggregate nominal demand and (b) inflation rate and changes in nominal demand. What are the "steady state gains" in each of these relations (long run impact)?
4. Discuss how cross-country comparisons could be used to test the model.
5. What are the implications of the model for the effectiveness of "aggregate demand management"?

Announces the publication of innovative educational materials in Business Administration, Economics and Political Science from leading scholars and universities.

Business Administration Reading Lists & Course Outlines
A new series of 14 volumes ranging from traditional subjects such as *Finance* and *Accounting* to less conventional ones such as *Business, Government & Society* and *Health Administration.*

Political Science Reading Lists & Course Outlines
Another new series whose 11 volumes range from *Political Theory* to *International Relations* and *Public Policy.* It includes the reading lists for Yale Ph.D. exams in 14 fields.

Economics Reading Lists, Course Outlines, Exams, Puzzles & Problems
This 25 volume series updates the original series compiled in July 1980, with the addition of exams, puzzles & problems, including preliminary examinations for graduate students in 16 fields at the Universities of Chicago, Michigan and Washington.

These paper bound volumes cover a sampling of both undergraduate and graduate courses at 72 major colleges and universities. They are designed to widen the horizons of individual professors and curriculum committees and to expand the possibilities for independent study and research. Some include suggestions for term paper topics, and many of the lists are useful guides for students seeking both topics and references for term papers and theses. They should enable faculty members to advise students more effectively and efficiently. They will also be useful to prospective graduate students seeking more detailed information about various graduate programs; to those currently preparing for field examinations; and to librarians responsible for acquisitions. Finally, they will be of interest to researchers and administrators who wish to know more about how their own work and the work of their department is being received by the profession.
The Economics exams, puzzles & problems include both undergraduate and graduate exams. They will be useful to professors in making up exams and problem sets, and to students studying for comprehensive exams.

Libraries and departments may wish to order entire collections, while individual professors and students may wish to purchase volumes in specific areas of interest.

All volumes have ISBN numbers and are listed in the Library of Congress catalog.

A partial list of Universities represented:

University of California, Berkeley
University of California, Los Angeles
University of California at Los Angeles
University of Chicago
Columbia University
Cornell University
Dartmouth College
Duke University
Harvard University
University of Illinois
Indiana University
Johns Hopkins University
London School of Economics & Political Science

Massachusetts Institute of Technology
University of Michigan
University of Minnesota
Northwestern University
University of Pennsylvania
Princeton University
University of Rochester
Stanford University
University of Toronto
University of Washington
University of Western Ontario
University of Wisconsin
Yale University

Economics Reading Lists, Course Outlines, Exams, Puzzles & Problems

Compiled by Edward Tower, *Duke University*

Volume 1 — **Microeconomics Course Materials** including oligopoly & game theory, theory of information, social insurance and the economics of technological change, 288 pages.

Volume 2 — **Microeconomics Exams, Puzzles & Problems** including the University of Chicago Ph.D. core exams in price theory 1967 - 1981, 290 pages.

Volume 3 — **Macroeconomics, Monetary Economics and Money & Banking Course Materials**, 301 pages.

Volume 4 — **Macroeconomics, Monetary Economics and Money & Banking Exams, Puzzles & Problems** including the University of Chicago M.A. comprehensive exams in micro and macroeconomic theory, Ph.D. core exams in the theory of income, and M.A. & Ph.D. preliminary exams in money and banking 1967 - 1981, 336 pages.

Volume 5 — **Development Economics Course Materials**, 208 pages.

Volume 6 — **Development Economics Exams, Puzzles & Problems**, 134 pages.

Volume 7 — **Industrial Organization & Regulation Course Materials**, 204 pages.

Volume 8 — **Industrial Organization & Regulation Exams, Puzzles & Problems**, 143 pages.

Volume 9 — **International Economics Course Materials**, 239 pages.

Volume 10 — **International Economics Exams, Puzzles & Problems**, 210 pages.

Volume 11 — **Public Finance Course Materials**, 211 pages.

Volume 12 — **Public Finance Exams, Puzzles & Problems**, 209 pages.

Volume 13 — **Comparative Economic Systems Course Materials** including economic anthropology, economic planning and the economics of socialism, 179 pages.

Volume 14 — **Comparative Economic Systems Exams, Puzzles & Problems, & the hit parade economics articles,** Ed Leamer's list of the most frequently cited economics articles 1895- 1976, 160 pages.

Volume 15 — **Labor Economics Course Materials** including economics of education and economic-demographic interrelations, 208 pages.

Volume 16 — **Labor Economics Exams, Puzzles & Problems**, including economic demography, 169 pages.

Volume 17 — **Econometrics Course Materials** including macro-econometric modelling, forecasting simulation, 175 pages.

Volume 18 — **Econometrics Exams, Puzzles & Problems**, 237 pages.

Volume 19 — **Mathematical Economics and Mathematical Models of Economic Growth**, 133 pages.

Volume 20 — **Public Choice, Political Economy, and the Economics of Public Policy & Law** including radical & utopian economics, economic models of the political process, income distribution, altruism & corruption, social choice & game theory, the economics of war, race and justice, 208 pages.

Volume 21 — **Economics of the Environment, Natural Resources and Energy** including fisheries economics and the economics of Middle East oil, 238 pages.

Volume 22 — **Agricultural Economics**, 222 pages.

Volume 23 — **Economic History** 249 pages.

Volume 24 — **History of Economic Thought**, 149 pages.

Volume 25 — **Urban and Regional Economics**, 194 pages.

Volumes 1, 3, 5, 7, 9, 11, 13, 15 and 17 contain reading lists & course outlines with exams & problem sets keyed to them. The even-numbered volumes between 2 and 18 consist of exams, puzzles & problems which are unrelated to the material in the odd-numbered volumes. Finally, volumes 19 - 25 contain all three types of material. 12% of the material in this collection is reprinted from the 1980 compilation.

Economics

☐ Vol. 1	$14	☐ Vol. 7	$12	☐ Vol. 14	$10	☐ Vol. 21	$13
☐ Vol. 2	$14	☐ Vol. 8	$11	☐ Vol. 15	$12	☐ Vol. 22	$12
☐ Vol. 3	$14	☐ Vol. 9	$13	☐ Vol. 16	$11	☐ Vol. 23	$13
☐ Vol. 4	$15	☐ Vol. 10	$13	☐ Vol. 17	$12	☐ Vol. 24	$12
☐ Vol. 5	$13	☐ Vol. 11	$13	☐ Vol. 18	$12	☐ Vol. 25	$12
☐ Vol. 6	$11	☐ Vol. 12	$13	☐ Vol. 19	$11	☐ Complete Set	$275
		☐ Vol. 13	$12	☐ Vol. 20	$12		

Political Science Reading Lists and Course Outlines

Compiled by Allan Kornberg, *Duke University*

Volume 1 — **Political Philosophy and Theory** including distributive justice and history of political theory, 224 pages.

Volume 2 — **Conduct of Political Inquiry** including formal logics and political arguments, research technique, theory construction, quantitative methods, and biological, sociological & psychological approaches to politics, 249 pages.

Volume 3 — **American Politics I:** the American congress, the presidency, and the American political system, 229 pages.

Volume 4 — **American Politics II:** American Political Parties, State Local & Urban Politics, Constitutional Law & Judicial Process, 268 pages.

Volume 5 — **Theories of International Relations** including science & technology in international affairs, current issues, nationalism & imperialism, 169 pages.

Volume 6 — **Foreign Policy, International Law, and the Politics of International Security** including Soviet and American foreign policy, defense policy, arms control, and evaluating nuclear strategy, 216 pages.

Volume 7 — **Comparative Politics** including comparative communism & totalitarianism, political participation & electoral behavior, and politics of ethnicity, immigration & cultural pluralism, 237 pages.

Volume 8 — **Area Studies in Comparative Politics** including Africa, Western Europe, Latin America, Canada, China and Japan, 224 pages.

Volume 9 — **Political Economy** including the politics of regulation and international political economy, 191 pages.

Volume 10 — **Political Economy of Development** including political development, problems of transitional societies, multinational corporations and underdevelopment, 165 pages.

Volume 11 — **Public Policy and Policy Analysis** including politics of the environment and media, 272 pages.

Business Administration Reading Lists and Course Outlines

Compiled by James W. Dean, *Columbia University* & *Simon Fraser University* and Richard Schwindt, *Simon Fraser University.*

Volume 1 — **Finance I** — Financial Theory, Financial Institutions and Money Markets, 131 pages.

Volume 2 — **Finance II** — Corporate Finance & Investments, 172 pages.

Volume 3 — **International Banking & Finance**, 145 pages.

Volume 4 — **International Business**, 130 pages.

Volume 5 — **Industrial Relations**, 163 pages.

Volume 6 — **Accounting I** — Financial & Managerial Accounting, 172 pages.

Volume 7 — **Accounting II** — Theory, Auditing, Taxation, History, Accounting for the Non-profit Organization & Multinational Firm, & Accounting Communication, 194 pages.

Volume 8 — **Marketing I** — Marketing Theory, Research, Management & Strategy, 192 pages.

Volume 9 — **Marketing II** — Product, Price, Place & Promotion, 221 pages.

Volume 10 — **Organizational Behavior**, 240 pages.

Volume 11 — **Quantitative Methods & Computer Applications in Business**, 181 pages.

Volume 12 — **Business Policy & Strategy**, 153 pages.

Volume 13 — **Business, Government & Society**, 134 pages.

Volume 14 — **Health Administration**, 315 pages.

Publication date: October 1981. 30% discount on multiple copies of the same volume for classroom use. Orders by individuals must be accompanied by payment. Institutions may request billing. Full refund if returned within 30 day examination period. Payment accepted in U.S. funds only. Outside North America add 10% for additional postage and handling.

Eno River Press
Box 4900, Duke Station
Durham, N.C. 27706
USA

Political Science

☐ Vol. 1	$13	☐ Vol. 7	$13
☐ Vol. 2	$13	☐ Vol. 8	$12
☐ Vol. 3	$13	☐ Vol. 9	$12
☐ Vol. 4	$14	☐ Vol. 10	$12
☐ Vol. 5	$12	☐ Vol. 11	$14
☐ Vol. 6	$13	☐ Complete Set $135	

Business Administration

☐ Vol. 1	$12	☐ Vol. 7	$12	☐ Vol. 13	$10
☐ Vol. 2	$13	☐ Vol. 8	$14	☐ Vol. 14	$15
☐ Vol. 3	$12	☐ Vol. 9	$14	☐ Complete Set $155	
☐ Vol. 4	$11	☐ Vol. 10	$14		
☐ Vol. 5	$13	☐ Vol. 11	$12		
☐ Vol. 6	$13	☐ Vol. 12	$10		

ISBN 0-88024-031-8